DATE DUE			

Shakespeare, Fletcher,
and *The Two Noble Kinsmen*

Shakespeare, Fletcher
and *The Two Noble Kinsmen*

Edited by Charles H. Frey

University of Missouri Press
Columbia, 1989

Library of Congress Cataloging-in-Publication Data

Shakespeare, Fletcher, and The two noble kinsmen / edited by
Charles H. Frey
p.   cm.
Bibliography: p.
Includes index.
ISBN 0-8262-0705-7 (alk. paper)
1. Shakespeare, William, 1564-1616. Two noble kinsmen.
2. Fletcher, John, 1579-1625. Two noble kinsmen.
3. Shakespeare, William, 1564-1616—Authorship.   4. Fletcher, John,
1579-1625—Authorship.   I. Frey, Charles H.
PR2870.S53   1989   88-27634
822.3'3—dc19   CIP

∞™ This paper meets the minimum requirements of
the American National Standard for Permanence of Paper
for Printed Library Materials, Z39.48, 1984.

To all the makers of this book

Acknowledgments

As explained further in the introduction, most of the essays collected herein were first drafted in connection with a seminar on *The Two Noble Kinsmen* that I conducted for members of the Shakespeare Association of America. Each member of the seminar read and commented on the first drafts of each other member, and revised drafts were prepared based on the many valuable suggestions received. Further revisions were made in preparation for this volume. I wish to acknowledge and express gratitude for the help I received from the other members of the seminar, and I want to record the collective expression of mutual appreciation voiced at the seminar. We became, I think, an unusually supportive group.

I want also to acknowledge with thanks the support of the Graduate School of the University of Washington, whose grant allowed Will Hamlin to research materials for the Bibliographical Guide and allowed me to complete work on the volume. Will Hamlin also read the manuscript and gave me many valuable suggestions.

I thank Thatcher Deane for his help with computer processing.

C.H.F.
October 1988

Note to the Reader

All Shakespeare quotations in this volume are from *The Riverside Shakespeare*, ed. G. B. Evans (Boston: Houghton Mifflin, 1974).

Contents

Introduction

Charles H. Frey

On 8 April 1634, there was entered in the Stationers' Register to John Waterson (a London bookseller) a "tragicomedy" entitled *The Two Noble Kinsmen* and identified as "by" John Fletcher and William Shakespeare. The first known text is a quarto dated the same year naming Fletcher and Shakespeare as its writers and stating that the play had been presented at the Blackfriars Theatre by the King's Men to great applause. The full history of theatrical and critical response to the play, which probably was written and first performed in 1613, is beyond the scope of this Introduction (see the Bibliographical Guide) but the weight of modern scholarship now attributes about half of the text to Fletcher, the rest to Shakespeare.

Despite the decided recognition of Shakespeare's hand in *The Two Noble Kinsmen,* relatively little interpretive attention has been accorded to it, at least until our time. But now, the play has been incorporated into several collected editions of Shakespeare; at least three major single-volume editions are in progress; the Royal Shakespeare Company produced the play in 1986; and there have been several recent productions in North America. Yet still *The Two Noble Kinsmen* might justifiably be termed an "embarrassment" not only to Bardolatry but also to Shakespeare studies generally. There are several reasons:

(1) The text is belated. Not part of the First Folio of 1623 or extant in Jacobean quarto or manuscript, it is our only Caroline first text of a Shakespeare play. It comes, in the 1634 Quarto, trailing a host of questions concerning its provenance. Assuming that *The Two Noble Kinsmen* was written some twenty-one years prior to publication in 1634, what sequence of theatrical managers, scribes, and compositors intervened between manuscript and Quarto? What history of the King's Men between 1623 and 1634 may be relevant to editing and understanding the Quarto text? What knowledge of promptbook practices and printing-house practices in that decade is needed? What study of the probable compositors for the 1634 Quarto would aid us in attribution study and in editing? Who will now undertake these unfamiliar and difficult questions? And with what results?

(2) The text probably is collaborative. That's a problem for study of this play and of the entire canon, because if Shakespeare collaborated in this play (roughly half of all Elizabethan and Jacobean plays appear to be collaborations), then he may have collaborated elsewhere, too. Does consideration of the collaborative nature of *The Two Noble Kinsmen* invite us to reopen questions of Shakespeare's possible collaboration on other plays? If we admit uncertainty

1

as to precisely which parts of *The Two Noble Kinsmen* Shakespeare authored, do we open the doors to vandalizing disintegrationists, to anti-Stratfordians, and to advocates of "new" works by Shakespeare? What may happen to Shakespeare's author-ity?

(3) The content of the play raises disturbing questions. It seems in some ways more disconsolate, more pessimistic, darker, than its sources in Chaucer, Boccaccio, and before. *The Two Noble Kinsmen* does not fit well with the other "Romances." It undermines the account of Shakespeare's development that leads to Prospero's radiant farewell (or to Cranmer's ebullient prophecy in *Henry VIII*). As "post-Romance," the play appears, moreover, distinctly mordant on subjects of friendship, nobility, and love. There are currents of sadness, harshness, and cynicism in *The Two Noble Kinsmen* that render it a most problematic final play.

Balanced against such enumerated "embarrassments" are the persistent flickers of bright appreciation accorded to *The Two Noble Kinsmen* by such critics as Coleridge, Lamb, De Quincey (who termed the play "the most superb work in the language"), Ward, Bawcutt, Edwards, and others (see the Bibliographical Guide). In recent years, moreover, the play has been mounted in well-received productions that demonstrate a very distinct theatrical viability and even modernity to be gleaned from *The Two Noble Kinsmen*.

Encouraged, therefore, by the tradition of such appreciations, the essays that follow meet head-on many of the embarrassments listed above. Most of the essays were prepared originally for a seminar on *The Two Noble Kinsmen* held under auspices of the Shakespeare Association of America. Those essays have been revised for this collection; a few new essays have been added; and the ordering follows the sequence of issues given above.

Addressing the text first as artifact, the opening essay complicates past discussions of the Quarto printing and assignments of authorial attribution. Paul Werstine studies patterns in spacing around punctuation and applies several tests to argue the presence of two compositors for the Quarto of 1634. He identifies the portions of text set by each compositor, and he surmises that the Quarto was set from a theatrical transcript employing scribal copy. By making much more certain an identification of two compositors and their respective contributions, Werstine opens the way for fresh considerations of the copy behind the text and for new attribution study. At the same time, he demonstrates how very tenuous may be methods of attribution that fail to take into account the many layers of managerial, scribal, and compositorial intermediaries that probably lie between authorial manuscript and Quarto print.

Widening the circle from Werstine's focus on provenance and compositorial attribution, the next three essays take up the problem of authorial attribution. The problem comes to us through tradition as a problem in identifying Shakespeare's "part" in the play, a problem of separating two possible, perhaps likely, collaborators: Shakespeare and Fletcher. The prevailing assumption has been that critics and readers would want to know which parts of the play to revere as Shakespearean, but the three essays by me, Donald Hedrick, and Michael Bristol question that assumption in various ways. In my essay I point to a shift in the Prologue from testing the purity of authorial contributions to requesting collaborative support from the audience and trace a similar shift from vertical, genetic inquiry to lateral, social authentication, a deflection in the action and language of the play and in the history of audience and reader response.

Widening further the significance of the play's interest in artistic and aristocratic rivalries, Hedrick suspends the assumption that Shakespeare and Fletcher collaborated on the play. He does so partly to consider the possibility that another playwright, neither Fletcher nor Shakespeare, wrote the play both to emulate one or more of the putative authors and to distinguish himself. The roughly equal division between single-authored and multiple-authored plays in Shakespeare's day (taken with additional theaters of male distinction and co-labor) suggests, for Hedrick, an authorial site of mixed competition and cooperation, a site inseparable from the many other arenas of homosocial collaboration and contest depicted in the play. Hedrick explores the astonishingly varied and complex systems of deference, emulation, rivalry, and social labor or production enacted in the text. He finds the play casting ironic light on the nature of artistic rivalry as well as on relations of collaboration and competition between friends and lovers. Viewed in its historical context, *The Two Noble Kinsmen* connects single authorship and heroic nobility, which it then contrasts against collaborative friendship and marriage. All four schemes are conceived as contrasting modes of production and life support.

Expanding on the critiques by me and Hedrick of Shakespearean authority, Bristol links the crisis of authority in Theseus's reign to crises of authority in our institutionalized idealizations of Shakespeare. Just as war and death threaten Theseus on his wedding day, so *The Two Noble Kinsmen* threatens the serene canonical closure offered by readings that celebrate *The Tempest* as Shakespeare's final and happiest play. The disease of unanimous judgment in Palamon and Arcite reveals that a creative authority needs to ally itself with a social energy of differentiation and renewal, an energy necessarily productive of disruption, struggle, and change.

Werstine points toward the bodily existence of *The Two Noble Kinsmen* as printed text and toward the historical substantiality of its producers. What we have now once failed to exist. Sparks of personal labor set words to ink and type. We want to know, inevitably, as much as we can about the precise terms and conditions of that labor. What exactly was made? Who made it? When? Under what conditions? Such questions almost hold off the terrible tide of significance. I, Hedrick, and Bristol address that tide as it sweeps the play toward us on massive waves of rumor and authority, interpretation and production. But behind that tide and the seemingly original authorial labor launched upon it, there lies an ocean of historical traditions.

Barry Weller places the play squarely in a tradition traced from Aristotle and other classical sources through Boccaccio, Chaucer, Thomas Elyot, and Shakespeare's earlier plays (particularly *The Two Gentlemen of Verona* and *The Merchant of Venice*). That tradition wrestles continually with tensions in male friendship, and Weller focuses on erotic components in the friendship of Palamon and Arcite. He shows how the play questions and requestions its own imperatives toward heterosexual collaborations in marriage. *The Two Noble Kinsmen,* as Weller sees it, explores patriarchal deformations of genuine mutuality and intimacy in marriage, and Weller speculates further on the play's frightening suspicions of intimacy in friendship as being self-mirroring and claustrophobic.

My second essay, on a grimacing skepticism in the play toward "nobility" in love, complements Barry Weller's essay on traditions of friendship. I focus particularly on that "sly obtruding of doubles" that continually deflects and compromises erotic possessiveness. In *The Two Noble Kinsmen,* loved ones arrive before lovers in a state of prior relation to earlier loves. Is the play saying: "If you would be loved, imitate your lover's preexisting object of desire"? Perhaps. But the play goes on to point toward disruptions of such imitation that accompany facts of gender and generativity. At war with the deadly differences of space (gender) and of time (generation), the play's instinct is, finally, to wince at the costs of submission.

Complementing my critique of gender-anxiety in the play, Susan Green analyzes the role of the Jailer's Daughter both in the play and in the trials of patriarchal criticism. She notes in the Prologue and elsewhere conflicting images of artistic and biological generativity, and she interprets the Jailer's Daughter as "the play's most potent figure of desire." Theseus becomes, for Green, a figure of anxiety concerning sexual identity and responsibility, an anxiety that would displace sensual experience into language and imagination, whereas the ardor of the Jailer's Daughter displaces language and imagination into sensual experience. Yet, argues Green, "an imagination like Theseus's *requires* a figure like the Jailer's Daughter." She is, perhaps, another of his "achievements."

Jeanne Roberts locates the figure of the Amazon in male western tradition and places *The Two Noble Kinsmen* in the context of a degenerating allegorical hierarchy of male/female attributes in Jacobean England. In the play, "Palamon and Arcite act out almost emblematically the Venus-Mars struggle in Theseus's mind and in the male progress toward adulthood." At the same time, Emilia and the Jailer's Daughter seek mediations between frosty Diana and rapacious Venus. Roberts finds, however, that, even to the end, disruptive female forces unsettle the patriarchal order and disturb the boundaries of gender in this "profoundly illuminating text."

Richard Abrams blends feminist, materialist, psychoanalytic, and formalist strategies to further the emergent theme of this collection: that, in *The Two Noble Kinsmen,* not only rivalrous personalities but also rivalrous systems of identity and value for artistic merit, gender relations, and social class oppose and mingle in curiously self-subverting ways. Abrams argues, more specifically, that the Prologue reconstitutes a nobility-seeking audience into bourgeois colaborers, that the would-be heroic language and relationships of the martial males are shot through with entrepreneurial fashion and desire, and that the subplot underclass succeeds and survives through a relinquishing of chivalric ideals in favor of middle-class comforts and content.

Needless to say, the glittering, often corrosive yet sometimes hopeful intricacies gleaned by contemporary critical acumen from *The Two Noble Kinsmen* have not been reflected much in the scattered stagings accorded to it over some 375 years. Insofar as the stage has responded to interpretation, it has tended not to revel in disjunctions but to rationalize solutions. Through performance history and analysis, Hugh Richmond documents how fully the theater has sought to extract varied unities of design from the play. The search for authority that is rendered problematic by Werstine, Hedrick, Bristol, and others is questioned also by Richmond as he contrasts reductive/redactive productions against the "multilayered," "oscillating," "counterpointing" performance values implicit in the full script. Richmond finds a congruence, however, in the "ritual recognition of abstract biological forces" featured throughout *The Two Noble Kinsmen,* and he argues for a "deliberately archaic style of production" to invoke rhythms of naive expectation evolving into stoic acceptance of seemingly arbitrary and unpredictable life forces. He concludes with a plea for less somber and gender-conflicted readings of the play and for more allowance given to staging orthodox morality and even a measure of providentialism in the play, values more accessible and pleasing, he opines, to most theater audiences. Does Richmond's perspective offer one more hint that readerly and theatrical arenas may contrast anti-collaborative yet charitable skepticism, on the one hand, and collaborative, social reaffirmations of collective norms, on the other?

Will Hamlin's Bibliographical Guide rewards close reading as it charts the play's critical and scholarly history. Opinions of editors and interpreters have proved surprisingly cross-grained as they have changed from era to era. Hamlin's work implicitly reveals the smoky coalescence of our readings-out and readings-in, all gamely pursued by dying generations at their Western work.

Taken together, the essays collected here gather toward a vision of "Shakespeare's" irresistible capacity to absorb our projections, to harbor our illnesses, and to embody our sacred dreams. *The Two Noble Kinsmen* truly *is* a superb dramatic work. It unmasks and mocks, remarks and remakes, many of our institutionalized emotions concerning maleness, friendship, war, authority, commerce, and love. It deserts the ideal of domination, and it embraces the problems of partnership. Its time is now. We hope that you find these essays helpful for your meditations upon this little known master-mystery of Renaissance and Modern culture.

1 On the Compositors of
The Two Noble Kinsmen

꛰⊙꛱⊙

Paul Werstine

In view of the considerable difference of opinion about the worth and authorship of *The Two Noble Kinsmen,* it is perhaps not surprising to find disagreement on the more technical question of compositor identification in the First Quarto of the play printed in the shop of Thomas Cotes in 1634.[1] Although purely a bibliographical matter in itself, compositor identification can, on occasion, turn out to be of some importance to the larger questions of authorship, attribution of scenes, and, especially, the nature of the manuscript used as printer's copy for a play-quarto. It may therefore be worthwhile to reflect briefly on the purpose, method, and potential uses of such identification.

On a theoretical level, compositor identification is an effort—always provisional, partial, and paradoxical—to recover a text (here a playtext), which is available to us only in printed form, from the material process of printing, which alone has made the text available to us. Identification remains provisional and partial because, in the absence of extant personnel records and production schedules for the printing houses in which such a playtext as *The Two Noble Kinsmen* was manufactured, compositor identification can never produce the historical identities of the workmen who set the play into type; nor can it ever draw exact margins around their individual contributions. Although we know that *some* typesetter(s) must have picked out of cases of type the pieces of metal that, when inked and applied to paper, have given us a playtext, we can never establish with certainty who these typesetters were, how many they were, or precisely which units of the playtext belonged to each. The compositor(s) of *The Two Noble Kinsmen* can exist for us today only at the level of inference; that is, a compositor is merely a pattern of typographical features and/or spelling variants located in certain bibliographical divisions of the printed text (part-pages, pages, formes, gatherings). We can speak of multiple compositors only when typographical features and/or spelling variants from different bibliographical divisions oppose each other. Without external records and printing schedules, however, we can never confirm that observable contrasts in typogra-

---

1. For my study in compositor identification, I have used *Shakespeare's Plays in Quarto: A Facsimile Edition of Copies Primarily from the Henry E. Huntington Library,* ed. Michael J. B. Allen and Kenneth Muir (Berkeley: University of California Press, 1981), 836–81. All my references to *The Two Noble Kinsmen* are to this 1634 edition.

phy and / or spelling must correspond to the actual division of labor between, or among, historical compositors. Without such confirmation, the best we can do is minimize the additional assumptions we make in the inferential construction of typesetters.

Ideally, when we are dealing with a single printed book for which the nature of the manuscript printer's copy is unknown, we should construct our compositor(s) only from purely typographical features—features that cannot have been taken over from printer's copy. With *The Two Noble Kinsmen* we are fortunate to find binary oppositions in patterns of spacing punctuation and the indentation of marginal stage directions—both typographical features. But this good fortune is not to be overemphasized: although distinctive on many of the 1634 quarto's pages, these patterns are not absolutely regular or uniform from page to page within a stint attributed to a particular compositor. The boundaries between the work of different typesetters are sometimes blurred. In this particular instance, as in general, compositor identification remains provisional.

Yet it does generate some explanatory power that can be brought to bear on observable anomalies in *The Two Noble Kinsmen,* and it does open up a space from which we can speculate about preprinting stages in the transmission of the playtext. Sometimes compositor identification can lead to quite straightforward explanations: for example, all the instances in which speech prefixes are stopped by commas (instead of periods as is usually the case in *The Two Noble Kinsmen*) are found in what seems to be, on quite other grounds, the work of a single compositor. Thus we can probably discount this anomaly in any attempt to reconstruct the preprinting history of the playtext; these commas cannot be assumed to be scribal or authorial slips, since printing-house agency provides a more immediate explanation. At other times, however, compositor identification exposes the possibility of considerable complexity in the transmission of the playtext. One such case concerns Richard Proudfoot's most useful observation that the name *Pirithous* was not only spelled differently but also pronounced differently (sometimes with three, sometimes with four syllables in verse) in different scenes; while the correlation between the different pronunciations (which cannot have been compositorial in origin) and the usual division of authorship for the play is exact, the correlation between the latter and the spelling variants is not. Can we then charge these spelling anomalies to the compositors? My analysis (provided in detail below) indicates otherwise, and so it opens up for speculation the possibility that other agents intervened between author(s) and compositor(s) in the transmission of the play into print.

Such speculation has its dangers, of course. But another danger is that we overlook the presence of compositors' hands in the transmission of the play, confuse differences in their handling of the manuscript with variations that derive from the manuscript, or dismiss features of the printed text as the errors of a single compositor, when, more probably, such features are common to the pages of more than one workman, with each merely reproducing what was in his copy. Without reliable compositor identification, we can err badly; with it, we can move on to other questions.

The first attempt at identifying compositors was F. O. Waller's in 1957. He limited himself to the following statement:

An analysis of certain spellings and of the spacings around punctuation shows that the quarto was set by two compositors, Compositor A doing B1-C1, C2v-E4, F3v-G2v, G4v, I1–14v, K3, and L4v-M2v, and Compositor B, C1v-C2, E4v-F3, G3-G4, H1-H4v, I4v-K2, K3v-L3v, M3v-M4v, and the Prologue and Epilogue on A1v and N1.[2]

In 1967 Paul Bertram offered this evaluation of Waller's contribution:

Waller publishes none of the evidence by which he arrived at these assignments. The amount and the complexity of the other material comprehended by his essay will perhaps justify the omission to some extent. Yet the assignment of 14v to both compositors and the failure to assign K2v, L4, and M3 to either compositor would surely seem to call for explanation or at least brief notice.

Bertram went on to offer his own analysis of the spelling pattern of the quarto, completely ignoring Waller's reference to spacing around punctuation, and concluded that there is "no reliable evidence sufficient to establish . . . a division" of the play between compositors.[3] Without reference to Bertram, G. R. Proudfoot arrived at the same conclusion in his edition of 1970: "The consistency of distribution of various spellings throughout the quarto suggests that it was set by a single compositor."[4]

Since, under the influence of Hinman's work on the Shakespeare First Folio,[5] compositor identification was understood as dependent on patterns of spelling variants alone, it is not surprising that Waller's reference to spacing was ignored. In the interim, T. H. Howard-Hill has discovered that Hinman's compositor attributions in the Folio can be confirmed and revised through attention to the compositors' habits of inserting spaces or omitting them after commas that appear in the middle of lines (medial commas) or before commas that appear at the ends of lines (terminal commas).[6] Hinman's Compositor B of the First Folio is now recognized as one who preferred to put a space after a medial comma, Compositor C as one who often put a space before a terminal comma, Compositor A as one who did not usually space either medial or terminal commas. It seems time now to return to Waller's observations about the spacing of punctuation in the quarto of *The Two Noble Kinsmen*. To do so is to come to share his belief in the presence of two compositors.

2. "Printer's Copy for *The Two Noble Kinsmen*," *Studies in Bibliography* 11 (1958): 78.

3. *Shakespeare and "The Two Noble Kinsmen"* (New Brunswick: Rutgers University Press, 1968), 82, 85.

4. *The Two Noble Kinsmen,* Regents Renaissance Drama Series (Lincoln: University of Nebraska Press, 1970), xxiv.

5. *The Printing and Proof-Reading of the First Folio of Shakespeare,* 2 vols. (Oxford: Clarendon, 1963).

6. "The Compositors of the Shakespeare Folio Comedies," *Studies in Bibliography* 26 (1973): 61–106.

I

The pages of *The Two Noble Kinsmen* Q1 may be divided into three groups: those on which a significant proportion of medial commas are spaced; those on which few are spaced; those that fall between the first two groups, because sometimes, but not always, there are too few commas for analysis. In Table 1, I have provisionally assigned the first group of pages to Compositor A, the second to Compositor B, and have left the third unassigned. In all cases I have ignored the spacing of commas in lines that extend the full width of the page because the compositors may have adjusted internal spacing in such lines in order to fit the type into their composing sticks—to "justify" the lines.

In the table, the principle of division of the pages between the compositors is to award Compositor A those on which at least 30 percent of the medial commas are spaced and to attribute to Compositor B those on which no more than 20 percent are spaced. The range on Compositor A's pages stretches from 30 percent (E3v) to 70 percent (N1), on Compositor B's from 0 percent (12 pages) to 20 percent (M3). The more commas that appear in short lines on a page, the greater the probability of the compositor attribution for that page; so we may be far more confident about page C4v, with thirty such commas, than about page G1, with seven.

Eight pages cannot yet be assigned: on C2, D1, D4, F1, F2v, F4v, and G3, the proportion of spaced medial commas is between 20 and 30 percent; on page L4 there is only one medial comma, nonspaced. We cannot then ignore the possibility that a single compositor set the whole quarto, his preferences for spacing varying from page to page, as sometimes he spaced commas and sometimes he did not, so that the proportions of spaced commas on his quarto pages extend all the way from 0 to 78 percent. Indeed we can never wholly eliminate this possibility; the best we can do is offer further evidence to corroborate the division of the quarto between workmen already proposed. It would be necessary to do so anyway because, as D. F. McKenzie has recently demonstrated, variations in the spacing of commas from page to page or gathering to gathering cannot alone persuade us that two compositors were at work. McKenzie examined an eighteenth-century book from a shop whose records are extant so that he could know from the beginning how many workmen set the book into type and what pages they set. He discovered that there was no correlation at all between the historical record and the very clear contrasts evident in the spacing of commas between different parts of the book. The same compositor was indeed responsible for whole gatherings in which few commas were spaced and other gatherings in which many were spaced; his fellows exhibited similar inconstancy in this habit and so remained indistinguishable from him.[7]

In the book McKenzie examined, the compositors were constant (and so again indistinguishable) in their spacing of the other punctuation marks—semi-

---

7. "Stretching a Point: Or, The Case of the Spaced-out Comps," *Studies in Bibliography* 37 (1984): 106–21.

Table 1. The Spacing of Commas: A Preliminary Survey

	Compositor A			Compositor B	
Page	Spaced Medial ,	Nonspaced Medial ,	Page	Spaced Medial ,	Nonspaced Medial ,
			A1v	2	16
B1v	4	5	B1	0	5
2	8	10			
2v	8	7			
3	7	12			
3v	7	9			
4	9	7			
4v	5	6			
C1	12	14	C1v	2	17
2v	10	11			
3	14	14			
3v	10	11			
4	9	9			
4v	16	14			
D1v	11	10	D2	3	12
2v	7	9			
3	8	13			
3v	6	5			
4v	4	4			
E1	9	11			
1v	7	6			
2	6	3			
2v	5	5			
3	8	8			
3v	3	7			
4	10	7	E4v	1	15
F3v	14	9			
4	7	13	F1v	1	24
			2	2	16
			3	1	26
G1	3	4			
1v	9	19	G3v	1	27
2	4	4	4	1	10
2v	8	12			
4v	8	14			
			H1	1	8
			1v	0	18
			2	4	22

(*continued on the following page*)

Table 1. The Spacing of Commas: A Preliminary Survey (*continued*)

	Compositor A			Compositor B	
Page	Spaced Medial ,	Nonspaced Medial ,	Page	Spaced Medial ,	Nonspaced Medial ,
			2v	1	20
			3	2	17
			3v	0	10
			4	3	16
			4v	1	14
I1	9	10			
1v	5	7			
2	10	5			
2v	12	13			
3	6	13			
3v	5	7			
4	13	16	I4v	0	10
			K1	0	21
			1v	1	28
			2	0	24
			2v	2	27
K3	17	19	3v	0	12
			4	1	23
			4v	1	22
			L1	0	21
			1v	1	26
			2	3	13
			2v	0	11
			3	0	6
			3v	0	10
L4v	8	12			
M1	6	13	M3	2	8
1v	9	7	3v	2	23
2	10	12	4	1	14
2v	8	8	4v	0	14
N1	7	3			
Totals	381	437		40	606

colons, colons, question marks, and exclamation marks.[8] The compositor(s) of *The Two Noble Kinsmen* Q1 was (were) not, and, remarkably, variations in the spacing of medial semicolons, colons, and periods coincide with the shifts already tabulated in the spacing of commas. While it is demonstrably true that a single compositor's habit can vary enormously in his spacing of commas, it is much less likely that a single compositor would on some pages appear entirely indifferent to his spacing of all medial punctuation marks, sometimes spacing them, as often not, and on other pages systematically omit spaces after medial commas but just as systematically insert spaces around most other punctuation. Yet just such a pattern can be discerned among the pages of Q1. The hypothetical Compositor A of Q1—the one who spaced about half the medial commas he set—was just as indifferent about inserting spaces before and after colons and semicolons—sometimes he did so, as often he did not, and, again as often, he inserted a space after the punctuation but not before it. The hypothetical Compositor B—the one who rarely spaced medial commas—seems to have strongly preferred to insert spaces both before and after colons and semicolons; when he did not insert a space before one of these punctuation marks, he rarely put one after it, instead leaving it nonspaced before and after. Table 2 depicts how these spacing habits corroborate those observed with medial commas and amplifies and corrects the assignments provisionally offered in Table 1. The ratio in the first column of each half of the table is the ratio of spaced medial commas to nonspaced ones (0/5, for example); the second column of each half of the table records the ratio of colons and semicolons spaced before and after to those spaced only after to those not spaced at all (5/2/4, for example, indicates that five of these punctuation marks are spaced before and after; that two are spaced after, but not before; and that four are not spaced at all).[9]

The hypothetical Compositor B's strong preference for spacing semicolons and colons, which is so consistently associated with his equally strong preference for not spacing medial commas, allows us to assign to him some of the pages that remained in doubt after only the spacing of commas had been tabulated. To him we can now give page F1, even though 22 percent of the commas are spaced, because the page shows an exclusive preference for spacing semicolons and colons. The same is true of pages F2v and G3, on which similar proportions of spaced medial commas appear but on which the ratios of spaced colons and semicolons to nonspaced and spaced-after are 8/1 and 6/2 respectively. We can even give him page L4, although with considerable doubt as yet, because all the available evidence on the page, little though it is, points to him. He can be ruled out of consideration for page D2, however; although only three of its fifteen commas are spaced, as we might expect from Compositor B, still the preference for not spacing colons and semicolons or for putting spaces only after them is Compositor A's, and I give this page to him. Also to Compositor A can go the

8. Ibid., 111.
9. I have not tabulated the very rare cases in which a colon or a semicolon is spaced before but not after. No discernible pattern is evident in the spacing of question marks or of any terminal punctuation, nor should we expect one.

Table 2. Compositors A and B of *The Two Noble Kinsmen*

	Compositor A			Compositor B		
Page			Page			
			A1v	2/16	3/0/0	
B1v	4/5	0/2/1	B1	0/5	0/0/0	
2	8/10	2/2/0				
2v	8/7	5/1/5				
3	7/12	4/2/2				
3v	7/9	1/1/0				
4	9/7	1/2/1				
4v	5/6	3/6/1				
C1	12/14	0/1/3	C1v	2/17	10/0/1	
2	3/8	2/1/2				
2v	10/11	0/5/3				
3	14/14	2/2/1				
3v	10/11	0/2/2				
4	9/9	0/2/2				
4v	16/14	2/1/0				
D1	3/10	2/4/1				
1v	11/10	5/2/3				
2	3/12	3/2/3				
2v	7/9	0/0/4				
3	8/13	2/6/1				
3v	6/5	1/1/1				
4	2/7	0/1/0				
4v	4/4	1/2/1				
E1	9/11	1/0/0				
1v	7/6	0/1/4				
2	6/3	1/4/5				
2v	5/5	1/0/2				
3	8/8	1/3/0				
3v	3/7	2/0/1				
4	10/7	4/5/0	E4v	1/15	8/0/0	
F3v	14/9	1/2/1	F1	4/14	8/0/0	
4	7/13	3/1/3	1v	1/24	10/2/0	
4v	6/17	2/5/2	2	2/16	8/1/2	
			2v	7/20	8/0/1	
			3	1/26	2/1/0	
G1	3/4	0/3/5	G3	4/14	6/1/1	
1v	9/19	4/3/4	3v	1/27	1/0/1	
2	4/4	0/2/2	4	1/10	7/1/3	
2v	8/12	0/2/1				
4v	8/14	1/0/2				

(continued on the following page)

Table 2. Compositors A and B of *The Two Noble Kinsmen* (*continued*)

Compositor A			Compositor B		
Page			Page		
			H1	1/8	4/0/1
			1v	0/18	6/0/1
			2	4/22	4/0/2
			2v	1/20	7/0/0
			3	2/17	4/0/1
			3v	0/10	7/1/3
			4	3/16	2/0/1
			4v	1/14	4/0/0
I1	9/10	2/1/4			
1v	5/7	1/0/1			
2	10/5	2/2/0			
2v	12/13	5/1/3			
3	6/13	1/1/0			
3v	5/7	1/2/3			
4	13/6	3/1/1	I4v	0/10	8/0/0
			K1	0/21	9/0/2
			1v	1/28	6/1/2
			2	0/24	6/0/2
			2v	2/27	1/0/3
K3	17/19	0/2/4	3v	0/12	6/0/1
			4	1/23	6/0/3
			4v	1/22	3/1/3
			L1	0/21	5/2/4
			1v	1/26	4/0/0
			2	3/13	4/0/3
			2v	0/11	1/0/0
			3	0/6	3/0/1
			3v	0/10	1/0/0
L4v	8/12	2/1/2	4	0/1	1/0/0
			M3	2/8	4/1/0
M1	6/13	1/5/2	3v	2/23	8/0/1
1v	9/7	3/3/1	4	1/14	15/0/0
2	10/12	7/4/0	4v	0/14	10/0/3
2v	8/8	4/2/2			
N1	7/3	7/0/1			
Totals	398/481	96/104/93		52/643	208/12/46
Simple Ratios					
	4/5	1/1/1		1/13	17/1/4

previously unassigned pages C2, D1, D4, and F4v. In each of these the proportion of spaced medial commas fails to reach 30 percent, but nevertheless each
shows evidence of the hypothetical Compositor A's indifference to the spacing
of colons and semicolons. There is other evidence too, although perhaps not as
much as we might ideally want, for these compositor attributions. Twice as
many periods are found on Compositor A's pages as on Compositor B's; the
first set sixty-three on his fifty-one pages (1.2 per page), the second only twenty-
three on thirty-nine pages (0.6 per page). Again a marked contrast arises from
the difference in the spacing of punctuation. Only nine of Compositor A's
periods are in lines that extend the width of the page—lines, that is, in which he
may have had to adjust spacing in order to get the whole line properly into his
composing-stick; these we should discount. Of the remaining fifty-four, only
thirty-two have spacing after them (59 percent), and only five are followed by
more than a single millimeter of spacing (9 percent). Just four of Compositor B's
twenty-three appear in long lines; eighteen of the other nineteen are spaced (95
percent), and sixteen have more than a millimeter of spacing after them (84
percent). Among the eighteen spaced periods on B's pages is one on L4, the
most problematic page in the quarto for compositor attribution in view of the
paucity of evidence it contains; this third bit of evidence associates with the
nonspaced medial comma and the spaced colon to indicate Compositor B's
hand.[10]

The two hypothetical workmen also appear to differ in their treatment of
marginal stage directions. By my counts, Compositor B set forty-one of these;
thirty-eight extend either exactly to the right margin of the page (Figure 1) or to
within a millimeter of the margin (93 percent); only one that he may have been
responsible for is inset from the margin by more than two millimeters (page
G3); the two other exceptions on his pages extend to within one to two millimeters of the right margin (both are on page K2). Of Compositor A's fifty-three
marginal stage directions, only eighteen come within a millimeter of the right
margin (34 percent); fourteen are short of the margin by more than two millimeters, another twenty-one are short by more than a millimeter. One example
("*Strew ¦ Flowers.*" [page B1v]) is inset eight millimeters, and "*Singes.*" (page I3)
is seventeen millimeters short of the margin. It would seem that the two workmen, if such they are, had quite different ideas about where stage directions
ought to go.

The two also may be differentiated in terms of their competence in maintaining a feature of Cotes's house style, the stopping of speech-heads, abbreviated
or not, with periods. Eighteen times on Compositor A's pages there are speech-
heads stopped by commas (16) or colons (2). Twice in Compositor B's work,
speech prefixes are not stopped by any punctuation (pages K1v and L2v), but it
is difficult to charge Compositor B with three cases in which prefixes are

10. Not included in this summary are periods after speech prefixes, abbreviations, or numerals
(most frequent as scene numbers). Usually the periods after scene numbers are spaced; both
exceptions (in lines not extending the full width of the page) occur, significantly perhaps, on
Compositor A's pages (C4v, G2).

70   *The Two Noble Kinsmen.*

Regiment;I have feene it approved,how many times
I know not,but to make the number more,I have
Great hope in this. I will betweene the paffages of
This project,come in with my applyance : Let us
Put it in execution;and haften the fucceffe, which doubt not
Will bring forth comfort.   *Florifh. Exeunt.*

Actus Quintus.

Scæna 1. *Enter Thefeus,Perithous,Hipolita, attendants.*
  Thef. Now let'em enter,and before the gods
Tender their holy prayers : Let the Temples
Burne bright with facred fires,and the Altars
In hallowed clouds commend their fwelling Incenfe
To thofe above us : Let no due be wanting,
                    Florifh of Cornets.
They have a noble worke in hand,will honour
The very powers that love 'em.
        Enter Palamon and Arcite,and their Knights.
  Per. Sir they enter.
  Thef. You valiant and ftrong harted Enemies
You royall German foes,that this day come
To blow that neareneffe out that flames betweene ye;
Lay by your anger for an houre,and dove-like
Before the holy Altars of your helpers
(The all feard gods)bow downe your ftubborne bodies,
Your ire is more than moreall; So your helpe be,
And as the gods regard ye,fight with Iuftice,
I le leave you to your prayers,and betwixt ye
I part my wifhes.
  Per. Honour crowne the worthieft.
                  Exit Thefeus,and his traine.
  Pal. The glaffo is running now that cannot finifh
Till one of us expire : Thinke you but thus,
That were there ought in me which ftrove to fhow
Mine enemy in this bufineffe,wer't one eye
Againft another : Arme opprest by Arme:

                                        I

Figure 1

stopped with commas, even though they appear on a page that has already been attributed to him on the basis of the spacing of punctuation presented above.

These three anomalies cluster together in lines 16–21 of page G3 and affect three successive speech prefixes (Figure 2). Line 25 on the same page is occupied by the only marginal stage direction inset more than two millimeters on a page attributed to Compositor B. It is difficult, then, to resist the possibility that the two compositors shared this page, with Compositor B setting some or all of the first fifteen lines as well as the last thirteen or so. Only two of the eleven medial commas in these lines are spaced, and all but two of the six medial colons are spaced both before and after—just what might be expected of Compositor B. The ten lines in the middle of G3, those characterized by irregularities in the punctuation of speech prefixes and placement of stage directions, may be Compositor A's; although only two of seven medial commas are spaced and the single medial colon is spaced before and after, the suspicion of Compositor A's hand remains because inferences based on spacing statistics for as small a sample as ten lines can scarcely be compelling.

The compositors seem to have slipped in their punctuation of stage directions in much the same way they did with speech-heads. Compositor A stopped two marginal stage directions (as well as the sixteen speech-heads) with commas instead of periods (pages D2 and E4); Compositor B omitted the period after a marginal stage direction on page L4, just as he left it out after two of his speech-heads. However, Compositor A also left out a period after *"Exit"* on G1v, and Compositor B set *"Exit. Daugh."* on K2v. In the ten lines on G3 that I have just reassigned from Compositor B to Compositor A is the only instance of a stage direction stopped with a colon: *"Winde Hornes:"*. Since Compositor A twice stopped speech prefixes with colons, again this error seems more likely his than Compositor B's. Although Compositor A may have erred in not following house style, he may, as we shall see later, merely have been following copy in stopping a stage direction with a colon.

Having now offered all the evidence I have been able to find differentiating two workmen in the quarto, I must now say that I hardly regard my compositor attributions as matters of fact, but I do regard them as more probable than the hypothesis that a single compositor set the whole quarto. It might be valuable to look briefly, however, at the objection raised by Paul Bertram to F. O. Waller's division of the quarto between compositors, a division almost exactly the same as mine, at which I have necessarily arrived independently, since Waller published none of his evidence. Bertram contended,

The proposed division, moreover, would mean [1] that the compositors, if pages had been set seriatim [that is, in reading order], would have exchanged labor no less than thirteen times, or if the quarto had been set by the forme, that they would have shared work on no less than ten formes [the inner forme of a quarto is pages 1v, 2, 3v, 4, printed on one side of the sheet at press, the outer, pages 1, 2v, 3, 4v, printed on the other side of the sheet].[11]

11. Bertram, *Shakespeare,* 82–83.

The Two Noble Kinsmen.   45

3. Ther's a dainty mad woman Mr. comes i'th Nick as
mad as a march hare : if wee can get her daunce, wee are
made againe: I warrant her, shee'l doe the rarest gambols.
  1. A mad woman? we are made Boyes.
 Sch. And are you mad good woman?
 Daugh. I would be sorry else,
Give me your hand.
 Sch. Why ?
 Daugh. I can tell your fortune.
You are a foole : tell ten, I have pozd him : Buz
Friend you must eate no white bread, if you doe
Your teeth will bleede extreamely, shall we dance ho ?
I know you, y'ar a Tinker: Sirha Tinker
Stop no more holes, but what you should.
  Sch. Dij boni. A Tinker Damzell ?   (play
 Daug. Or a Conjurer: raise me a devill now, and let him
Quipassa, o'th bels and bones.
  Sch. Goe take her, aud fluently perswade her to a peace:
Et opus exegi, quod nec Iouis ira, nec ignis.
Strike up, and leade her in.
  2, Come Lasse, lets trip it.
 Daugh. Ile leade;   (*Winde Hornes* :
  3. Doe, doe.
 Sch. Perswasively, and cunningly : away boyes,
                    Ex. all but Schoolemaster.
I beare the hornes : give me some
Meditation, and marke your Cues
Pallas inspire me.
            Enter Thes. Pir. Hip. Emil. Arcite : and traine.
 Thes. This way the Stag tooke.
 Sch. Stay, and edifie.
 Thes. What have we here ?
 Per. Some Countrey sport, upon my life Sir.
 Per. Well Sir, goe forward, we will edifie.
Ladies sit downe, wee'l stay it.   (*Ladies.*
 Sch. Thou doughtie Duke all haile : all haile sweet
 Thes. This is a cold beginning.
 Sch. If you but favour; our Country pastime made is,
                    G 3   We

Figure 2

Bertram's objection amounts to a demand, common in the time at which he wrote, for a pleasing symmetry in the division of pages between workmen, one setting the first half of a book, the other the second; or the two alternating in the setting of whole gatherings (one doing gatherings B, D, F and so on, the other doing gatherings C, E, G). It was for the latter pattern of division, for example, that P. W. M. Blayney looked when he attacked the collection of Shakespeare quartos, some of them apocryphal, printed by Thomas Pavier in 1619.[12] Assumptions such as this one persisted for a long time, in spite of D. F. McKenzie's observation that "wherever full primary evidence has become available it has revealed a geometry of such complexity that even an expert in cybernetics, primed with all the facts, would have little chance of discerning it" and his warning that "bibliography will simply have to prove itself adequate to conditions of far greater complexity than it has hitherto entertained."[13] More recent compositor studies, such as Blayney's with the First Quarto *Lear*, regularly assign compositors shares of the same pages as well as the same formes.[14]

II

If the compositor attributions I propose can be accepted, at least provisionally, they can explain some of the peculiarities in the printing of Q1 and even reveal some features of the manuscript that lay behind the printed text. A minor anomaly in the printing is the absence of signatures from the bottoms of leaves F3 and L3. In every other gathering, the first three leaves are signed in the form, for example, "C," "C2," and "C3." Both the omissions occur on pages assigned, on quite other grounds, to Compositor B, who can thus be identified as the source of the errors. Some irregularities in catchwords may also be traced to the division of the quarto between compositors. Ideally, the form of the catchword, the word set on the last line of a page below the text, ought to be replicated in the first word on the following page. As Table 3 indicates, the ideal is not always achieved in Q1.

There are eighty-eight catchwords in the quarto, eight errors (as Table 3 shows), and fifteen exchanges of labor between the compositors. If the errors in catchwords were distributed throughout the quarto merely by chance, then exactly 1.3 of the eight should have coincided with an exchange in labor. That three coincide seems more than coincidence and, instead, another indication of the presence of two compositors.

Of textual, rather than merely bibliographical, interest are variations in the placement and font of stage directions. Critics have found most noteworthy those printed in the margins of the quarto, generally, but not always, in small

12. "'Compositor B' and the Pavier Quartos: Problems of Identification and Their Implications," *The Library*, 5th ser., vol. 27 (1972): 179–206.
13. "Printers of the Mind: Some Notes on Bibliographical Theories and Printing-House Practices," *Studies in Bibliography* 22 (1969): 60.
14. *Nicholas Okes and the First Quarto*, vol. 1 of *The Texts of "King Lear" and Their Origins* (Cambridge: Cambridge University Press, 1982), 181–87.

Table 3. Catchwords with Variant Referents

Page	Catchword	Compositor	Page	First Word	Compositor
B3	Lie	A	B3v	Ly	A
E2	*Keeper*	A	E2v	*Keep.*	A
G1v	Against	A	G2	Against.	A
G4	*Arcite.*	B	G4v	*Arc.*	A
H3v	Beside	B	H4	Beside,	B
K2v	*Iaylor.*	B	K3	Iay.	A
K3	Regiment,	A	K3v	Regiment;	B
M1v	*Cornets,*	A	M2	*Cornets.*	A

roman type (in contrast to the italic customarily used for directions in the body of the text). Those in the margins are of two different kinds, the first is "advisory" while the second calls for sound and action. The first sort—the "advisory" or warning notes to have properties and/or actors ready for entrance many lines later—are found only in pages set by Compositor A: "2. Hearses rea- ¦ dy with Pala- ¦ mon: and Arci- ¦ te: the 3. ¦ Queenes. ¦ Theseus: and ¦ his Lordes ¦ ready" (C3v, all required about forty lines later); "3. Hearses rea- ¦ dy" (C4, properties needed about twenty lines further); "Chaire and ¦ stooles out" (G2v, in readiness for those playing Theseus and his company to use them about thirty lines later).[15] None of the stage directions that Compositor B put in the margins is of this sort; all of his signal immediate action or sound effects: "Florish" (A1v, set in ordinary roman type at the beginning of the Prologue); "This short flo- ¦ rish of Cor- ¦ nets and ¦ Showtes with- ¦ in" (E4v, opposite the opening stage direction to II.v); "Cornets in ¦ sundry places. ¦ Noise and ¦ hallowing as ¦ people a May- ¦ ing" (F2, opposite the act division between 2 and 3); "Knocke for ¦ Schoole. Enter ¦ The Dance" (G3v); "They bow se- ¦ verall wayes: ¦ then advance ¦ and stand" (H1v, opposite a line of dialogue containing an asterisk that, presumably, marks the point at which the direction should be read).

The last of these may be authorial, for in Beaumont and Fletcher's *The Captain* printed in the Folio of 1647, there are again asterisks in the text to indicate the positions of marginal stage directions; directions in *The Captain* that are so marked seem to originate with the author(s), but perhaps with Beaumont, rather than with Fletcher.[16] All critics agree, however, that with the possible exception of the last direction quoted, all those printed in the margins of Q1 derive from the theater, not the author(s); we know that in the playhouses stage

15. The only other stage direction set in the margin by Compositor A is "*Sing.*" (G1v); twice the same compositor set "*Singes.*" as a conventional stage direction (I3, I3v), rather than in the margin. Commentators have not associated this anomaly on page G1v with the other directions set in the margins, probably because it alone is in italic. They are likely right in making this distinction because on G1v there was no room for a stage direction in the conventional position on the first line of the song, so there is no need then for us to resort to copy for an explanation of the placement of this direction.

16. Waller, "Printer's Copy," 64 n. 6.

directions were sometimes rewritten in the margins of manuscripts for greater visibility to whichever member of the company held book during a performance. Noticing the colons used to separate the names of roles in the first of those printed in the margin on Compositor A's pages and observing the similar use of colons in the extant transcript of *The Honest Man's Fortune* in the hand of Edward Knight, book-keeper for the King's Men from circa 1628, Waller followed Greg in maintaining that Knight may have inscribed in the margins of the manuscript printer's copy for the quarto the directions now found in the quarto's margins.[17] Further evidence of a book-keeper's hand is found in the appearance of the names of two actors in other stage directions printed in italic in the body of the text: "*Enter Messengers. Curtis*" (I4v); "*Enter Theseus, Hipolita Emilia Perithous: and some Attendants T. Tucke: Curtis*" (L4v). Waller also claimed to detect Knight's style in what he regarded as an addition to the beginning of one more direction: "*A Battaile strooke withim* [*sic*]: *Then a Retrait: Florish. Then Enter Theseus (victor) the three Queenes meete him, and fall on their faces before him*" (C4). According to Waller, the author's direction began with the word *Enter,* which the author capitalized, as did the compositor, who was following copy.

In the belief that printer's copy for the quarto may have been, at least in part, a holograph, Waller was reluctant to grant theatrical provenance to any other stage directions, but there are at least three reasons to associate considerably more with the theatrical annotator or scribe. By Waller's own criterion, syntactically disjunct elements punctuated by colons in any stage direction may be theatrical additions. These may then include any or all of the following:

stage direction	possible addition
E4v *Enter Theseus, Hipolita Pirithous Emilia*	:*Arcite with a Garland, &c.*
G3 *Enter Thes. Pir. Hip. Emil. Arcite*	:*and traine.*
L4v *Enter Theseus, Hipolita, Emilia, Perithous*	:*and some Attendants: T. Tucke: Curtis.*
M2v *Enter Palamon and his Knightes pyniond*	:*Iaylor, Executioner &c. Gard.*

Three of these four suspected additions address a single problem, the possible failure to provide for attendants to the royal Theseus upon his entrance. That such provision was a concern for the book-keeper, if such he was, who inscribed the stage directions that now appear in the quarto's margins can be gauged by comparing his advisory direction on page C3v (quoted above) for the upcoming fourth scene of the first act with the opening stage direction for that scene in the body of the text. The first indicates that "Theseus: and his Lordes"

17. Ibid., 64–65; W. W. Greg, *The Shakespeare First Folio* (Oxford: Clarendon, 1955), 98.

are to be ready; the relevant part of the second calls only for the entrance of "*Theseus (victor)*" (C4). The colons used to punctuate two calls for sound and action, proper subjects for a book-keeper, may also raise suspicion that these are his: "*Hornes within: they stand*" (H2); "*Showt, and Cornets: Crying a Palamon*" (M1v). Since these, like the suspected additions charted above, are divided between the pages of the two hypothetical compositors, the colons do not represent an individual typesetter's preference.

The peculiar stage directions printed in small roman in the margins that so strongly suggest a book-keeper's hand are also, as has been noted, divided between the compositors, but each compositor set a different kind. It becomes possible then to hazard the following narrative about the treatment of such stage directions in Cotes's printing house. The only directions that Compositor A kept in the margins were advance warnings, which could not logically be included in the text opposite which they occurred because, even to the dullest of typesetters, it would be obvious that there was no relation between text and direction. Yet we cannot infer that Compositor A set in the margins of the printed text all the directions that he may have found in the margins of his copy. Indeed we can readily see that his pages contain within the body of the text exactly the same kinds of directions that Compositor B set in the margins. Compare Compositor A's "*Winde hornes of Cornets*" (F3v, apparently an inexpert conflation of author's and book-keeper's directions) or "*Cornets. a great cry and noice within crying a Palamon*" (M1v), neither set in the margin, with Compositor B's "*This short florish of Cornets and Showtes within*" (E4v), set in the margin. Almost all the sound calls set by Compositor A are either too early or, occasionally, too late; perhaps, I am suggesting, these were written in the margins, where Compositor B set some of his, and Compositor A erred in his placement of them when he moved them into the text.

All the directions that Compositor B set in the margins occur among the first fourteen pages that he set; there are none in his last twenty-five. Yet twice in the latter half of his work there are grossly misplaced sound cues. On his page K3v, he ended a scene with the Jailer, the Doctor, and the Wooer with "*Florish. Exeunt,*" then set "*Actus Quintus,*" between rules, followed by the entrance of Theseus and his company. Obviously the "*Florish*" was to announce the entrance of Theseus, not the exit of the subplot characters, but Compositor B may well have misplaced the direction as a consequence of its placement in the margin of his copy, probably the same place the sound call introducing the third act was also inscribed because Compositor B put that one in the margin of the quarto. On page L4 Compositor B replicated the mistake by setting the "*Florish*" introducing 5.3 before the exit for 5.2. It would seem, then, that Compositor B, although initially faithful to his copy in the placement of directions, grew impatient with the aggravation of using the margins and began to follow Compositor A's practice of moving stage directions into the body of the text. If so, we must suspect that there may have been many more book-keeper's directions in the margins of printer's copy than there are in the margins of the quarto itself. Possibly printer's copy was not simply annotated in the theater but transcribed there.

The two errors in the quarto's numbering of scenes, when examined in relation to compositor attributions, offer further indications that printer's copy may have been a theatrical transcript. The first of these errors is the easier to dismiss. Scenes 4 and 5 of act 2 are both numbered "Scaena 4," although the scenes open on consecutive pages (E4, E4v); a compositor would be dull indeed if he made this error. But the error can be explained by the hypothesis presented here that two different men each set one of the pages. The duplication in numbering is probably then the responsibility of Compositor B, who set page E4v, especially since he numbered the next scene correctly ("Scaena 6") on F1v. Very different circumstances govern the second error, the numbering of three successive scenes in act 3 as "4" (G1v), "6" (G2), and "7" (G4). Compositor A set the first two of these scene openings, and so one might simply accuse him of possibly misreading "v" as "vi" on G2, but this explanation is apparently ruled out by Compositor B's numbering the last of the three scenes "7," not "6." Unless we believe two workmen colluded in error, we must assume that both were following their copy. Perhaps then a scene (3.5) had been cut from it—not all that unlikely in a theatrical manuscript.

The compositors may well have been responsible for the duplication of Emilia's entrance on pages I4 and I4v. Her first entrance (on I4) was set by Compositor A; when Compositor B took over printer's copy to compose I4v, he first set the last ten lines of Emilia's soliloquy, probably with no idea who the speaker was. Then he came to an exchange between Emilia and a Gentleman, which may have been headed in his copy by the entrance only of the latter. Confronted immediately thereafter by a speech by Emilia, the compositor *may* have added her name to the existing direction.

But the compositor(s) have also been charged with inconsistencies of which they may sometimes have been innocent. Richard Proudfoot, in preparing his Regents Renaissance Drama edition of *The Two Noble Kinsmen*, usefully identified a linguistic feature that seems to put beyond reasonable doubt the case for collaboration on the authorship of the play that earlier investigators made largely on the basis of parallel passages in the works of Fletcher and Shakespeare (of course, Proudfoot did not close the argument about the identity of the collaborators). As noted before, he observed that the name *Pirithous* is not only spelled differently between the scenes usually assigned to Shakespeare and those given to Fletcher but also pronounced differently. The discovery indicates the presence of two individual dramatic poets, each forming verse according to his own ear. Because the variant spellings of the name do not exactly coincide with the usual division of authorship, Proudfoot charged the compositor(s) with the discrepancies in the pattern charted in Table 4.[18]

18. "Speech Prefixes, Compositors and Copy: Illustrated from the SPs in Plays from the Shakespeare *Apocrypha*" (Shakespeare Association of America Seminar Paper, Montreal, March 1986), xix, 1.

Table 4. Pyrithous / Pirithous / Perithous

Act, scene	Author	Spellings	Compositor
1.1	Shakespeare	Pyrithous (2) Pirithous	A
1.3	Shakespeare	Pirithous (2) Pir. (4) Pirothous	A
2.2	Fletcher	Pirithous	A
2.5	Fletcher	Pirithous Pirith. Per. (4) Perith. Perithous	B
3.5	Fletcher	Pir. Per. (4)	B
3.6	Fletcher	Perithous Per. (7)	B
4.1	Fletcher	Perithous	A
4.2		Perithous Per. (9)	B
5.1	Fletcher	Perithous Per. (2)	B
5.3	Shakespeare	Perithous (2) Per. Pir.	A
5.4	Shakespeare	Pirithous Pir.	B

Proudfoot concludes that Shakespeare's manuscript spelling had a medial -i- or -y- and Fletcher's a medial -e-, and it is hard to gainsay him, for the -i- and -y- spellings predominate 13 to 3 in the Shakespeare scenes and the -e- 32 to 4 in Fletcher's part. Both compositors set both spellings, and so the variation does not originate with them. But how are we to explain the three anomalous -e- spellings in Shakespeare's portion and the four anomalous -i- spellings in Fletcher's? Compositor A may well be responsible for the first -i- in Fletcher's 2.1, for the -i- spelling was the one Compositor A had already set ten times, and so he is likely to have used it again, regardless of what was in his copy. No such explanation is available, however, for the three -i- spellings set by Compositor B in Fletcher's scenes. In 2.5, this compositor was seeing the word for the first time and would probably then have followed his copy. Nor is it at all easy to explain why Compositor B would suddenly revert to the -i- spelling in 3.5 after he had set -e- a half dozen times or why Compositor A would set the -e- spelling in Shakespeare's 5.3 when he had seen it only once before (in his copy for Fletcher's 4.1)—unless both compositors were following copy. If Proudfoot's reasonable conclusion about Shakespeare's preference for *Pirithous* and Fletcher's for *Perithous* is to be preserved, it must include the corollary of a scribal transcript that intervened between authorial manuscript and printed text and in which the pattern of authorial preferences was overlaid with a scribe's halfhearted attempts to regularize his copy. (The possibility remains, of course, that the conventional division of authorship is in error: perhaps, for example, Shakespeare wrote the part of 3.5 in which the spelling *Pir.* occurs, even though this spelling is immediately followed by two *Per.* spellings in the next five lines. But such inferences become more and more dangerous as the evidence accumulates that the printed text stands at two or more removes from the author's papers; one would be reluctant to rely on isolated spelling anomalies as indications of the division of authorship. Perhaps, however, the anomalous *Pir.* spelling in 3.5 is Compositor A's, rather than B's, since there are some indications, already observed, that Compositor A may have had a hand in this page—the limits of a compositor's share in a single page are often indeterminable.)

A more significant problem for editors is line-division in the quarto of *The Two Noble Kinsmen*. Most comments have focused on the mislining of two entire scenes as verse when the most cursory examination shows that they are prose (2.1, 4.3) and on the reduction to prose of the verse speech that begins 3.5 (lines 1-21 in the Riverside edition), yet there are numerous isolated cases of mislineation and particular concentrations of the problem in 2.3, 3.3, and 3.5. A good deal of what troubles modern editors may not have bothered the authors of the play, from whose own manuscripts some of the mislineation may derive. Another set of difficulties probably arises from the compositors. Even after both these categories are identified, however, a considerable amount of residual mislineation remains.[19]

One feature of authorial dramatic manuscripts is the running together of a half-line of verse with the full line that precedes or follows it. The best-known examples are evident in the Hand-D pages of *The Booke of Sir Thomas More* usually assigned to Shakespeare, but the habit is by no means uniquely Shakespearean.[20] Since the printed page can accommodate far fewer words on a single line than the manuscript page, compositors are often forced to redivide

19. In this discussion of mislineation in the Quarto, I attend only to the alleged cases that are emended by all four of the most recent editors of *The Two Noble Kinsmen*: Proudfoot; Clifford Leech, in *The Signet Classic Shakespeare* (Toronto: New American Library, 1966); G. Blakemore Evans, in *The Riverside Shakespeare* (Boston: Houghton Mifflin, 1974); N. W. Bawcutt, in *The New Penguin Shakespeare* (Harmondsworth: Penguin, 1977).

20. Transcribed in *The Riverside Shakespeare*, 1686-94.

the verses according to their own lights or run the verse on as prose. Repeatedly such errors turn up in Q1, as, for example, I4v; 4.2.64–65:

> *Theseus.* Bring 'em in quickly,
> By any meanes, I long to see 'em.

Editors now divide the lines at "in | quickly." Scattered throughout the Quarto—between the scenes usually assigned to Shakespeare and those awarded to Fletcher, between the stints of Compositors A and B—there are about two dozen cases of such erroneous verse divisions.[21]

Some kinds of error are unique to the pages of just one of the two compositors and therefore, perhaps, are the responsibility of the individual compositor. Compositor B alone divided certain single lines of verse into two. He split one line between pages L2 and L2v (5.2.11) and cut in two another on M3 (5.4.36)—he did not have room for the whole of this second line after he had set the unabbreviated speech prefix "*Iailor.*" We need not look beyond the compositor for the origin of these errors. Peculiar to the pages of the other compositor, Compositor A, is the apparently needless mislineation of Theseus's speech at 1.1.149–50 (B3v in Q1):

> It is true. [*sic*] and I will give you comfort,
> To give your dead Lords graves:
> The which to doe, must make some worke with *Creon;*

The most probable solution to this error is the one offered by Evans in the Riverside, in which the last two lines are divided at doe, | must. The compositor, it seems, ended the line when he got to the end of the clause, not of the verse. Compositor A may again have needlessly shifted words from one line to the next on page F4, but not at the end of a clause this time (3.1.121–22). Both compositors sometimes mislined verse in order to accommodate stage directions, Compositor A on pages G1v–2 (3.4.25–26), Compositor B on G3 and G4 (3.5.93–94, 157–59), on both of which the stage directions in question are misplaced.

Even after these possibly compositorial errors are discounted, a number of occasions remain in the stints of both compositors on which either verse is set as prose or prose as verse. Most of the verse set as prose occurs in Compositor A's pages: E3, 2.3.42–49, 51–54; G2, 3.5.1–21. Particularly in 2.3, but occasionally elsewhere as well, Compositor A has run together lines of verse as if they were prose but kept the convention of capitalizing the first words of his lines, as for example:

21. Possible authorial mislineation: 1.1.95–96; 1.1.96–97; 2.3.33–34, 36–37; 3.3.18–19, 19–20, 20–21, 21–22, 22–23, 23–24, 24–25, 26–27, 35–36, 41–42, 45–46, 46–47; 3.5.83–84, 84–85, 86–87; 3.6.201–2, 255–56; 4.1.34–35, 42–43;, 4.2.64–65; 5.2.27–28 (line numbers here and elsewhere are cited from *The Riverside Shakespeare*). It is disturbingly inexplicable for me, however, that so many of these errors are concentrated on so few pages.

Weele see the sports, then every man to's Tackle: and
Sweete Companions lets rehearse by any meanes, before
The Ladies see us, and doe sweetly, and God knows what
May come on't.

(E4, 2.3.55-58)[22]

It would be tempting to suppose that the compositor on these occasions simply kept adding words into his stick until he had filled it, before he became aware that he had gone beyond the end of the verse line; having found out his error only after he had justified the line, he chose simply to persist in it. Yet a similar error also occurs on one of Compositor B's pages, even though B was far less prone than A to set verse as prose, doing so only once (G3, 3.5.72-75). Compositor B also ran verses on until his stick could hold no more when he set the Wooer's speech on L2 (5.2.3-6) and, like Compositor A in the example quoted above, B too set a capital at the beginning of each line. Since such errors are common to the pages of both typesetters, they probably originate in printer's copy. A scribe intervening between the authors and the typesetters is the more likely source of these errors.

The most remarkable instance of a shared error in line division occurs with 4.3, a verse scene set almost entirely in prose. The scene occupies four pages (K2-3v), three of them set by Compositor B (K2, 2v, 3v), the fourth set by Compositor A. There is scarcely room to doubt that this error derives not from the compositors misconstruing their copy but from scribal copy itself.

III

When Cyrus Hoy attacked the problem of assigning to the collaborative authors of *The Two Noble Kinsmen*, Shakespeare and Fletcher according to the title page, their shares of the play, he encountered two major problems.[23] First, he found it difficult to establish purely linguistic grounds as a basis for determining Shakespearean authorship of any play; second, he had to account for the relative infrequency in *The Two Noble Kinsmen* of Fletcher's linguistic preferences—particularly the pronoun *ye*. Hoy's study established a significant match between the frequency of such elided forms as *y'*, *'em*, *i'th'*, and *o'th'* in the scenes usually awarded Shakespeare in *The Two Noble Kinsmen* and their frequency in a number of other plays of undisputed and, presumably, unaided Shakespearean authorship. These latter consisted of *The Tempest, The Winter's Tale, Timon of Athens* (perhaps not of Shakespeare's unaided authorship), *Coriolanus, Antony and Cleopatra, All's Well That Ends Well,* and *Cymbeline.* Even as long ago as the early 1960s, when Hoy wrote, the first two of these

---

22. The other cases occur at 2.3.38-39, 40-41, 55-59; 4.1.147-49.
23. "The Shares of Fletcher and His Collaborators in the Beaumont and Fletcher Canon (VII)," *Studies in Bibliography* 15 (1962): 71-90. For simplicity's sake, I have often referred to the shares of authorship in the play as matters of fact rather than conjecture. However, I do believe that they are only conjectural.

plays were widely regarded as having been set into type from transcripts by Ralph Crane; only the last five were thought to have been printed from their author's manuscripts, although Greg allowed that printer's copy for *Cymbeline* might have been a transcript.[24] Now the possibility has been raised that *Timon, Coriolanus, Antony,* and *All's Well That Ends Well* may all have been printed from scribal copies.[25] What Hoy may have established then is a correlation between the allegedly Shakespearean portions of *The Two Noble Kinsmen* and scribal transcripts of Shakespeare's other plays.

When Hoy failed to find nearly as many *yes* in the allegedly Fletcherian parts of *The Two Noble Kinsmen,* he was forced to account for the deficiency by arguing that, like *Bonduca, The Two Noble Kinsmen* had been transcribed and that this transcript had served as printer's copy. In arguing for Shakespeare's sole authorship of *The Two Noble Kinsmen,* Bertram pointed to the tight circularity of Hoy's reasoning: the paucity of *yes* indicates a transcript behind the quarto; the use of a transcript as printer's copy explains the paucity of *yes*.[26] This essay supports Hoy's conclusion and attempts to break the circle of his reasoning by showing that there are various grounds—stage directions, spellings of a proper name, mislineation—that point independently to a scribe's hand in the transmission of the text of *The Two Noble Kinsmen.*

This essay makes no claim, however, to being an exhaustive bibliographical study of the quarto's printing. It is merely a tentative excursus that leaves much undone. Since *The Two Noble Kinsmen* has lingered on the fringes of the Shakespeare canon, its printing and printer have received little attention compared to that lavished on Jaggard of the Shakespeare First Folio, or Creede, Simmes, and Okes of the early Shakespeare quartos. One would have considerably more confidence in the conclusions drawn in this essay if there were available a study of Cotes's printing house in the 1630s or even a distinctive-type analysis of the *The Two Noble Kinsmen* quarto alone or of any other Cotes quarto. These remain necessary tasks.[27]

---

24. Greg, *First Folio,* 427.

25. For evidence that *Timon, Antony,* and *Coriolanus* may have been set from transcripts, see my "Line Division in Shakespeare's Dramatic Verse: An Editorial Problem," *Analytical and Enumerative Bibliography* 8 (1984): 73–128; for evidence that *All's Well That Ends Well* also was, see T. H. Howard-Hill, *Ralph Crane and Some Shakespeare First Folio Comedies* (Charlottesville: University Press of Virginia, 1972), 183 n. 88.

26. Hoy, "Shares of Fletcher," 74–83.

27. While this essay was in manuscript, three editions of *The Two Noble Kinsmen* were in progress. I am grateful to the editors of these, Fredson Bowers, William L. Montgomery, and Eugene Waith, for their consideration of my essay in the introductions to their editions. I am grateful to Bowers for allowing me to see the relevant part of his introduction in manuscript and to Montgomery for sending me the proofs of his piece in *The Textual Companion* as soon as they became available. Bowers and I share the view that *The Two Noble Kinsmen* was probably printed from a scribal transcript. Montgomery believes that the manuscript was a heavily annotated and somewhat revised holograph; Montgomery and I failed, in our exchange of views, to convince each other.

Table 5. Alleged Collaborators and Compositors

Act, scene	Pages	Alleged author	Alleged Compositors
1.1–2.1	B1–D2.9	Shakespeare	Compositor A: B1v–C1, C2–D2
2.2–6	D2.10–F2.17	Fletcher	Compositor A: D2–E4
			Compositor B: E4v–F2
3.1–2	F2.18–F4v.14	Shakespeare	Compositor A: F3v–4v
			Compositor B: F2–3
3.3–5.1.33	F4v.15–K4.16	Fletcher	Compositor A: F4v–G2v, G4v,
			I1–4, K3
			Compositor B: G3–4, H1–4v,I
			K1–2v, K3v–4
5.1.34–173	K4.17–L2.23	Shakespeare	Compositor B
5.2	L2.24–L4	Fletcher	Compositor B
5.3–4	L4v–M4v	Shakespeare	Compositor A: L4v–M2v
			Compositor B: M3–4v

Epilogue

Only after completing this study did I have an opportunity to consult F. O. Waller's "A Critical, Old-spelling Edition of *The Two Noble Kinsmen*."[28] His compositor attributions, based on the spacing of medial commas and colons, and some spellings, are almost exactly the same as mine, but not quite. We differ on the assignment of four pages: B1 (the first page of the play itself), N1 (the Epilogue), and two pages we both had difficulty assigning, C2 and L4. The coincidence is the more remarkable because of the very different ways in which we compiled evidence. In tabulating spaced and nonspaced commas, I excluded all those in lines stretching the full width of a page, on the now widely accepted assumption that the spacing of these commas may have been influenced by difficulties in justification of such lines. Waller employed much more subjective criteria in allowing for justification: "In all cases the count excludes punctuation at the ends of lines as well as instances where the spacing seems to have been affected by the compositor's justification of the line"; "I have excluded from my count all instances where I thought the spacings (or lack of them) represented an accommodation to the line length."[29] As a consequence our counts of spaced and nonspaced commas agree for only seventeen pages. Waller also used morphologically related groups of spellings—different words containing the same sequences of letters or the same final letter, for example, *receive, perceive, deceive* or *trie* and *crie*. This practice was criticized by T. H. Howard-Hill, who demonstrated, with reference to the scribe Ralph Crane's spelling habit, that the same individual could and did spell morphologically related words in different ways—for example, *many* but *bewtie*.[30] Waller paid

28. Ph.D. diss., University of Chicago, 1957.
29. Waller, "Critical, Old-Spelling Edition," 68, 69.
30. "Spelling and the Bibliographer," *The Library* 5th ser., vol. 18 (1963): 1–28.

no attention to some of the evidence considered here, such as the spacing of marginal stage directions or of medial periods.

Waller was also concerned, as Bertram was in criticizing Waller's results, to minimize the number of changeovers between the compositors. This would seem to be his chief reason for assigning page B1 to Compositor A, who, we both agree, set the rest of sheet B. The two spellings that Waller charted on B1—*odour* and *smel-lesse*—if they have any validity as evidence at all, point to Compositor B, who preferred *-our* endings to *-or* endings in the ratio of 3/2, and *-esse* to *-es* in the ratio of 9.7 / .3. Compositor A's preference for *-our* to *-or* was stronger than B's (9 / 1), but Compositor A, according to Waller, preferred *-es* to *-esse* by 4 to 1. Granting less significance to minimizing changeovers, I give page B1 to Compositor B. In the introduction to the forthcoming edition of *The Two Noble Kinsmen* in the Cambridge University Press Dramatic Works in the Beaumont and Fletcher Canons, Fredson Bowers, who read this essay in manuscript, points out that the inset marginal stage direction on page B1 ("*Musike*") is characteristic, according to my findings, of Compositor A, to whom Bowers assigns the page. I must acknowledge then that, like Waller's evidence, my evidence for the attribution of B1 is divided against itself: the nonspaced medial commas suggest Compositor B, the inset marginal stage direction Compositor A.

Spelling evidence, like spacing evidence, is also divided for page C2. Waller finds two *-y* endings (I find three: *quality, mercy, Fury*) and two *-our* terminations—*terrour* and *dishonour*—all somewhat more characteristic of Compositor A than B, since A had an almost exclusive preference for *-y* (98.2 percent) while Compositor B's was weaker (64 percent). Yet C2 also contains two *-esse* endings, Compositor B's preferred form, if "forms" of spelling can be relied on at all. Waller felt that if Compositor B had set page C1v, as the evidence indicates, then he also would have set a second page of the inner forme of sheet C and so gave Compositor B page C2. I prefer Compositor A as a candidate for C2 on the basis of the spacing of colons and semicolons, but the page must remain in doubt.

The same is true of page L4, on which there is practically no evidence. There are five *-y* endings on this page (one in a long line), suggestive of Compositor A to Waller, and two *ile* spellings. I find little to choose between the two compositors in their spellings of *ile* or *Ile,* and neither did Waller. Compositor A is completely indifferent to the capital, about half his spellings employing it, half not; Compositor B has only the slightest preference for the capital (64 percent). I give Compositor B this page, again on the basis of spacing of punctuation, and again with considerable reservations.

On page N1, Waller found no spelling evidence. I give this page to Compositor A, in spite of the number of spaced colons and semicolons, because there are more of these in the pages set later in the quarto by A than in his earlier pages. I have more confidence in assigning page N1 than B1, C2, or L4, but I insist on none of these attributions; nor did Waller. In spite of this small handful of problems, I share with William L. Montgomery the impression that "a consensus appears to be emerging" about the compositors of *The Two Noble Kinsmen*.[31]

31. Montgomery is author of the chapter on *The Two Noble Kinsmen* in the forthcoming *Textual*

2 Collaborating with Shakespeare
After the Final Play

Charles H. Frey

Collaborate has two main meanings for us: (1) to work with another on a project to be jointly accredited; and (2) to cooperate with the enemy. If Shakespeare collaborated in the writing of *The Two Noble Kinsmen* (as the title page of the Quarto tells us he did), then to what degree should the project be "jointly accredited"? "Hardly at all" has been the main modern response to this question, for most of the scholarly energy, if not total human energy, devoted to this play has been concerned with separating out the respective contributions of the collaborators. This very effort *not* to "jointly accredit" suggests that the coauthors are in some crucial way dissimilar. The presumed collaborator of Shakespeare's is often described as a wretched contriver of vastly inferior verse and drama. As a typical commentator in the nineteenth century put it: "In *The Two Noble Kinsmen,* the degradation of Shakspere's work by the unclean underplot of Fletcher is painful, and almost intolerable."[1] Such description renders Fletcher tantamount to Shakespeare's enemy. Shakespeare, at least, is often treated as if he risked severely tainting his own labor by joining it to another's.

It is amusing that the precise seams between Shakespeare's work and that of his presumed collaborator are often unrecognizable in the sense that, after more than a century of effort, scholars still cannot agree as to which author or authors wrote which parts of *The Two Noble Kinsmen.* Some say Shakespeare wrote all of it; some say he wrote none of it; many divide the play between Shakespeare and Fletcher, but few agree as to the precise division. And whether the two presumed authors would have kept their fingers or suggestions out of each other's scenes may be doubted. Still, the conviction that any collaboration by Shakespeare must in part bear the opprobrious taint of collaborating with the enemy, or at least with an undesirable, remains widespread.

But if we think of Shakespeare as collaborating only to his and our detriment, because we think that whoever he collaborated with necessarily compromised the purity of his unique genius, then do we also assume by probable implication that other persons in Shakespeare's working environment—actors in his company who limited his conception and, possibly, persuaded revision of parts; audiences whose comprehension and taste limited Shakespeare's otherwise infinite range; colleagues or source authors or court authorities whose ideas were

---

1. Edward Dowden, *Shakspere: A Critical Study of His Mind and Art* (New York: Harper, 1881), 360.

cruder than the Bard's yet still influenced him—do we assume that such persons were also alien to or restrictive upon Shakespeare's otherwise unhampered expression of genius? Was Shakespeare, a free spirit capable of moving beyond the collaborations of tradition and ideology, forced nonetheless or even quite willing perhaps to collaborate with the enemy of limitation by coauthority? Or might such colabor, on the contrary, often have rendered "Shakespeare's" contribution less page-bound, more active, accessible, and public? less high-and-mighty in diction and skepticism, more body-voiced, and more emotionally real and grounded than possible from a silent authorial text? Any playwright of other than closet drama *chooses* to be a collaborator (even a closet dramatist collaborates with the audience he imagines), and if Shakespeare chose to collaborate not only with scribes, copyists, actors, other share-owners, varied audience cliques, and so on, but also with a specific or several specific coauthors, who are we to single out the coauthor or authors for special opprobrium and for separatist treatment? Do we know no other ways to give power, coherence, allegiance, credit to a work product than to trace it to an individuating source?

In the case of other kinds of work products, surely, we do jointly credit our labor. Indeed, probably most human labor is jointly credited in significant ways. We look at a road, a car, a building, at most of the things we use, and we jointly credit their makers. We look at each other or at ourselves and jointly credit pairs of parents for our being. Only in certain, specialized classes of labor can we retain any, if often a false, sense of authorship. The word *collaborate* derives from the Latin verb *laborare,* to labor, and this word seems to connect not only with ancient imagery of grasping but also with a whole host of loosely related terms derived from an "l-e-b" stem, terms that suggest a rhythm of grasping and letting go, terms like *lap, lip, labial, lapse, lobe, slump, slab, slip,* and *sleep. Labor* in many associations seems to connect to actions influenced by gravity or other forces beyond personal control or will—as in the labor of love and labor of birth where the sense of individually willed effort fuses with the mandates of extrapersonal forces. Birth labor is straining work and at the same time a gift of nature whereby one mother is made two (or more) persons and two parents are made three (or more) persons. Still, despite the colabors of love and birth and their joint accreditings, we beholders of birth take up attribution study the moment the child issues. We say the new child, or work of art, has one parent's eyes, or another's nose, or voice. By analogy, then, a collaborative literary work may be considered, in our culture, connected in each part to a single authorial parent.

The Prologue to *The Two Noble Kinsmen* works with several images of colabor, including that of the play itself as child of various breeders. Before such an image is reached, however, the play is compared not to the child but to, of all things, the maidenhead of the child's mother:

New plays and maidenheads are near akin—
Much follow'd both, for both much money gi'n,
If they stand sound and well . . . .
                    (Pro. 1–3)

The potential mother's maidenhead—both her virginity and, more literally, her hymen—is valuable if it stands sound and well, if under the stress of "first night's stir" (Pro. 6) it really stands up to the push of breeding and thus constitutes proof of virginity, because then any child that results from the "stir" should have a known paternity. That is, new plays are like hymens in a patriarchy: men may be assumed to value them when they give proof of authorship. The very first lines of the play, then, raise a question of collaboration: how can one know whether the issue held forth by paired collaborators really is the product of each? This question could, of course, apply to declared coauthors of a play, such as Shakespeare and Fletcher, but here it applies in the first instance to a different pair of collaborators: the "new play" itself as wife and the audience as husband who seeks proof of authenticity in the play.

Now, "much money" is given, I assume, not to the play itself or, in terms of the metaphor, to the virginal wife, but rather to the one(s) who present and guarantee the play or maid to the husband. And that underlying or covert assumption naturally directs attention, in the patriarchal economy of the metaphor, to the status of the "breeder" (Pro. 10) of the play/maid. Would the breeder(s) be likely to have produced honest, modest, chaste offspring? What is the status of the breeder?

As if this last question had been raised explicitly, the Prologue immediately identifies not the playwright(s) but an ancestor, Chaucer, as the pure and noble "breeder" (Pro. 10) of the play that now is both "like her" (the virgin) and also "our play." As the new play evolves, in the Prologue from "maidenhead" to "her" to "our play" with Chaucer as its breeder, the implicit image widens from the audience as husband giving "much money" for the new, virginal play toward Chaucer as breeding "it" (Pro. 10) and then to Chaucer as giving not the play but rather the "story" that itself lives, like a chaste wife, "constant to eternity" (Pro. 14). Just where the playwright(s) may fit into this procreative tangle remains mysterious, however, for, insofar as the playwright(s) may be identified with the father who takes "much money" for being able to provide a virgin daughter, the playwright(s) may seem quite the patriarchs, but, insofar as the playwright(s) may be identified with the play itself, "our play," or with the "story" as "constant to all eternity," then to that extent the playwright(s) would seem feminized to the special maternal source and sole knower(s) of legitimacy. As the Prologue proceeds, this feminized role for the playwright(s) seems to be the one that is developed:

If we let fall the nobleness of this,
And the first sound this child hear be a hiss,
How it will shake the bones of that good man . . . .
                    (Pro. 15-17)

Now the play is a "child" whom the "writer" (Pro. 19) or writers must protect from bastardizing hisses by refusing to "let fall" the nobleness of "this" (breeder? story? child? retelling?). It sounds as if the writer(s) may control the

nobleness of the play in some way analogous to the way in which the maid
controls the "honor" of the first night.

An alternative reading of the Prologue could place the writer(s) of this new
play as male(s) sub-breeding the play from the "constant" female story sired by
Chaucer. This seems the direction taken by the continuing Prologue:

> For, to say truth, it were an endless thing
> And too ambitious, to aspire to him,
> Weak as we are, and almost breathless swim
> In this deep water.
>
> (Pro. 22–25)

This sounds like male emulation of a progenitor. The focus has shifted from
inquiring whether the new play, as maiden, catches up the nobility and purity of
her ancestor, Chaucer, to inquiring whether "we"—writer(s) and, perhaps,
actors—may gain some strength to compete with Chaucer.

Such strength is to be gained here not from coauthorial collaboration but
rather from collaboration with the audience. Whereas at first the audience was
invited to judge the quality of the play by the purity and nobility of its
authorship, now the audience is invited to participate in providing "breath" or
inspiration:

> Do but you hold out
> Your helping hands, and we shall tack about
> And something do to save us . . . .
>
> (Pro. 25–27)

One could summarize the argument of the Prologue thus: "You in the
audience would like to know for certain the paternity of a new play such as
ours, wouldn't you? Well, it does have a particularly famous and noble ancestor,
and it would be a shame if his nobility were somehow compromised in our
retelling. But, really, we can't emulate him exactly, so you'd better decide you
will help by applauding and appreciating what you get here. Let Chaucer sleep,
and you be content."

I am arguing, obviously, that the Prologue to *The Two Noble Kinsmen* anticipates, indirectly, the major critical debate on the play, namely, the debate over
the nobility of its authorship. While later generations of readers have pondered
the relative merits of two possible coauthors, the Prologue sets up a rivalry
between two generational levels of authorship—Jacobean and medieval—and
then submerges that rivalry through an extended plea for a supervening collaboration, that between the immediate producers of the play and the watching
throng. This argument, that the basic strategy of the Prologue is to deflect
attention and inquiry from one pair of collaborators to other pairs (and specifically from authorial collaboration to responsive collaboration), informs the
more extended argument of my essay: that a dominant internal strategy of the

play is to deflect our attention from the "right" collaborative couple to a "wrong" one and that a potentially useful external strategy for our treating the play is to deflect attention from the "right" collaborative couple, the presumed coauthors and their relative merits, to the "wrong" collaborative pair, modern productions of the play (including texts, performances, teachings, and criticism) and their varied audiences.

The play opens with the wedding celebration of Theseus and Hippolyta, whom Theseus has conquered and who now collaborates with her former enemy. The first character we actually see is Hymen, god of marriage but also god of the "maidenhead" proposed first for examination by the Prologue. At issue, then, is issue: whether the "firstborn child" (1.1.7) and "Nature's children sweet" (1.1.13) will bless the royal couple and be free from "the sland'rous cuckoo" (1.1.19).

Somewhat as inquiry into the relations of the new play and its "husband" shifted to inquiry into the status of a third party, the bride's breeder, so now attention on ritually banishing any taint from the royal coupling shifts to Theseus's "gentility" (1.1.25), to Hippolyta's "mother's sake" and Hippolyta's wish that her "womb may thrive with fair ones" (1.1.27), and on to a third focus (or couple), Emilia and "the love of him whom Jove hath mark'd / The honor of your bed, and for the sake / Of clear virginity" (1.1.29–31). In equational terms, the Prologue's "husband" is to Theseus as the new play is to Hippolyta, and as attention is deflected in the Prologue from the maidlike new play to its noble breeder and then onward from purity of authorial collaboration to collaboration of a third party (the audience), so here in the opening scene attention is deflected from Hippolyta to her "mother's sake" and then onward from the royal progenitive pair to a distinctly "third" relation, the bride's *sister* and her as yet unknown husband, a relation that turns out to be the true focus of interest.

As, in the Prologue, the test of "goodness" for the play/maid turned from her physical virginity to the nobility of her paternal breeding, so in the opening scene attention turns from the panoply of physically present signs—Hymen, the wheaten garlands, white robes, and so on (all suggesting virginity)—to the wider context of noble breeding. Purely physical virginity may help the husband to feel assured of his paternity, but beyond that assurance lies the desire to be assured of gentle or noble offspring. In the Prologue, that desire evolved into a registry of the play/maid's male ancestral line; in the opening scene, that desire evolves, via the Theban Queens, somewhat more comprehensively into mention both of Theseus's "gentility" (1.1.25) and of Hippolyta's "mother's sake" (1.1.26). According to the Queens, if Theseus would demonstrate the nobility of his breeding ("gentility" as "extraction" as in Orlando's usage in the opening scene of *As You Like It*), then he must heed the Queens' demands for help. If Hippolyta would give sign to the world that her mother bore noble offspring and if Hippolyta would hope herself to do so, then she must heed the Queens' demands. Gentility and nobility are not just secrets in the blood, for they are made manifest only through behavior, action. As Duke Vincentio says in *Measure for Measure:* "if our virtues / Did not go forth of us, 'twere all alike

/ As if we had them not" (1.1.33–35). There must be some outward and visible sign of the inward condition, a sign signaling beyond physical beauty toward a volitional virtue.

To recapitulate my argument thus far: (1) attention to *The Two Noble Kinsmen* has centered on the issue of collaboration and, more specifically, the question of to what extent Shakespeare's authorship may be in evidence; (2) the play's Prologue almost anticipates that question when the Prologue interrogates the ancestry, authorship, and breeding of the piece in terms showing how naturally we tend to test aesthetic or artistic merit by our conception not merely of immediate purity or virginity of the piece itself but also of its patriarchal bloodlines (if Chaucer made it, it must be good); (3) intermediary breeders between the noble grandauthor (Chaucer) and the present incarnation or child can prevent the nobleness from "falling," prevent it not by themselves aspiring to claim authorial or genetic nobility but rather by soliciting the enthusiasm of the contemporary audience and letting the child play to that; (4) the play's opening scene sets up a similar dynamic in that the initial focus on Hippolyta's maidenhead or hymen as guarantor of noble progeny widens into a focus on her and her husband's nobility of ancestry and then into a focus on the deeds that must be done to give outward signs of the inward nobility.

One of the things this argument may have obscured is the imprecision of analogies between artistic collaborations and procreative couplings. Theseus and Hippolyta are man and woman, capable of engendering offspring (though Hippolyta as an Amazon would catch up attributes of the male gender). By verbal sleight of hand, the Prologue inserts differential sexuality into the authorship of the play: first the new play is likened to a maid whose husband seems to be the audience following and giving money; then the new play turns into the offspring of Chaucer. The missing term becomes the play's mother. Implicitly, the playwright(s) would occupy that position if the metaphor of human sexual procreation were to remain in mind. Sexual difference thins out, however, from the Prologue as he proceeds to convert the playwright(s) to the masculinized force that could blast Chaucer's bays (Pro. 20) and to the male writer(s) who could "aspire to him" (Pro. 23). The audience, moreover, asked to help the play-producing swimmers or sailors (again plainly men), would also seem to be imagined as men in a male environment. Compare the Epilogue's final words: "Gentlemen, good night" (Epi. 18).

The shocking, even brutal, invocation of the hymenal site as source and test of siring standards becomes subordinated first to a consideration of patriarchal bloodlines or gentility and then to an almost parthenogenetic vision of men— Chaucer and the writer(s)—seeking to create what is worthy through their own actions and presenting it to other men. This movement away from what might be called heterosexual anxiety toward what might be termed homosocial hoping is a movement of the main action of the play where the initial view of Hymen and the bride and groom seems to slip out of focus as attention turns to Emilia and Flavina and then to Palamon and Arcite and the bonds of their brotherhood.

The essential collaboration for the extension of the human race is between men and women, as is evident in the opening images of both Prologue and play. The image of the two different sexes collaborating equally in essential creation may underlie much of our cultural imagery of colabor—as when the Prologue first posits a two-gendered origin for the play or when critics such as Dowden distinctly feminize the "beauty" of "the young Fletcher in conjunction with whom Shakspere worked upon *The Two Noble Kinsmen*."[2] Thus searching for the Shakespearean portion of the play is also searching for the man's (or "real man's") part.

Apart from making babies, however, much of the most revered colabor in Shakespeare's society (if not also our own) took place among same-sex groups, and the colabor or action that was deemed ennobling as the proof of high blood was, in that patriarchal context, the colabor of men in the church, in legal institutions, or in battle. Thus, to prove his "gentility," Theseus (who has already "shrunk" the Amazon Hippolyta back into the woman's bound she was overflowing [1.1.83]) will take his army of men to attack Thebes. Emilia, furthermore, declares that she will never "take a husband" (1.1.205) unless Theseus takes the petitioned action, as if the war against Thebes were an act emblematic (or even productive) of man's progenitive honor, an act allowing Emilia to choose a worthy mate. Palamon and Arcite, similarly, mull over causative connections between male actions—infamous or heroic—and their impact on male blood. The Theban tyrant Creon is one, says Palamon, who subsumes the heroism of others into his own bodily substance, "who only attributes / The faculties of other instruments / To his own nerves and act" (1.2.67–69). Arcite would have the pair leave the court:

for our milk
Will relish of the pasture, and we must
Be vile, or disobedient—not his kinsmen
In blood unless in quality.
(1.2.76–79)

Here is made explicit not only the notion that male heroic action directly influences nobility of blood but also the notion that male blood catches up the essential defining power for the quality of offspring. Palamon and Arcite are like two mother cows concerned for their calves and fearful that their environment will taint their "milk," which controls the worth of their physical and spiritual inheritance and bequest.

Both the Prologue and the developing play (as well as traditional criticism of the play) are founded on the grossly patriarchal paradox that the qualities of biological (and artistic) offspring are to be judged, ultimately, not on their own merits or on the apparent merit (virginal status) of any mother but only on the noble breeding of the male ancestors of both mother and father. Such breeding

2. Ibid., 379.

is proved, however, not simply through blood relationships but rather through heroic (martial) male action that ennobles the hero's "milk," that purges and purifies the hero's "blood" (1.2.72, 109). The quest for being, for knowing who the ancestors are, turns to a quest for doing, for knowing what the ancestors (male) have done to qualify themselves as noble, so that the outcome of all heterosexual collaboration can be judged, finally, only on the basis of prior homosocial collaboration in heroic (all-male) action.

It is true that *The Two Noble Kinsmen* presents in its first scene a brief and tantalizing glimpse of noble worth and purity of breeding established not through all-male action but through heroic struggle directly with the female (the Amazon), but this possibility is elided, as it were, through the recycling of Theseus, to prove his "gentility," into battle with a male antagonist. Still, does not the glimpse toward the society of the "most dreaded Amazonian" (1.1.77) constitute a quicksilver admission or presupposition for the play that women may relish their own society, just as men may relish theirs, and that the business of breeding could be reframed as a subordinate kind of collaboration in life? Hippolyta comes to Theseus not alone but paired with a sister—as if Amazonian society were not quite atomized—and not just with a sister, but with a sister who (unlike the standard marriage-eager sister of much comedy) prefers members of her own sex, declaring "the true love 'tween maid and maid may be / More than in sex dividual" (1.3.81–82).

Further subverting the centrality of cross-gendered collaboration is the friendship or doubling between Theseus and Pirithous. If this were a standard romance, the bride's sister, Emilia, would fall in love with and marry the groom's best friend, Pirithous. But here the main collaborative energy of each is distinctly same-gendered. The "knot of love" between Theseus and Pirithous "may be outworn, never undone" (1.3.41). "Love"—among these Greeks, if not elsewhere—centers itself ambiguously among cross-gendered and same-gendered pairs. The hymenal imperative, the command to breed bravely, seems to motivate the main physical action, but the emotional and spiritual centers of love seem to slip between same-gendered pairs.

How to reconcile the patriarchal dictate for a colabor of man and woman toward noble offspring with the supervening demands of same-sex friendships becomes a central problem of the play as it fusses over the meaning of the love between its titular heroes. Though they are true cousins, the sons of sisters, Palamon and Arcite are first presented as "dearer in love than blood" (1.2.1). The twinning of their souls makes them almost one and leads to strange locutions of oneness. Arcite says to Palamon in prison: "The sweet embraces of *a* loving wife . . . shall never clasp *our* necks" (2.2.30–32); "Were we at liberty, / A wife might part us lawfully" (2.2.88–89): "We are one another's wif*e*, ever begetting / New births of love" (2.2.80–81).

After Palamon spies Emilia and falls for her, Arcite exclaims: "am not I / Part of your blood, part of your soul? You have told me / That I was Palamon, and you were Arcite." Palamon answers, "Yes." And Arcite continues:

Am not I liable to those affections,
Those joys, griefs, angers, fears, my friend shall suffer?
  Pal. Ye may be.
  Arc.   Why then would ye deal so cunningly,
So strangely, so unlike a noble kinsman,
To love alone?

(2.2.186–91)

Arcite's question, out of context, sounds funny, perhaps, but the play seems
seriously to be asking: If two males think of themselves almost as identical
twins and also as soul mates, then will they not share an identity of desire? Just
before seeing Emilia, Palamon says to Arcite: "Is there record of any two that
lov'd / Better than we do, Arcite?" Arcite replies:

Sure there cannot.

  Pal. I do not think it possible our friendship
Should ever leave us.
  Arc.   Till our deaths it cannot,
    Enter Emilia *and her* Woman [*below*].
And after death our spirits shall be led
To those that love eternally. Speak on, sir.
  [*Emil.*] This garden has a world of pleasures in't.
What flow'r is this?
  Woman.   'Tis call'd narcissus, madam.
  Emil. That was a fair boy certain, but a fool
To love himself.

(2.2.112–21)

The inward-looking love of Palamon and Arcite for each other may be a kind
of narcissus-like self-love. Just as Palamon raises the issue of whether anything
could part their friendship, Emilia enters the garden of time and its worldly
pleasures. Arcite continues to affirm a spiritual love between himself and Palamon that will join them in an eternal company. But Palamon has launched his
desire now into the garden. When Arcite follows him there, "falling" also in
love with Emilia, Arcite quite seriously seems to imagine an equality of love
capable of being shared by the two kinsmen, at least for a moment. Since
Palamon is made to assume an exclusivity in love the question is soon dropped
whether three persons could ever share in an identity, a singleness, of love.

Arcite for an instant hints, however, at a way that both he and Palamon could
share a love for Emilia. He says to Palamon: "I will not [love her] as you do—to
worship her / As she is heavenly and a blessed goddess; / I love her as a woman,
to enjoy her. / So both may love" (2.2.162–65). But Palamon does not really love
so spiritually. He insists that he has taken "possession" of all Emilia's beauties.
And of course the kinsmen imagine heterosexual love in the context of wives
and issue. When Arcite pictures neither of the two kinsmen having a wife, he

laments, and perhaps laments primarily, that then, as he says, shall "no issue know us" (2.2.32). Still, Palamon and Arcite could conceivably collaborate in a love for Emilia, in a ménage à trois that produced issue. She herself makes no persistent distinction between them and cannot choose one over the other "but must cry for both" (4.2.54). What makes such a solution repellent, finally, is the anticollaborative convention of paternity that is assumed on all sides. When Arcite in prison laments the prospect of having no wife and no issue, he describes such issue as "figures of ourselves" (2.2.33), sons who could remember what their fathers were (2.2.36). As images of particular selves, garnered in necessity from only one man's sperm, children cannot have collaborative biological fathers. Yet any number of collaborative parenting arrangements could be imagined. Arcite's concern for identifiable paternity is at base an economic convention of ownership; he wants to be able to say (even though he never can be sure) what issue he can assume belong to him as extensions of his physical being. Thus, when the Prologue of *The Two Noble Kinsmen* speaks of the play as a child with Chaucer as breeder and the author(s) implicated in the breeding process, it invokes and we pursue our deep assumptions about impossibilities of collaborative fatherhood in one sense and improprieties of it in another. That a play is not literally a child, that any spermatic analogies between artworks and children are extremely questionable, and that possible collaboration on a play may indeed challenge our assumptions about the nature of fatherhood, breeding, and authorship seem to be issues that the Prologue taken together with the action of the play invites us to consider.

It so happens that another triangle of lovers in the play comments on the colabors of Palamon and Arcite over Emilia as well as on the possible colabors of producers of this play. The Jailer's Daughter loves Palamon, and she in turn is loved by the character known only as her Wooer. Palamon does not, so far as we know, return her love. The heavy middle of the play is dominated by the very physical passion of the Jailer's Daughter, who longs to lose her maidenhead only by Palamon: "Let him do / What he will with me, so he use me kindly, / For use me so he shall, or I'll proclaim him, / And to his face, no man" (2.6.28-31). In her madness, her talk becomes increasingly bawdy: "I must lose my maidenhead by cocklight" (4.1.112); "I'll warrant ye he had not so few last night / As twenty to dispatch. He'll tickle't up / In two hours, if his hand be in" (4.1.137-39); "now direct your course to th' wood, where Palamon / Lies longing for me. For the tackling / Let me alone" (4.1.144-46). Insofar as the Jailer's Daughter fails to retain, in the terms of the Prologue, much maidenly modesty, she seems to become sexually initiated in the course of the play. When her Wooer substitutes himself for Palamon, and when the couple exits with the mad Daughter plainly intended to go to bed with the Wooer (on Doctor's orders), then we are presented with a strangely collaborative love triangle. The Wooer collaborates, acceptably to the Daughter, with her image of Palamon (as the Wooer's friends all collaborate in her projection). Whose child might she consider any issue to be? Palamon's? Her love gives and hence finds nobility where it wills? Nothing is good or bad but that her thinking, to adapt Hamlet's phrase, makes it strangely so? This is a version of marriage plus sex à trois.

Consider now a different analogy among the triangles. As the Jailer's Daughter yearns for Palamon, so Palamon yearns for Emilia. And as the Wooer steps in for Palamon, so might Arcite step in for Emilia. The notion of Arcite as Palamon's "wife" might seem farfetched were it not for Arcite's explicit mention in prison of them being one another's wife. Arcite, furthermore, though he prays to Mars and wins the fight with Palamon, is consistently imaged as feminine in his beauty. Emilia says of him: "His mother was a wondrous handsome woman, / His face, methinks, goes that way" (2.5.20–21). He has a "sweet face" (4.2.7); his brow is "arch'd like the great-eyed Juno's" (4.2.20); he is "gently visag'd" (5.2.41). Arcite, in praying to Mars, speaks, moreover, of winning a garland described as the "queen of flowers" (5.1.45). And Emilia specifically compares Arcite to Ganymede (4.2.15), Jove's page, who "set Jove afire" (4.2.16). Palamon, furthermore, brings to the final combat a group of helpers who are distinctly feminine in appearance. One has thick-curled yellow hair and the face of a "warlike maid" (4.2.106), pure red and white and with no beard. Another is white-haired with arms that gently swell "like women new conceiv'd, / Which speaks him prone to labor" (4.2.128–29). Is it not thus suggested that Palamon's friends resemble male brides? If he could not accept Arcite as collaborator in his love for Emilia, might he accept Arcite as himself an equivalent love? When Arcite dies, Palamon says to Emilia: "To buy you I have lost what's dearest to me" (5.3.112); Emilia thinks of herself as having cut from Palamon "A life more worthy . . . than all women" (5.3.143). And Palamon at the end laments that "we should things desire which do cost us / The loss of our desire!" (5.4.110–11).

A further analogy applies that lament to the probable collaboration of Shakespeare and Fletcher. We might think of ourselves as readers or viewers of the play in a position analogous both to that of the Jailer's Daughter longing for Palamon and to that of Palamon longing for Emilia. If we so strongly and singly desire only Shakespeare in the play and will accept no collaborators, then we may find ourselves desiring what costs us the loss of our desire. Our desire need not be primarily to identify our author and his intents. In some important way, all our origins are collaborative. Recognizing that fact, we are freed to make what we can and will out of our own state and being. As interpreters, if we search for intention or original meaning, we may resemble children questioning their paternity. If we concern ourselves less with an authority embedded in history or in tradition and more with what we now make of the little we can know of that authority and tradition, then we may accept, like the Jailer's Daughter, an object of our desires who may be counterfeit but who also responds to those desires with genuine reward.

One result of such thoughts is, I believe, a felt imperative to make real for oneself the play's emphasis on the emptiness of possessive desire. Desire to know authority, to have authority, to obtain power, is seen as laughably inane in

The Two Noble Kinsmen. Theseus speaks of the gods "who from the mounted heavens / View us their mortal herd" (1.4.4) as if we were simply ridden and driven by overmastering and uncontrollable forces, and this despite the counterdrive of characters in the play to "master" their own affections and make them bend (1.1.229). The Jailer's Daughter decries "What pushes are we wenches driven to / When fifteen once has found us!" (2.4.6–7). Theseus speaks of Palamon and Arcite having "the agony of love about 'em" (3.6.219). And, in one of the greatest speeches in the play, the address of Palamon to Venus, Palamon refers to the lead-heavy yoke of love that stings like nettles (5.1.97) and to the way Love makes its chase this world "and we in herds thy game" (5.1.132). Though in this aspect the play seems bleak and sad, a moral it teaches is, I think, to question and resist, when possible and appropriate, the neediness of desire, the wanting to own, the promotion of self-interest over collaboration, and the desire for authority, all of which puts us in power struggles, rivalries, and other appetitive uses of our energy. At the end of the play, Theseus advises: "Let us be thankful / For that which is" (5.4.134–35). Such ungreedy emotional expenditure has not been prominent in the play save perhaps in Theseus's charity to the three Queens and in the mad largess of the Jailer's Daughter toward the captive Palamon. Still, the play seems to laud loving as giving, and I would use that notion to commend a similar relationship between us and Shakespeare.

Just as the Prologue turned from an inquiry into the noble breeding of the play toward a plea for collaborative help from the audience to authenticate the play's "content," so current readers and watchers of the play might usefully turn from inquiring mainly into the play's authorship toward collaborative creation of its contemporary significance. Instead of seeking, worshiping, or emulating Shakespeare's authority, why should we not instead give of ourselves to his plays in the spirit of accepting collaboration? When we read or watch silently, for example, do we behave primarily as consumers, taking it all in, voyeuristically, as if we were not really part of it, but only observing and soaking up the authority of the master author or of professional performers? I would encourage a wholly different stance toward the reading and seeing of Shakespeare, a stance of much more active colabor with Will.

One example of such collaboration would be voiced reading, particularly the sort of voiced reading that relishes the capacity of interjections, oaths, expletives, nonsense words, soundplay, meter, freely chosen tonalities, and all the paralinguistic features of Shakespearean speech to force our own collaborative creation of significance.[3] Another example of such collaboration would be to read aloud while standing or walking. Or if one ventured to try out or figure forth certain gestures, postures, or actions in the text, one could immeasurably increase one's sense of life there. In the words of the Prologue: "Do but you hold out / Your helping hands" and greater "content" shall follow.

---

3. See Terence Hawkes, *That Shakespeherian Rag: Essays on a Critical Process* (London and New York: Methuen, 1986), 73–91.

In the field of English studies, we have barely begun to emulate the great collaborative shift from authorial inquiry to our own psychosomatic, helping-hands response so plainly mandated by the Prologue and perhaps also indicated as a megatrend by the many contemporary decenterings of traditional sources of authority ("man," Western canonical tradition, God, nature, patriarchalism, and so on). Ironically, as readers we are much less inhibited from holding out our hands in the creation of significance than we are as spectators. Yet I would argue that, against the recognition of what might be created through genuine, living collaboration between spectators and actors, modern Shakespeare audiences tend to be much too observant of conventions relevant only to viewing TV, film, and representational theater where the audience pretends it isn't there. Elizabethan audiences wrote down lines in their table books, made faces and joked at the actors, cried out, wept loudly, laughed uproariously. Nuts were cracked, hands were clapped, apples were thrown, hisses were common, and, at the play's end, audiences would sometimes sing and dance.

Such carryings on might be thought terribly intrusive upon the actors' concentration and any sense of rapt communication with the throng. And there were, certainly, moments of utter silence and stillness. The Elizabethan actors did take a lot of abuse, but also they received from the audience an incredible tide of real, full, warm attention and energy. Each side, performers and spectators, opened itself to the other and collaborated in a vital way. It is hard for us to picture the difference between modern playing conditions and Shakespearean ones. As Bernard Beckerman has written:

Today as much as possible the actor will try to maintain the illusion that he is facing a fellow actor and not facing the audience. The flat picture frame of our theater encourages this illusion. In the Elizabethan theater the actor had to turn out, that is, orient himself to the circumference of auditors, if he were to be seen at all. This condition reinforced the conventional or ceremonial manner in acting.

By turning out, the actor emphasized the stage as a setting behind him rather than an environment around him. This was in accord with the demands of the plays. . . .

On stage, he shared his experience directly with the audience. He was part of an elaborate pageant taking place in a far-off land against an opulent backdrop. Yet on an emotional level he communicated intimately and directly with the audience. In more or less unrestrained utterance he portrayed extremes of passion.[4]

Each side, in other words, presented itself to the other, through voice contact, movement, and interchange of energies. Today, if a modern Shakespeare audience would seek more than a tepid experience of mild, quiet Bardolatrous reverence, such an audience could hardly do better than to agree to seek maximum openness and mutual commitment to vulnerability with the acting troupe as expressed through direct eye contact, appropriate sound interchanges, and relaxed, small-scale gestural mimicries or incorporations of the actions performed. If we would explore the potential emotion in Shakespeare's

4. *Shakespeare at the Globe: 1599–1608* (London: Macmillan, 1966), 129, 156.

plays, we must reappropriate their life and their significance in dynamic debate with cultural authorities of presumed authorship, scholarship, or stage professionalism. Shakespeare can live fully only in our eyes, our voices, our bodies and in the feelings stored and working there. Shakespeare inheres in the full, participatory collaboration between the page, the stage, and our capacities to give, to go forth from ourselves in forms of charity and good humor that are not only learned or socially constructed but also unlearned or deconstructed. Let Shakespeare collaborate and merge with his colaborers. Let us collaborate and colabor with Shakespeare. After the final play, what else is left?

3 "Be Rough With Me"
The Collaborative Arenas of
The Two Noble Kinsmen

Donald K. Hedrick

To the extent that necessity is socially dreamed, the dream becomes necessary. —Guy Debord, *Society of the Spectacle*

I. Collaboration versus Authorship

In describing *The Two Noble Kinsmen,* one might well follow Pierre Macherey's prescription that a literary work be treated as "the product of a specific labor," thereby avoiding an account of artistic creativity that in humanist fashion "omits any account of production."[1] I want to provide such a description, however hindered by the formidable obstacle that the historically specific circumstances of the labor producing this work—usually assumed to be a collaboration of Shakespeare and Fletcher—are wholly lost, as are for the most part the circumstances of collaboration between any Elizabethan playwrights. As indexes to such practices, we have but a few, scattered facts together with the plays themselves. *The Two Noble Kinsmen* may be our best theoretical index.

The account I want to provide is neither an attribution study nor a thorough "reading," but rather a selective analysis based on my interest in the audience strategies or rhetoric of Renaissance spectacle. By the "spectacular" I refer to the economy of visual practices constituted by the agency of all participants (including managers, actors, patrons, texts, artists, audiences, judges, administrators), practices whose end is in decision and judgment. These decisions take different forms, such as taste in artistic spectacle, "calls" in athletic spectacle, and consent in political and legal spectacle. The prizes respectively conferred on the spectators—genius, fanhood, and citizenship—may be as substantive as any of those for the performers.

I propose that this play represents the general practices and perhaps the immediate circumstances of its production. It may even be that it is designed for its historical audience, or at least part of the audience, to recognize these circumstances through the play "translucently,"[2] although such a possibility could

---

1. Pierre Macherey, *A Theory of Literary Production* (London, Henley, and Boston: Routledge, 1978), 51, 58.
2. Donald K. Hedrick, "The Masquing Principle in Marston's *The Malcontent*," *English Literary Renaissance* 8 (1978): 24–42.

hardly be confirmed from the chiefly "internal" evidence and interpretation I give. Along the way I will make several claims useful to a "reading" and to attribution study. Specifically, I claim that the play thematically explores the nature of artistic rivalry, in such a way as to suggest strongly that one of its collaborators was not, as is customarily thought, Shakespeare.[3] The former analysis is not dependent on this incidental claim, whose value depends on an unincluded analysis on new stylistic grounds—rejecting Shakespeare on the basis of speech act theory, by demonstrating that Fletcher's unidentified coauthor is wholly unskilled in the degree and kind of indirect, inferential, second-order speech acts characteristic of Shakespeare. These sorts of acts constitute the informal logic of natural conversation, where speakers reconstruct, reinterpret, and draw inferences from each other's words; where speech acts appear as other forms (assertions as questions, requests as assertions, and so on); and where conversational "maxims," such as the principle requiring one to

---

3. The version of this paper presented at the seminar on *The Two Noble Kinsmen* in 1985 is largely unchanged with respect to its subsidiary claims against Shakespeare's coauthorship on stylistic and thematic grounds. I want to thank Charles Frey for his critique of the reading, but especially for challenging me at that time to provide an alternative candidate. Although I believed that the kind of study I had done relieved me of the obligation to seek a different author, I began to study evidence about one of the candidates mentioned in the "Coda," Nathan Field. I learned that he had never been considered, that other collaborations of his had been only recently identified, and, most striking, that the nineteenth-century stylistic foundation of the case for Shakespeare—a supposedly thorough comparison of the text's style with all other authors of the period—while still treated as authoritative and relied on by serious scholars and editors of the play, had never actually been carried out.

I have left the fanciful "Coda" virtually unrevised, to reflect my original thinking. If Field was Fletcher's coauthor, its conjectures nevertheless remain surprisingly apt, except that Field would have been younger than his collaborator, hence more aspiring and less a professional equal. The "Coda" remains fanciful, of course, in its fiction of a kind of playwriting contest with Shakespeare as judge, but I think there may be a larger, nonliteral truth to it. We have more work to do in understanding the institutional base of the drama of the time.

Nathan Field, ambitious artistic upstart in Jacobean theater, a self-confessed aspirant to write tragicomedy like that of his friend Fletcher, and the only major actor-playwright immediately following Shakespeare, was working with Fletcher, as we now know, at the time of *Kinsmen*. He had already tried his hand at adapting Chaucer for the stage, unlike Shakespeare, and had done so working with Fletcher. His poetic style was the only remaining one like Shakespeare's, whose influence is readily argued from plot borrowings, neologizings, and from Field's having memorized Shakespeare in order to act in his plays. Recognized stylistic features of Field, such as "clotted" rhetoric and uncertain tone, have been consistently remarked in the non-Fletcherian parts of *Kinsmen*. The lengthy actor-oriented stage directions we find in *Kinsmen* are a signature, as are other themes, motifs, bawdy style, sexual themes, and Jonsonian misogyny. Major metrical and vocabulary tests (including double endings, *o'th'*, *'em*, *hath* and *doth*, and unique inventions) support the claim. Field's theatrical connections to Henslowe and others, his move to Shakespeare's company (where he may have received Shakespeare's shares), and his early disappearance support his candidacy as Fletcher's collaborator on this play. His cheeky personal spirit of outrageously noble gestures, his self-fashioning as Bussy D'Ambois (the character he starred as), all imbue *The Two Noble Kinsmen*. The thematic concerns I first recognized in the play turned out to be his "identity themes." In his self-fashioning to fill the gap left by Shakespeare, Field, I believe, deserves study as the first Shakespearoid writer.

The evidence I summarize here was presented in a paper given at the Shakespeare Association Meeting in Montreal, 1986: "The Politics of Attribution: Authorial Image and the Competitive Field of *The Two Noble Kinsmen*."

be relevant to the topic at hand, are often violated for effect and meaning. (See Appendix for examples and discussion.)

Conversation is, not coincidentally, the consummate form of a collaborative practice that includes a competition or rivalry. As such, it too participates thematically in a play about a rivalry between friends. In addition to its reliance on speech act theory—introduced as a language model that vastly improves upon the models grounding earlier style study—the present analysis uses the feminist theory of "homosociability" in order to read systematically the play's representation of collaboration as a professionalist subtext, a reading that adds further weight to the case against Shakespeare as coauthor. Finally, another detachable section—a speculative "Coda"—advances the case by a circumstantial scenario based on the theme.

As a detective enterprise in collaborative work, attribution study typically locates discoverable stylistic differences resulting from two writers combining efforts to produce a spectacle. For *The Two Noble Kinsmen,* aside from the disputes about the names of the writers, there has been some consensus along these lines: (1) the play is written in two distinct styles, (2) one of the styles is more Shakespearean than the other, and (3) there is some rough parity in their quality.[4] I propose to recuperate the collective force of these views by seeing them not as the discoveries of scholars but rather as the special features of the spectating experience for the historical audience, including the writers themselves. The motivating question is this: What if such features of writing were meant to be seen? What if dual authorship does not merely *produce* the show, but *constitutes* the show? The scholarship on this question has provided important insights while evading their force—that the play presents its differences as spectacle. I propose that *The Two Noble Kinsmen* is less significant as a collaboration on spectacle than it is as a spectacle of collaboration.

Collaboration itself, I want to show, appears as a subject for scrutiny in the play. This obsessive topic corresponds, moreover, to the play's valorization of a certain nobility, whose representation is the chief addition to Chaucer and which is always accompanied by a radical anxiety concerning any collaborative production of meaning and value. That is, when *The Two Noble Kinsmen,* unlike *The Knight's Tale,* strives to idealize friendship and nobility, it reflects an anxiety about the way they are produced—specifically, in an artistic, competitive, and "homosocial" labor. This specific mode of labor is at the same time the mode of production of the two noble collaborators of *The Two Noble Kinsmen.* The play is their title match.

The rivalry of Palamon and Arcite for the hand of Emilia is, of course, the central action, shared by both Chaucer's tale and *The Two Noble Kinsmen.* The major thematic shift is signaled by the term *noble* in the play's title, since the rivals' nobility and magnanimity are continually studied, as if transposing

4. For the development of the consensus, see David V. Erdman and Ephim G. Fogel, eds., *Evidence for Authorship: Essays on Problems of Attribution, with an Annotated Bibliography of Selected Readings* (Ithaca: Cornell University Press, 1966), 486–94.

the story's arms contest into a Renaissance magnanimity contest. Noble gestures, which are selfless and unnecessary, punctuate the entire story—from Theseus's willingness to interrupt his wedding at the pleas of the three widowed Queens for noble burials of their husbands, to Palamon and Arcite's decision to fight for their own kinsman Creon despite his moral inferiority, to the fraternity-style, charitable collection of the knights contributing to the madwoman's dowry. The most spectacularly magnanimous gesture is undoubtedly the scene of the two kinsmen arming each other for their combat, a scene vastly enlarged from the wordless event merely mentioned by Chaucer. Here again we see the play's added fascination with the dramatic ironies of honor between antagonists. What the play chiefly adds, then, is an exaggeration of the paradoxicality of the rivalry, fluctuating as it does between reluctance, assertiveness, nostalgic goodwill, and hostility.

With this addition, the play raises the question of differences in nobility between the two without ever fully clarifying, fixing, or dramatizing those differences. (Hence the interpretive debate about their distinguishability.) For Chaucer the differences were more thematic, functioning more as instantiations of courtly love questions such as "Who loves truly? the one who loves his object as a human or the one who loves his object as a goddess?"; or, "Who is worse? the imprisoned one who sees his beloved, or the free one banished from his beloved?" For *The Two Noble Kinsmen,* we seem to be invited only to search for differences in noble style, as Emilia searches for them, as if constructing an indecisive though discriminating audience. Stressing the paradoxical rivalry, the play reduces the consequentiality of any differences. It does this not only by the trick ending in which the military victor dies while the loser wins the girl, as in Chaucer, but especially by its changes. Emilia's indecision, for instance, is as anguished as her preference is fickle. In the play's added subplot, moreover, the Jailer's Daughter does see difference between Palamon and Arcite, but the difference is inconsequential since in her madness she accepts the unnamed Wooer as the surrogate Palamon and is thus fooled into sleeping with him. In both plots there is an ultimate failure—through indecision or through madness—to establish differences. A female failure resolves male rivalry.

In its deliberate exaggeration of the themes of noble indifference, selection by destiny, and courtesy between rivals, the play approaches self-parody, an internal pressure best defined and completed by the play's reception in Jonson's contemporaneous *Bartholomew Fair.* Jonson's allusion signals the main direction of the change from Chaucer, in the rivalry between Winwife and Quarlous for the hand of Grace Wellborn. Interrupting their sword fight, Grace coolly describes both her Emilia-like indecision and its solution: she will also let fate decide, but in a literary way, having each of them write down ("conceive") a word, one of which the next random passerby is to mark. Quarlous picks his word "out of the *Arcadia,* then: 'Argulus,'" and Winwife "out of the play: 'Palamon'" (translating their competition into a competition between literary works). Their absurd hostility-cum-courtesy is a condensation of *The Two Noble Kinsmen.* The situation in which one helps the other produce one's own defeat—a chief paradox of *The Two Noble Kinsmen*—is the ground of Jonson's amusement at Grace's cheery mediation: "Because I will bind both your endeavors to work together, friendly and jointly, each to the other's fortune, and have myself fitted with some means to make him that is forsaken a part of amends."⁵ This world is so noble that no one ever loses in it.

The reluctance of the rivalry, and the simultaneous heightening and dissolution of difference, corresponds to the play's elevation of nobility defined as a kind of collaboration among the noble.⁶ To understand this "collaboration," however, it is useful to interrogate the term, its uses and associations. Current interest in the subject spans the arts and may be part of a general cultural project of overcoming a textual ideology linked to Romantic and modern notions of individual authorship and genius. Allied to such interests are recent, poststructuralist interrogations of authorship itself, including the "death" of the "author" and his replacement by textuality, or by an "author-effect" in which his identity is institutionally and ideologically constituted, his roles or practices dispersed.⁷ Coincidentally, such theoretical claims correspond to recent shifts in Shakespeare studies, where author-centered meaning is reduced by comparison with the meanings produced by the institution itself. Shakespeare's art accordingly can be seen as more of a workshop product of the theatrical company and, bringing in the other side of the stage, as the collaborative product of interchange with the audience, a view growing out of Collingwood's aesthetics.⁸ But all such shifts, I believe, demonstrate a premature mystification of collaboration, particularly insofar as, by stressing cooperation, they filter out an oppositional character to the term, one that is revived in the European association of *collaboration* with subversion or treason. In a word, we will soon require more of Jonson's critique of mystified collaboration, expressed in his parody of *The Two Noble Kinsmen*.

How broadly may the term be applied to Elizabethan drama? G. E. Bentley, on the subject of collaboration, concludes, "Every performance in the commercial theatres from 1590 to 1642 was itself essentially a collaboration; it was the joint accomplishment of dramatists, actors, musicians, costumers, prompters (who made alterations in the original manuscripts) and—at least in the later theatres—of managers."⁹ Although this is a persuasive view, we need not stop at a consideration of practices exclusively "internal" to the theater companies.

5. Ben Jonson, *Bartholomew Fair*, in *Drama of the English Renaissance: The Stuart Period*, ed. Russell A. Fraser and Norman Rabkin (New York: Macmillan, 1976), 4.3.71–74.

6. In the visual arts of the Renaissance and modern eras, see for example *Collaboration in Italian Renaissance Art*, ed. Wendy Stedman Sheard and John T. Paoletti (New Haven: Yale University Press, 1978), and Cynthia Jaffee McCabe, *Artistic Collaboration in the Twentieth Century* (Washington, D.C.: Smithsonian, 1984).

7. See Roland Barthes, "The Death of the Author," in *Image-Music-Text* (New York: Farrar, 1977), and Michel Foucault, "What Is an Author?" in *Textual Strategies: Perspectives in Post-Structuralist Criticism*, ed. Josue V. Harari (Ithaca: Cornell University Press, 1979).

8. R. G. Collingwood, "The Artist and the Community," in *The Principles of Art* (1938; rpt. New York: Oxford University Press, 1972).

9. G. E. Bentley, *The Profession of Dramatist in Shakespeare's Time: 1590–1642* (Princeton: Princeton University Press, 1971), 198–99.

We might also include involvement by the nobility and royalty—positive as in commissioned performances and texts, negative as in censorship. This mixture of encouragement and control, cooperation and competition, had an unofficial form as well, if we can believe Dekker's mention of tavern "revels masters" whose criticism influenced playwriting and revision.[10] Indeed, the Elizabethan theater seems to have been as oppositional as it was cooperative. There was cutthroat competitiveness among rival companies at the very beginning of the institution, not to speak of the rivalries among actors, between men's and boys' companies, and between public and private theaters. Plays combated plays, in arenas where bears combated dogs, and fencers combated each other. We have not yet thoroughly explored the implications of a situation in which dramatic texts were themselves arenas for actors, in a setting where wagers were sometimes placed on competing actors, who may have supplemented their salaries by bets that they would outdo others in some role.[11]

The term *collaboration,* with its current positive associations, was not the term applied to the joint authorship of plays, nor did we have the term until two centuries later. Henslowe, recording payments to collaborators, doesn't call them that but simply registers their names with their full or installment payments during or after the composition.[12] Yet we have a recoverable technical term for "coworker" from Jonson himself. The term is *co-adjutor,* significantly used by him in the prologue to *Volpone,* where he demotes this and corollary terms in a boast that he wrote the play all by himself in only five weeks:

From his owne hand, without a co-adiutor,
Nouice, iourney-man, or tutor.[13]

As an index to the times, Jonson may be less representative because of his role as a self-classicizing playwright writing on the side of individual genius in a bookish theater.[14] But his remarks nevertheless carry general significance, even though it may be vain, as Bentley asserts, to speculate about procedures of collaboration from this list. The list presupposes, we might say, a range of possibilities rather than a standard method; more importantly, it signals a power differential and a potential rivalry between coworkers, proceeding from the more equitable to the more power-differentiated relationships. Bentley, in his discussion of what is known about Elizabethan collaboration, argues there must have been a standard procedure and that collaboration itself was the standard mode of authorship, on the grounds that as many as half of the plays were coauthored. But Bentley's claims evade the force of the brute evidence he fur-

10. Thomas Dekker, *The Gull's Hornbook,* in A. M. Nagler, *A Source Book in Theatrical History* (New York: Dover, 1952), 135.

11. B. L. Joseph, *Elizabethan Acting,* 2d ed. (London: Oxford University Press, 1964), 94.

12. Bentley, *Profession of Dramatist,* 199ff.

13. *The Works of Ben Jonson,* ed. C. H. Herford and Percy Simpson (Oxford: Clarendon, 1937), vol. 5, Pro. 15–18.

14. Timothy Murray, "From Foul Sheets to Legitimate Model: Antitheater, Text, Ben Jonson," *New Literary History* 14 (1983): 641–64.

nishes—that if half of the plays were coauthored, half were not. What we can infer is not the existence of some procedural norm, but the existence of a system in which modes of production are themselves in competition for privilege. Authorship competing with collaboration was the Elizabethan theatrical situation thematized, as we shall see, in *The Two Noble Kinsmen*.

II. Conversation and Contest,
or How Men Do Things with Words

Among all the productive modes of collective effort, perhaps the most common is the practice of conversation, that is, the joint production of utterances among at least two participants. One of the singular accomplishments of Shakespeare that has received little sustained attention among scholars is his ability to represent natural conversation naturally. Throughout the canon he is increasingly attentive to the informal logic, and indeed the collaborative nature, of ordinary talk, including its capacity for the anticollaborative or competitive construction of meaning (best exemplified by Hamlet, or by fools).[15] It is this informal logic with its attendant violations of conversational maxims, as indicated earlier, that led me to conclude that the non-Fletcherian portions of the play were quite un-Shakespearean—that speakers in these portions simply did not do to each others' words as much as Shakespeare can have his speakers do. (See my Appendix for more on this stylistic criterion to add to those such as vocabulary, image clusters, and metrics.)

For the present purposes, it is sufficient to observe the general phenomenon that conversation is a mode of the production of meaning in which team cooperation and individual competitiveness are in a positive tension. This aspect of conversation enables it to participate significantly in the matrix of competitive-cooperative forces in the play. But the notion of conversation as a form of contest requires translation into a narrower context here: namely, in *The Two Noble Kinsmen* conversation is to be understood as masculine conversation in specifically masculine contexts. The reason for this will become clearer when the concept of conversation is linked to a thematic reading of the play in terms of "homosociability."

Competing readings of *The Two Noble Kinsmen* yield the customary themes of humanist literary studies. One such reading—that the play exemplifies the (late Shakespearean) theme of the passage from innocence to a joyless experience—is especially relevant to the present concerns.[16] The timeless theme of passage, however, here acquires a gendered form. A feminist version of this narrative paradigm is provided in Eve Kosofsky Sedgwick's concept of "male

15. For Shakespearean conversational analysis, see my "Merry and Weary Conversation: Textual Uncertainty in *As You Like It*, II.iv." *ELH* 46 (1979): 21–34; or Keir Elam, *Shakespeare's Universe of Discourse: Language-Games in the Comedies* (Cambridge: Cambridge University Press, 1984).

16. Philip Edwards, "On the Design of *The Two Noble Kinsmen*," *A Review of English Literature* 5 (1964): 89–105.

homosocial desire," by which she means all forms of male bonding, located within a standard cultural narrative of a "male path through heterosexuality to homosocial satisfaction," a path that while compulsory in most cultures is nevertheless a "slippery and threatened one."[17] Mapping this cultural narrative onto the action of the play brings into relief the way in which the contest over Emilia later becomes a contest among all chivalric values. Since those are presumably male values, this path corresponds to Sedgwick's theory of "homosocial desire." Finally, I want to translate this "desire" into the terms of a specifically artistic desire.

More evident in *The Two Noble Kinsmen* than the theme of lost innocence is the play's pervasive representation of the male world of contests. Their frequency has been noticed by Paul Bertram, who thereby deduces thematic unity and the play's single authorship by Shakespeare.[18] (The argument is flawed in its assumption that a main theme could not be jointly achieved.) He notes, for example, that the wedding festivities and the war against Creon are "sports craving seriousness and skill." There are also the "games of honor" that Palamon and Arcite say they will miss, Arcite's wrestling at the May "pastimes," and Theseus's hunting expedition in the third act. Even the morris entertainment becomes a contest for exhibiting skill and prowess, with the schoolmaster Gerrold (who has difficulty when forced to collaborate with rustics) in something like Theseus's role in the final tournament. Other games and sports include the Wooer's fishing after being deserted by the Daughter, the couples' chase game of "barley-break" (known also as "last couple in hell"), and the Wooer's invitation to supper and cards. While noting the relation of such contests to the interest in heroic values, Bertram is finally content to generalize about the enduring significance of play in all human cultures.

What is lost by this generalization is the problematization of gender-specific play throughout *The Two Noble Kinsmen,* where the paradoxes of a self-defeating victory are foregrounded, simultaneously defining and threatening the male world of collaboration and contest.[19] Early in the play we observe this fascination with paradox, in Palamon's comments on the military veterans now begging in the streets of Thebes: "scars and bare weeds / The gain o' th' martialist, who did propound / To his bold ends honor and golden ingots, / Which though he won, he had not; and now flurted / By peace, for whom he fought" (1.2.15–19). And Emilia, lamenting the loss that wins her a husband, concludes the spectacle: "Is this winning?" (5.3.138). Palamon universalizes, "O cousin, / That we should things desire which do cost us / The loss of our desire!"

---

17. Eve Kosofsky Sedgwick, "Sexualism and the Citizen of the World: Wycherly, Sterne, and Male Homosocial Desire," *Critical Inquiry* 11 (1984): 228–29. See also Sedgwick, *Between Men: English Literature and Male Homosocial Desire* (New York: Columbia University Press, 1985).

18. Paul Bertram, *Shakespeare and "The Two Noble Kinsmen"* (New Brunswick: Rutgers University Press, 1965).

19. For a gender-specific reading of the play's world, see Charles Frey, "'O sacred, shadowy, cold, and constant queen': Shakespeare's Imperiled and Chastening Daughters of Romance," in *The Woman's Part: Feminist Criticism of Shakespeare,* ed. Carolyn Ruth Swift Lenz, Gayle Greene, and Carol Thomas Neely (Urbana: University of Illinois Press, 1980), 305–12.

(5.4.109–11). And Arcite makes the paradox an economic one: "Emily, / To buy you, I have lost what's dearest to me, / Save what is bought; and yet I purchase cheaply, / As I do rate your value" (5.3.111–14). Such paradoxes require, I believe, a more gender-specific consideration.

Working from an unswerving humanist essentialism,[20] Bertram simplifies the play's treatment of noble values. But he does so in an instructive way when observing the theme of "admiration-turning-to-emulation." We identify the theme in 1.3 when Emilia tells how she and her childhood friend imitated one another in everything. Its fullest treatment, however, is the dialogue between Palamon and Arcite in which, as they arm each other, they recall earlier encounters:

> *Pal.* Methinks this armor's very like that, Arcite,
> Thou wor'st that day the three kings fell, but lighter.
>   *Arc.* That was a very good one, and that day,
> I well remember, you outdid me, cousin;
> I never saw such valor. When you charg'd
> Upon the left wing of the enemy,
> I spurr'd hard to come up, and under me
> I had a right good horse.
>   *Pal.*   You had indeed,
> A bright bay, I remember.
>   *Arc.*   Yes. But all
> Was vainly labor'd in me; you outwent me,
> Nor could my wishes reach you. Yet a little
> I did by imitation.
>   *Pal.*   More by virtue.
> You are modest, cousin.
>   *Arc.*   When I saw you charge first,
> Methought I heard a dreadful clap of thunder
> Break from the troop.
>   (3.6.70–84)

To concentrate on a theme of emulation of the dialogue, however, is to risk losing sight of the deliberate way that the escalating compliments begin to perform the very rivalry bringing Palamon and Arcite to combat in the first place. As Arcite describes how Palamon "outwent" him in the arena of battle, both begin to transform their conversation into another arena, each outdoing the other by competitive memory and by the one-downsmanship of humility. What follows after the passage Bertram cites is therefore crucial, for Palamon appropriates Arcite's metaphor of thunder in order to say that Arcite was actually first in the charge, just as lightning comes before thunder:

---

20. I follow the critique of this intellectual tradition offered by Jonathan Dollimore in *Radical Tragedy: Religion, Ideology and Power in the Drama of Shakespeare and His Contemporaries* (Brighton, U.K.: Harvester, 1984), 156ff.

Pal   But still before that flew
The lightning of your valor. Stay a little;
Is not this piece too strait?
Arc.   No, no, 'tis well.
Pal. I would have nothing hurt thee but my sword,
A bruise would be dishonor.
Arc.   Now I am perfect.
Pal. Stand off then.

(3.6.84–89)

In complimenting each other they disarm each other while arming each other, acting out an emulation bound up in principle with a rivalry both constructive and destructive. A speech about competition, in the homosocial recursive economy of language, itself becomes a competition. Not accidentally, the scene also figures as an aesthetics of military equipment, a discriminating evaluation of war materials by joint recollections of former armor and former horses. The conversation builds to its natural conclusion in action—a military fashion show of sorts, with Palamon admiring how well his assistance has adorned Arcite.

In recapturing the past, this dialogue echoes other reminiscences in the play, notably in 3.3 when Palamon, having just been released by the doting Jailer's Daughter, is eating the food Arcite brings to strengthen him for their fight. Jarring to critics because of its snickering, locker-room tone, the scene portrays Palamon and Arcite gossiping about former girlfriends, about getting wenches pregnant, and about "hunting" in the woods. Here they employ what socio-linguists term the "topping constraint" in competitive story chaining.[21] They license this competitive discourse with an initial agreement to police their conversation by having "no more of these vain parleys" over Emilia. And they agree to have "no mention of this woman" and to "argue that hereafter" (3.3.5ff.). But they cannot keep cooperation and competition apart. Their nostalgia immediately sours when the topic of Emilia comes up "naturally"—that is, as a result of the logic of competitive conversation. Once again they are at each other's throats with insults and threats as memories of conquest intrude on present cooperation.

An even more important instance of the collaboration/competition matrix is found in the scene in which the rivalry begins:

Pal. I saw her first.

. . .

Arc. I saw her too.

(2.2.160–61)

The issue of who went into battle first will repeat this issue of who saw Emilia first. In the logic of the spectacle, a competition is countered by an emulation,

---

21. Livia Polanyi, "The Nature of Meaning of Stories in Conversation," *Studies in Twentieth Century Literature* 6 (Fall 1981–Spring 1982): 59.

itself another competition. Chaucer's debate about which lover loves truly is emended into a seeing contest or spectacular competition. Thus, women produce not only *sight* but also *sighting*, or competitive male work. They are the agency through which the claims of *seeing first* and *seeing too* are pitted against one another, juxtaposing competition and collaboration.

Aggressive vision is also assigned to the Jailer's Daughter, who is quick to distinguish between the two prisoners in another spectacular moment: "No, sir, no, that's Palamon. Arcite is the lower of the twain; you may perceive a part of him. . . . It is a holiday to look on them. Lord, the diff'rence of men!" (2.1.49–54). Her unfeminine, unhesitant vision is reprimanded by her father, who tells her not to point at them because they would not do so to her. In contrast to Emilia, she is not reluctant to distinguish noble men in competitive and hierarchical terms. But that reluctance is, in Emilia, a positive force, a noble indecision. Indeed, the Jailer's Daughter's failure to be thus reluctant seems allied to her very madness. True nobility makes men difficult to distinguish. Emilia's indecisiveness honors the homosocial community of noble men; the other woman's decisiveness disrupts it. The latter imagines distinctions between Palamon and Arcite that aren't there, while failing to see those that are there between Palamon and the Wooer.

Because of its anxiety about collaborative speech and vision, the play intermittently must present a frictionless conversation, different from its idealization of a "rough" one. This style is by and large a female one, signaled at the outset by the resolutely cooperative entreaties of the three Queens. We also find it in the prison scene when, before the men see Emilia, they are collaborating together on a meditation, a resignation to a fate that will keep them not only from corruption but also from either "business" or a "wife [who] might part us lawfully," followed by a list of natural evils such as sickness (2.2.88ff.). Arcite compares women to "liberty and common conversation, / The poison of pure spirits" (2.2.74–75), insofar as both seek to mislead youth. Accordingly, he goes on to imagine the opposite of "common conversation," that is, a high-minded conversation of further collaborative meditations. This future talk is thought of as the product of an all-male generation:

Arc.   What worthy blessing
Can be, but our imaginations
May make it ours? And here being thus together,
We are an endless mine to one another;
We are one another's wife, ever begetting
New births of love; we are father, friends, acquaintance;
We are, in one another, families;
I am your heir and you are mine; this place
Is our inheritance . . .

(2.2.76–84)

Despite the imagery of this, we need not look for a homoerotic or homosexual subtext, if we acknowledge the governing structure of "male homosocial desire." Arcite is daydreaming an idealized arena of labor that dissolves all other social structures but that lacks usual competitive forces. The vision is one of artistic collaboration between comparably talented coadjutors, a vision that is itself collaboratively produced as the two men work together on an acceptable metaphor for their present enclosure. (Arcite begins, "Let's think this prison holy sanctuary" [2.2.71].) But the entire play will move toward its proper enclosure—the field—as the true metaphor for male homosocial satisfaction and its "new births of love." The momentary vision of sanctuary, like other nostalgias for a pure cooperation, will not survive conversation.

In its representation of arenas for speech, vision, and love, *The Two Noble Kinsmen* inevitably focuses on *titles,* a theme that has been well demonstrated by Bertram. In its primary sense *title* signifies a victory, as in Palamon's prayer to Mars that he "be styl'd the lord o' th' day" (5.1.60). The adjunct sense of ownership is also included, as Palamon uses the term when he accuses Arcite of being as "false as thy title to" Emilia (2.2.172), and as Arcite uses the term, responding that his is "as just a title to her beauty" (2.2.180, ownership of spectacle). In a later scene he reasserts the claim of "good title" (3.1.112). One of the Knights will describe the shifts of "Fortune, whose title is as momentary / As to us death is certain" (5.4.17-18). Theseus will tell one of the Queens that to be mastered by the senses is to "lose our human title" (1.1.233) and will later tell Emilia that she must attend the final spectacle since she is "the price and garland / To crown the question's title" (5.3.16-17). Allowing Theseus's metaphor of herself as the "treasure" that "gives the service pay," she will nevertheless deny that she must be present at the homosocial arena: "Sir, pardon me, / The title of a kingdom may be tried / Out of itself" (5.3.32-34). Emilia is reluctant to be a spectator, fearing that she will influence the outcome of the contest if she herself becomes a spectacle for the two rivals as they fight. Hippolyta alludes to other "title" matches, lamenting that she would rather see a fight for a different prize: "They would show / Bravely about the titles of two kingdoms" (4.2.144-45). The metaphor of contested kingdoms echoes Arcite's description of the horses Emilia gave him as fitting to be "by a pair of kings back'd, in a field / That their crowns' titles tried" (3.1.21-22).

The title-seeking of the two "bold titlers" (5.3.83) is represented also at the important level of conversation and language, where we again find the struggle between collaboration and competition. Rivalry mixed with respect motivates, moreover, the exchanges of the two men when they select titles of address for one another. "Noble kinsmen," "sir," "cousin," and proper names alternate in their polite address in the arming scene, where the shifts between formal and informal address again signal their bond and their distance. Palamon even adopts an old, punning form of address to embody the dilemma: "Cozener Arcite" (3.1.44). Turning address itself into yet another contest, their final farewell before the tournament again turns magnanimously competitive:

Pal.   You speak well.
Before I turn, let me embrace thee, cousin.

This I shall never do again.
Arc.   One farewell.
Pal. Why, let it be so; farewell, coz.
Arc.   Farewell, sir.
(5.1.30–33)

But to win a title is, in the arena of the play, for the other to lose a title, a "paradox" emblematized in the tournament's un-Chaucerian rule that the loser shall die. Fame and the memory of name are contrasted to the forgetting of a name, as Arcite describes:

Arc.   I am in labor
To push your name, your ancient love, our kindred,
Out of my memory, and i' th' self-same place
To seat something I would confound.
(5.1.25–28)

When they speak of who loses, the talk again acquires its competitive edge, where to praise the other requires one to debase oneself. Thus, in the arming scene Palamon first wishes an honorable place for whichever man is defeated, offering forgiveness in advance if he himself is killed:

Pal.   If there be
A place prepar'd for those that sleep in honor,
I wish his weary soul that falls may win it.
(3.6.98–100)

After a handshake, however, the conversational rivalry continues, as Arcite competes by announcing an even more spectacular resignation to fate: if he loses, he will accept from his opponent what would be a patently unjust title:

Arc.   If I fall, curse me, and say I was a coward,
For none but such dare die in these just trials.
Once more farewell, my cousin.
Pal.   Farewell, Arcite.
(3.6.104–7)

The absurdity of such exchanges, with Palamon not reacting to this outrageous request, can be accounted for as a desperate artistic attempt, bordering on self-parody, to imagine a transcendent *Sprezzatura*.

Just as title and form of address are used as weapons in the collaborative-competitive arena, so are the speech acts of praise and blame. When Palamon and Arcite first meet after prison, the rapid shifts between flattery and insult may seem an impoverished psychological verisimilitude, but the intention seems to be to represent the paradox of productive rivalry. When Arcite gener-ously offers to bring files to remove Palamon's shackles, to feed, clothe, and even perfume him until he's ready to fight to the death for Emilia, Palamon momentarily demands that the rivalry be conducted with *fitting* conversation, that is, with a hostility to match the forthcoming combat:

> *Pal.*   Most certain
> You love me not; be rough with me, and pour
> This oil out of your language. By this air,
> I could for each word give a cuff, my stomach
> Not reconcil'd by reason.
>
> (3.1.101–5)

Proceeding with invincible politeness, Arcite begs pardon that his language is not rough, using polite language to apologize for polite language. He explains that he does not even chide his own horse to spur him. Palamon has located language itself in the system of a homosocial labor aesthetic, as a rough "spur" to inspire an escalating greatness in both opponents. To request to be used roughly is the paradigmatic magnanimous gesture of this competitive-cooperative arena. The entire play dreams of a contradictory speech act—"[Please] be rough with me"—as the figure of ideal social relations, the social dream noted in the present essay's epigraph. This is what men do with words.

We see the female antithesis of this complex mode of speech when the deluded Jailer's Daughter goes off to sleep with the man she thinks is Palamon, requesting to him, "But you shall not hurt me," and replying to his assurance, "If you do, love, I'll cry" (5.2.111–12). The pacific mode of action and discourse, linked to women and to madness, is specifically devalued by its juxtaposition with the male dream.

Collaborative-turned-competitive discourse also dominates the prison scene, where the dialogue upon the sighting of Emilia shifts from iteration to one-upmanship:

> *Arc.* She is wondrous fair.
> *Pal.*   She is all the beauty extant.
>
> (2.2.147)

As they have produced collaborative warfare, meditations, and viewings, so Palamon and Arcite here create collaborative judgment and value. Here, as elsewhere in the play, it is difficult to distinguish between the cousins, and their competitive descriptions increase the stakes in the rivalry at the same time they constitute the value of its object:

> *Pal.* What think you of this beauty?
> *Arc.*   'Tis a rare one.
> *Pal.* Is't but a rare one?
> *Arc.*   Yes, a matchless beauty.
> *Pal.* Might not a man well lose himself and love her?
> *Arc.* I cannot tell what you have done; I have,

Beshrew mine eyes for't! Now I feel my shackles.
  Pal. You love her then?
  Arc.   Who would not?
                    (2.2.153-58)

    The tone of this scene is hard to grasp, probably because it is a version of the artificial conversation game known as the "vapors," or sustained contradiction or nonacceptance of whatever your partner says—the game that Jonson spoofs in the same play wherein he spoofs *The Two Noble Kinsmen*. At once imitative and adversarial, such collaborative labor proceeds almost tentatively, as if the production of value is too important to be assigned to a single member of the team. It may be that the love judgments of the men are undermined in the scene, as if neither would be in love if the other were not, but it seems rather that we are invited merely to admire their high masculine spirits. Indeed, this collaborative work seems more a sign of nobility than a deviation from it. Dependence on the other's judgment does not by itself seem to be the object of an implied critique, at least not in the parallel circumstance of Emilia's indecisiveness about the two men. Her indecision is another collaboration. Choice is not simply choice for her but choice in an arena, even when she is alone, soliloquizing over their two pictures in yet another spectacular contest. While she debates their looks—now preferring Arcite's sweeter face, now Palamon's more sober face—at one point she indicates that her choice is not merely influenced, but actually constituted, by the audience observing the choice. Significantly, the choice is gender specific, so that for the male audience she says she loves Arcite, the worshiper of Mars, and for the female audience she says she loves Palamon, the worshiper of Venus:

For if my brother but even now had ask'd me
Whether I lov'd, I had run mad for Arcite;
Now if my sister—more for Palamon.
Stand both together: now, come ask me, brother—
Alas, I know not! Ask me now, sweet sister—
I may go look! What a mere child is fancy,
That having two fair gauds of equal sweetness,
Cannot distinguish, but must cry for both!
                    (4.2.47-54)

Emilia in her anxiety of choice focuses on the aspect of the arena that makes choice impossible—its bifurcated audience. To seek common values in such a situation is ultimately delusory. The spectacle is constituted by the spectator; the answer to a question depends on who is asking. Along with her own reluctance to be a spectator at the tournament, for fear of becoming a distraction, Emilia's representation of the power of the audience reflects the authors' similar ambivalence toward their audience—an ambivalence, it might be added, far more Jonsonian than Shakespearean, tending more toward hostility than toward generosity. In the audience's power, we learn from the Prologue and Epilogue, rests the play's victory, or its defeat.

III. Nurturing Competition: Beyond the Spectacular Arena

Having located a gender-specific thematization for *The Two Noble Kinsmen,*
we might expect some direct correspondence of cooperation with the female,
competition with the male. But this equation breaks down in the play's more
complicated versions of spectating. Ultimately, the play presents not a gendered
division of labor and identity but rather a purified labor and identity that, by
balancing cooperation and competition, usurp the realm of the female, who
accordingly disappears as the requisite audience constituting the male homosocial arena. The purified or idealized arena is always endangered by a non-
idealized, specifically bifurcated audience for whom every performance will
always carry a specifically bifurcated significance. Men and women, seeing two
different shows in the same arena, place bets on different contestants. In such a
spectacle, winning is always losing. The male appropriation of the two oppositional terms—emulation and competition, or oily and rough language—forms
the spectacular dream of a nurturing competition, hence raiding the customary,
envied social slot of the female. No wonder that Emilia is an anxious, unwilling
audience. Reduced, or elevated, to being the contested "kingdom," she is
included as a spectator only to be excluded as a judge or collaborator, not only
"guiltless of election" but also denied the construction of value. Emilia leaves
the arena to the men, letting "the event," which Arcite calls "that never-erring
arbitrator" (1.2.114) and which is doubtless a male version of Fortune, decide.

The Two Noble Kinsmen is largely about differentiating and electing men by
their qualities. This activity is carried out aside from the main plot in a rather
odd extension of Chaucer's descriptions of the assistant knights at the final
tournament. In this undramatic section of the play we hear lengthy descriptions
of the men's features and clothing, from which we are apparently, as implied
spectators, to judge manliness. Many of the details are drawn from Chaucer,
but the features are distributed among three instead of two men, as if specific
actors may have been intended. The descriptions involve such an exerted delicacy of distinction that judgment itself becomes a noble performance, a skill
best exemplified in the ability to read paradox: "when he smiles / He shows a
lover, when he frowns, a soldier" (4.2.135-36). The slightest shades of color are
deployed in the judgment, demonstrating noble discrimination: "He's white-
hair'd, / Not wanton white, but such a manly color / Next to an aborn"
(4.2.123-25). The arena is significantly a male aesthetic one, a decadent
patriarchal aesthetics.[22] We have observed that the indecision of Emilia
acknowledges the community and variety of male virtues while at the same time
stereotyping her feminine inconstancy. Still worse is the Jailer's Daughter, who,

---

22. For an account of the Renaissance view of performance judgment as just another kind of
performance, see Frank Whigham, "Interpretation at Court: Courtesy and the Performer-Audi-
ence Dialectic," *New Literary History* 14 (1983): 623-39. For insight into the relation of masculinist aesthetics and warfare I am indebted to poet Jonathan Holden's studies of contemporary
sensibilities, especially the essay on the ways American boys satisfy the "aesthetic impulse" with
warplanes: "Boyhood Aesthetics," *Iowa Review* 12 (1981): 135-46.

unintentionally inconstant, chooses too soon and gullibly accepts cheap substitutes. Failing at noble judgment, these women are inferior audiences.

The men, of course, differentiate themselves through combat, which is itself
a mode of spectacle. When Theseus interrupts Palamon and Arcite's duel in the
forest, he merely defers it; by ordering a tournament, he shifts the mode from
private duel to public spectacle. (For the audience, however, it is the second
combat that, because offstage, is "private.") The stakes are the same but medi-
ated differently: the loser expects to lose life and title, but only in the private
spectacle will he die by the other's hand, the destructiveness unmediated. In
spectacular terms the viewing of a contest is itself a contest of viewing, reminding us of the rivals' obsession about who saw the beloved one first. Public
spectacle is an arena of audience bifurcation constructed by the male value of
priority, where rival viewing replaces rival combat. The issue for the two
kinsmen is chiefly whether Palamon's seeing Emilia first counts as a victory, an
idea rejected by Arcite with this military analogy:

> *Arc.*   Because another
> First sees the enemy, shall I stand still,
> And let mine honor down, and never charge?
>   (2.2.193-95)

What is not at stake is whether the event counts as a contest. That is, no one
asks if love is really like a contest or not. Maintaining the question within the
terms of a contest, Arcite only muddles the issue by substituting military conventions, but he does so by devaluing spectating and by locating a mimetic
component within a competition. In its spectacular economy, the enemy is
exchanged for the loved one.

Fight in *The Two Noble Kinsmen* is invariably allied to sight, a conjunction
we see in a repetition of phrases by different speakers anticipating the final
tournament: the Messenger warns the Doctor that he may "lose the noblest
sight / That ev'r was seen" (5.2.99-100), to which the Doctor promises, "I will
not lose the fight" (5.2.103; some later editions emend this to "sight"). The
following scene begins with Pirithous asking Emilia, "Will you lose this sight?"
(5.3.1). Emilia's indecision figures as a self-contesting vision:

> . . . I
> Am guiltless of election. Of mine eyes
> Were I to lose one, they are equal precious,
> I could doom neither. . . .
>   (5.1.153-56)

The idea of an internal visual contest rehearses the values of the homosocial
arena, and accordingly the figure of her fear is reversed by Palamon when he
expresses his absolute willingness to destroy the enemy, even if it were a part of
himself: "were't one eye / Against another, arm oppress'd by arm, / I would

destroy th' offender, coz, I would, / Though parcel of myself" (5.1.21–24). The dream of the arena is thus repeated in and on the male body. The cultural narrative of an achieved homosocial satisfaction is accompanied by anxiety about the proliferation of arenas, which create competitive viewing, even within one subject. The anxiety is relieved by a desire to reduce the internal violence of competitive viewing by reducing the event either to a private spectacle or to a public spectacle viewed by a unified, noble audience capable of drawing distinctions but for whom choice remains a rough, noble performance. The dream of homosocial performance requires a homogeneous audience. Appropriately, the Epilogue to the whole play is addressed only to the "gentlemen."

A version of the nostalgia for a single audience is found in the prison scene when Palamon, lamenting that they can't see Thebes, speaks of spectacle lost: never again to see "the hardy youths strive for the games of honor, / Hung with the painted favors of their ladies, / Like tall ships under sail" (2.2.10–12). Palamon collaboratively reminisces about a race, another of the play's numerous contests, in which he and Arcite outran their competitors as well as the audience of ladies:

> . . . then start amongst 'em
> And as an east wind leave 'em all behind us,
> Like lazy clouds, whilst Palamon and Arcite,
> Even in the wagging of a wanton leg,
> Outstripp'd the people's praises, won the garlands,
> Ere they have time to wish 'em ours.
>
> (2.2.12–17)

This vision reconciles collaboration and competition by turning a public race into a private one, unifying the spectators by erasing them. To erase the spectators is to erase the fact of Palamon and Arcite's own competition. Since we never hear which of the two won, their rivalry has been substituted by the rivalry with others. Rough with each other, they spur each other's victory beyond the others, and beyond the competitive judgments of the bifurcated spectators. Like Emilia, the audience is denied the power of observing winning. Especially noteworthy is the play's inclusion of a scene in which the dominant male homosocial vision is explicitly contrasted with the extramural, female alternative. I refer to Hippolyta and Emilia's commentary praising the friendship between Theseus and Pirithous, which, with differences, reminds the women of the childhood friendship between Emilia and a certain Flavina. Hippolyta pictures the men's friendship as a world of sport and labor, describing their having "cabin'd / In many as dangerous as poor a corner," "skiff'd / torrents," and fought together (1.3.35–40). She pictures their ideal male friendship as a self-supporting but self-contesting bondedness: "Their knot of love / Tied, weav'd, entangled," and not to be unwoven (1.3.41–42). Anticipating the imagery of the arming scene, Emilia compares the men's friendship to women's own: "Theirs has more ground, is more maturely season'd, / More buckled with strong judgment, and their needs / The one of th' other may be said to water / Their intertangled roots of love" (1.3.56–59).

In her extended description of her own friendship, Emilia emphasizes a different sort of collaboration, if it can be called collaboration. She pictures this female friendship as a mirror rather than a knot, emulation rather than self-contestation. In their innocent admiration, the two girls would imitate each other in specular spectatorship:

> *Emil.*   What she lik'd
> Was then of me approv'd, what not, condemn'd,
> No more arraignment. . . .
>   (1.3.64–66)

Her idealized memory constitutes a homosocial aesthetics when she describes a flower she would put between her breasts, with Flavina longing to do just the same: she would "commit it / To the like innocent cradle, where phoenix-like / They died in perfume" (1.3.69–71). Cradled, these flowers are both children and works of art. Emilia and her friend would copy each other's fashions ("On my head no toy / But was her pattern"). And they would copy each other's music, both copied or "stolen" tunes ("Had mine ear / Stol'n some new air") as well as original ones ("or at adventure humm'd [one] / From musical coinage, why, it was a note / Whereon her spirits would sojourn (rather dwell on) / And sing it in her slumbers" [1.3.71–78]). The images of friendship are consistently those of artists working together.

Friendship, a given in Chaucer, is the subject under investigation by *The Two Noble Kinsmen* through juxtapositions with artistic labor, originality, and collaboration. Both female-female and male-male friendships are thus explicitly idealized and at the same time subjected to an implicit comparison or competition. The play adds a new love-debate to Chaucer by asking: "Which friendship is best?" Emilia, introducing this rivalry between friendships, suggests the priority of the female, claiming, "the true love 'tween maid and maid may be / More than in sex [dividual]" (1.3.81–82). Broadly speaking, a self-contesting but collaborative mode is pitted against a narrowly imitative one lacking priority or leader. The former will turn out to be the preferred mode, as we might expect when we hear Palamon declare that he will never imitate bad manners because he never stoops to any imitation whatsoever: "Either I am / The fore-horse in the team, or I am none / That draw i' th' sequent trace" (1.2.58–60). Scorning the textual realm of the sequent trace, his speech diminishes in advance the mimetic values of female friendship, while the female mode of reproductive "sequent traces" is nevertheless given its due, however anxiously.

Fear of the imitativeness idealized in the Flavina-Emilia relationship takes a different form in another of the play's literalized artistic collaborations—the dance. When the Jailer's Daughter declares "I'll lead" (3.5.90) and presumably dances the Third Countryman (who replies "Do, do") offstage after her last

line, her madness is gender defined, or gender violating. Her aggressive desire
not to be a "sequent trace," allied to the hopeless madness of electing Palamon
as her lover, signals an invasion of the homosocial arena that at the same time
validates the male traits she appropriates. She is accordingly represented as a
kind of mad artist, whose audience admires her mad pageants and especially
her originality—as the Doctor exclaims, "How her brain coins!" (4.3.40). Her
artistic assistant is the fantasy horse that she says can dance, read, and write
(5.2.47ff.). This gift, which she believes Palamon has given her for releasing him
from prison, is nicely contrasted to the pair of horses given by Emilia to Palamon and intended for use in military collaboration. But the Jailer's Daughter
suffers spectacular indignities, ranging from sleeping with the mere image of
Palamon to being herself an image appropriated for the performance of the
rustics, who decide that she is just the right thing for a winning show:

> 3. *Coun.* If we can get her dance, we are made again.
> I warrant her, she'll do the rarest gambols.
>   1. *Coun.* A mad woman? We are made, boys!
>   (3.5.74–76)

Where the sequent trace or copy is not idealized as in the Flavina passage, it is
denigrated and again linked to a version of artistic production. When the Doctor advises that the nameless Wooer pretend to be Palamon by adopting his title
("Take upon you, young sir her friend, the name of Palamon") and by singing
the songs Palamon sings (4.3.75ff.), the imposture taints the very ideal of copy.
That this imposture is connected to the realm of art, and even to inferior art, is
more noticeable in a later scene when, at the Wooer's protest that he has no
voice to sing like Palamon, the Doctor advises him to sing anyway: "That's all
one, if ye make a noise" (5.2.16). In another example, Emilia, walking outside
the prison just before the rivalry is initiated, speaks with her waiting woman
about the flower Narcissus and its story of self-mimetic exclusion: "a fair boy
certain, but a fool / To love himself. Were there not maids enough?" (2.2.120–21).
Emilia asks the woman if she can "work such flowers in silk" for a "gown full of
'em" and admires their color (2.2.127). But to "take out" or copy in this way is,
of course, a devalued female and schoolboy labor. It will figure as such in the
brute sexual jesting of the countrymen, who prescribe a male folk remedy to
cure another problem woman, a jealous wife, by handing her one's erect penis:

> 3. *Coun.*   Ay, do but put
> A fescue in her fist, and you shall see her
> Take a new lesson out, and be a good wench.
>   (2.3.33–35)

In this joke, female art is performed by means of male technology; that is, the
woman is temporarily both armed and disarmed by the masculine instrument
of copy.

Despite such superficially evenhanded evaluations of both male and female forms of homosocial friendship, *The Two Noble Kinsmen* works to "ground" or privilege male friendship and the collaborative arena in which spectating is purified of a female emulation, or emulation is purified of a female spectating. The purification takes the final form of nurturing competition. We are tempted to conclude from such a play that women are the objects of this male rivalry. And our conclusion would be supported by a literalized reading of Theseus, for example when he urges Emilia's attendance at the tournament, saying, "You are . . . the price and garland / To crown the question's title" (5.3.16–17). In spectacular rather than metaphorical terms, however, we see them not as valued objects but as empty circles enclosing value, like the numerous garlands, arenas, and other round enclosures of the play. By spectacular inversion, women stand for the dream of a purified male arena.

I have tried thus far to show the ways that collaboration and competition "intertangle": in speaking, in spectating, in being either performer or audience, in love and friendship. But in these examples of the paradoxes of a noble male rivalry, we have repeatedly encountered specifically artistic constructions of that rivalry. In other words, the category of artistic labor has swallowed up or included all other categories of practice, revealing the entire play as a study of the satisfactions achieved from a male labor that is specifically artistic. Moreover, the labors of *The Two Noble Kinsmen* are quite pointedly theatrical, spectating events so that the play is self-referential and, more significantly, self-endorsing. The conditions of dual authorship, then, are represented within the play as a residue of anxiety and perhaps as the intentional effect of spectacular translucency. If the effect is intentional, then some specific audience—the theater audience, the company, the managers, or the writers themselves—is intended to wonder at the writers' high, competitive collaboration. (The sustained effect of this attempt to enforce wonder may even account for the responses of some modern readers who find the play insufferable.)

The arming scene in act 3, continually circled about and reviewed by the present study for various purposes, turns out to be even more crucial for the professionalist subtext of the play since it exhibits not only the paradoxes of a nurturing rivalry but also a specifically male technology in a backstage performance of a *tekhne* or skill. The scene's clever premise is the alternation of polite discourse with the stage business of arming each other to kill—and what is more ironic, to kill one another. The dialogue is obsessed with the aesthetics of weapons and armor. The muted (or inept) comic effect is one of cumulative, involuted ironies, resulting from the participants' exaggerated, well-meaning, and temporary deference. We have already observed moments of an emulation that arouses spectacular virtue and competitions of humility. Palamon, in order to outdo Arcite's generous wish for an honorable "place" for the loser, whoever it should be, offers to accept the title of *coward* should he himself lose in order to show that these are "just trials" (3.6.105). His humility legitimates, just as brashness does, the entire male arena. We might once again formulate the speech act here as a *request to be rough,* an act reconciling collaboration and competition in speech and action. The conversation of the scene is punctuated with physical gestures that contain and license, like the conversation itself, whatever is rough:

> *Arc.*   Do I pinch you?
> *Pal.*   No.
> . . .
> *Arc.*   I'll buckle't close.
> *Pal.* By any means.
> . . .
> *Pal.*   Good cousin, thrust the buckle
> Through far enough.
> *Arc.*   I warrant you.
> . . .
> *Pal.* Thank you, Arcite.
> How do I look? Am I fall'n much away?
> *Arc.* Faith, very little. Love has us'd you kindly.
> *Pal.* I'll warrant thee, I'll strike home.
> *Arc.*   Do, and spare not.
> I'll give you cause, sweet cousin. . . .
> *Pal.* Is not this piece too strait?
> *Arc.*   No, no, 'tis well.
>   (3.6.55–86)

I will not examine the dialogue's sexual innuendo, assuming that is what is operating in these double entendres, although I would argue that the probable tone of this passage is intended to produce a homosocial locker-room snickering for the male audience rather than a homosexual reference to the characters. For the present purposes, one sees that their conversation embodies both the visions as well as the tensions of the collaborative arena in which the two contests of private victory and collaborative victory are entangled. The involutions brought about by this idealized magnanimity are evident enough here and once again bound up with art.

When Arcite begins by offering, "I'll arm you first" (3.6.53), we observe how important priority is to these collaborative competitors as artist-soldiers. We are perhaps expected to notice that the more one helps one's opponent to arm, the greater the risk to the self, and the more noble one's victory will be in the end. Politeness is radically consequential: the better, more confident fighter facilitates, through his nobility, his own defeat. What is more, in this rough use, the fight stands for the friendship, as Arcite implies when he responds to Palamon's wish that he could thank him for his services with embraces rather than blows: "I shall think either, / Well done, a noble recompense" (3.6.23–24). Blows and embraces are interchangeable, both capable of being artistically "well done."

Watching these artist-figures, as it were, behind the scene, we conclude that more important than the choice of women (ultimately decided merely by fate, not by skill) is the choice of arms. The latter is performed in delicate negotiation:

Pal. I am well and lusty: choose your arms.
Arc.   Choose you, sir.
Pal. Wilt thou exceed in all, or dost thou do it
To make me spare thee?
Arc.   If you think so, cousin,
You are deceived, for as I am a soldier,
I will not spare you.
Pal.   That's well said.
Arc.   You'll find it.
                    (3.6.45-49)

To choose first in this game (like being the starting player in collaborative art) is to confess a desire for better arms, thereby conceding one's inferiority. But cooperation and competition threaten to cancel each other out in a comedy of painful deferentiality where competitive magnanimity trips over itself. A new convention deconstructs gender division by dictating that the more deferential contestant is the more masculine contestant. On the other hand, an act of deference—letting the other choose first—could just as well be read as a strategy for victory, which implies that the other must repay, or outdo, the gesture by letting up in combat. All this male comedy depends on an awareness of the self-interfering character of a collaborative, competitive magnanimity. It addresses a male audience, assumed to be both amused and obsessed by such rituals of deference.

At the end of the cited passage the temporary dispute is resolved by a return to the first rule—contractual roughness—followed immediately by Palamon's aesthetic judgment of Arcite's conversational move. Deference, the spectacular acknowledgment of another's authority, again contains within it a potential alternative reading: to acknowledge the authority is to authorize it, and by authorizing one becomes its author. In this arena politeness threatens to subvert, and speech turns on noble gesture to disarm it. With Emilia, Palamon, and Arcite we might ask, "Is this winning?" as they tangle themselves within the involutions of a mimetic and competitive magnanimity. To "defy in fair terms" (3.6.25) is the oxymoron upon which both the play and its discourse are constructed.

IV. Men's Tournament of Art

To view the men's final tournament is not only to be a part of it, as Emilia fears, but also to constitute it as a tournament, which, Theseus tells her rather unconvincingly, could not exist as a private contest: "You must be there; / This trial is as 'twere i' th' night, and you / The only star to shine" (5.3.18-20). In her absence the event is perhaps only semipublic. In any case, if viewed, this "deed of honor" becomes a work of art:

> *The.* She shall see deeds of honor in their kind,
> Which sometime show well, pencil'd.
>
> (5.3.12–13)

Whether this means (1) "a mere sketch will represent them," or (2) "as long as they are depicted in word or image," his comment valorizes the event as public spectacle of men's art.

The desire to reconcile rough behavior with cooperative behavior ultimately determines Theseus's novel ground rules for the tournament—a game that requires critical explanation beyond what it has so far received.[23] For the contest he orders that a "pyramid" or obelisk be constructed and that each man, with the assistance of his three knights, attempt to force his opponent to touch the pillar first. While Chaucer stages a bloodless, ordinary tournament between Palamon and Arcite and their one hundred knights, *The Two Noble Kinsmen* creates a peculiar contest with significant structural relations to the many other contests of the play. Among the "games of honor" about which the two men are most nostalgic are racing and combat. Theseus interrupts their actual combat, changes the game, and adds an audience. The form of the new game is significant: the fight around an object mirrors the rivalry over the love-object. Beyond that, the new game is a synthesis of relations: the contest whose object is a common goal (love) and the contest whose object is the elimination of the other (war) are combined in the form of the pillar spectacle, which is an inverted race—by forcing the other man toward a single object that he resists, one *escapes* rather than *seeks* the "goal." Fighting not to touch the column is a physical embodiment of the deferential or self-defeating rivalry characterizing the male arena and its goal of homosocial satisfaction. The game reflects and reverses the play's obsessions. On the one hand, to spur the other on with rough talk and opposition, thus reconciling competition and collaboration, is to reverse the game of the obelisk, in which one resists with all one's strength moving in the direction that one's opponent is pushing. On the other hand, the game is a remarkable embodiment of the idealized rivalry: it replaces swordsmanship's more single-directed thrusting with the tactical give-and-take of something more like wrestling. In such a contest momentary cooperation or passivity, like a polite gesture, can be a feint in order to use, as in the martial arts, an opponent's full momentum against him. Passivity is not the opposite of power, but just one more of the tools in its box. On the other hand, full cooper-

---

23. The strongest and most illuminating discussion of the form of the contest is by Paula S. Berggren, "'For what we lack, / We laugh': Incompletion and *The Two Noble Kinsmen*," *Modern Language Studies* 14 (1984): 3–17. Berggren recognizes the physical character of the game as "strength working against itself" (7) and as a reversal of phallic assertion in having a goal one loses by touching. Her investigation of possible sources of the game identifies it as historically unique to the play.

ation, or cooperation at just the wrong moment, is fatal. Thus, this tournament figures both the idealized form and the attendant anxiety of a collaborative-competitive enterprise. The project of *The Two Noble Kinsmen* is twofold: the construction of a dream arena for homosocial labor, and the design of just the right dream game to play in it.

A metaphor for artistic collaboration, the pillar contest contrasts with the singing contest that Theseus uses for the play's ultimate figure of the rivalry between Palamon and Arcite. Summarizing the fight as a nurturing competi-tion, Theseus narrates an aspiring, self-undoing contest that proceeds toward undifferentiation and absence of priority, a knot of love rendering useless the judgment of spectators, like the race that left all the spectators behind:

> I have heard
> Two emulous Philomels beat the ear o' th' night
> With their contentious throats, now one the higher,
> Anon the other, then again the first,
> And by and by out-breasted, that the sense
> Could not be judge between 'em. So it far'd
> Good space between these kinsmen, till heavens did
> Make hardly one the winner.
>   (5.3.123–30)

The play returns to the circumstances of its production through the striking analogy of a singing contest. A bold tale in which the heavens intervene to make losing into winning, in which the power of spectating to decide a contest is neutralized, and in which an audience is too noble to assign either man victory, is a tale serving as the ideal vehicle for an artistic project in which group and individual success are both interdependent and at odds. The final tournament is, ultimately, an inverse spectacle of fame, since the obelisk, the icon of eternal fame, is to be avoided rather than sought. More precisely, the pillar of fame is what one spurs the other to touch by working in selfless collaboration. By the special rules of the contest, however, to touch the male monument is to lose girl, friend, and life, in a repetition of the play's paradoxes of losing by winning, and vice versa. By a complicated representation of nobility and noble contests, *The Two Noble Kinsmen* rereads Chaucer as a stalemate dream permitting con-tinued life within the contradictions that produce value and meaning in an arena of artistic, competitive, and male homosocial labor. Circumstances, not people, conspire to reconcile collaboration and competition perfectly.

But the idealizations of male production, and the consequent reduction and exclusion of female spectatorship, do not tell the full story. *The Two Noble Kinsmen* outdoes its own representations by an even more extravagant mysti-fication of its own artistic labor. In the last degree of mystification of this labor, art takes on the character of the radical other, the mimetic female kingdom in which differentiation and competition with the other dissolve. The highest representation of a mystified homosocial labor, what such representation dreams to become a metaphor of, is paradoxically female labor, whose product is a child who is also a work of art but not a victory. The hyperidealized work, then, inevitably draws a physically sensuous imagery from lovemaking, like the flower imagery of Emilia and Flavina. We have already noted how Palamon and Arcite's collaborative meditation is regarded as their child: "We are one another's wife, ever begetting / New births of love" (2.2.80–81). In another instance, when we hear a description of physical male beauty such as the messenger gives of the freckle-faced knight attending Palamon, and when that description strives for its most mystified status, the imagery again turns toward pregnancy:

> . . . his arms are brawny,
> Lin'd with strong sinews; to the shoulder-piece
> Gently they swell, like women new-conceiv'd,
> Which speaks him prone to labor, never fainting
> Under the weight of arms. . . .
>
>   (4.2.126–30)

The Two Noble Kinsmen desires to be another "new birth of love" of a collaborative homosocial labor. Accordingly, it produces at the end a boy, who appears to be a child actor (comparing himself to a "schoolboy" in his dumbfounded fear) to deliver the Epilogue, which is conventionally apologetic and which teasingly calls for a judgment of the entire spectacle. The homosocial arena surrounds both story and play as the boy addresses his "good night" only to men—unlike typically Shakespearean epilogues addressing both sexes.

The Prologue (whether or not it is a later addition) also introduces the ideal of a homosocial birth by comparing the staying power of the play to the staying power of a wife's modesty after the marriage day ("New plays and maidenheads are near akin" [Pro. 1]), before turning to an announcement of the play's source and competitive patriarch, Chaucer ("a poet never went / More famous yet 'twixt Po and silver Trent" [Pro. 11–12]), who is significantly termed the play's "noble breeder and a pure" (Pro. 10). The Prologue reinforces the desired, collaborative nobility of the writers by expressing the fear that if they fail ("if we let fall the nobleness of this") Chaucer himself will lose fame: "O, fan / From me the witless chaff of such a writer / That blasts my bays and my fam'd works makes lighter / Than Robin Hood!" (Pro. 18–21). Originality and unoriginality are reconciled, as are the productive modes of competition and collaboration. In the spirit of the play, the Prologue thus constructs a selflessness by which one noble assists and advances the other. The fear of an aspiring artistic epigone is also uttered: "it were an endless thing / And too ambitious, to aspire to him, / Weak as we are, and almost breathless swim / In this deep water" (Pro. 22–25). Repeating the motif of athletic effort, while transferring it to the realm of writing, the Prologue goes on to ask for its own assistants ("your helping hands" [26]), to rescue it from drowning.

Representing itself as a collaborative birth of homosocial satisfaction, of "noble breeders" who bond together even across time to do noble things with each other's words in conversation, *The Two Noble Kinsmen* thus translucently represents the circumstances, and reveals the anxieties, of an idealized collaboration and, by extension, of the specific collaboration of its two authors. My interpretation, in sum, suggests a collaborative contest between rivals and friends of more comparable professional stature—not between the retiring master impresario and the young playwright who was replacing him. This particular professionalist subtext would be odd for a retiring, but not for an aspiring, playwright.

In any case, whoever dreamed it, the play is a compulsory dream for a masculinist theater, a masque of labor for reconciling collaboration and authorship. The inescapable deconstructive conclusion is that its oppositions interanimate one another—that collaboration is the ground of individual authorship, as individual authorship is the ground of collaboration. Let us escape from such a conclusion. We do so by recognizing that the special tension is only significant insofar as the binaries are not logical but historical. That is, this writing occurs at a time when half the plays were produced in one mode, half in the other, and when their interdependency was institutional and gender-specific rather than always rhetorical. Grounded in these facts, even a fanciful conjecture is more historical than an endless play of figures.

In this spirit I offer such a conjecture, having concluded that *The Two Noble Kinsmen* is a title match and spectacle of professional collaboration with some rules, some spectators, some judge, and some prize.

V. Coda

A play that presents art as the children of men's labor imagines a system devoid of paternity or legitimacy questions; yet, ironically, its own paternity has been most seriously in doubt. The play touches on paternity suits of its own—from the Prologue, in which the writer or writers defer to Chaucer, mentioning him only as its "noble breeder," to Palamon's odd prayer before battle to Venus, whose power enabled a gouty, deformed, eighty-year-old man to have a child by his child-bride—or so it is said:

> This anatomy
> Had by his young fair fere a boy, and I
> Believ'd it was his, for she swore it was,
> And who would not believe her?
> (5.1.115–18)

The madness of the Jailer's Daughter raises other paternity questions. She praises Palamon because all the maids of the town are supposedly in love with him, and she muses that he has made "at least two hundred" of them pregnant (4.1.129). If she swears they are his, who would not believe her? When we last see her, she goes off to sleep with the nameless Wooer, about whom she says,

"We shall have many children" (5.2.94). Those children may get different answers from mother and father when they inquire as to their paternity. Who you are depends on who is asking.

The title page of the first and only published quarto of *The Two Noble Kinsmen* indicates Shakespeare as its breeder, along with Fletcher. But the publisher twelve years later sold his copyright without Shakespeare's name. Title pages were often inaccurate, and dispute still exists about the play's style or styles.[24] The inaccuracy of title pages at the time reinforces the present claim that the era was as divided as its plays were between the values of single authorship and those of collaboration. Writers of Shakespeare's time, like poststructuralists, were groping toward concepts of authorship. Title pages are sites of conflict over sovereignty and must have been subject to whatever forces of circumstance and competition existed in each case. Jonson shows us the territorial thinking when, in order to keep his single-title authorship of *Sejanus*, he painstakingly rewrote all his collaborator's passages, in what he implies is a generous prevention of a "usurpation," as he calls it. The title page is thus yet another arena where we often find the residues of some power relation: there, a coauthor might somehow lose his title; or writers who contributed different amounts (if the records of differing payments are indicative), not to mention different qualities, might win equivalent titles as authors.[25]

Let the reluctant rivalry of *The Two Noble Kinsmen* represent its writers' competitive and collaborative feelings, an anxious and intertangled knot of ambition to promote the self, the other, and the play. Stage a tournament for writing, and let the splendid choice of arena for the tournament be Chaucer's tale of deep play between friends where everything is at stake. Expand the old tale with considerations of a collaborative artistic nobility and, risking your own defeat, spur on your co-adjutor. Dwell on these paradoxes for your spectators, who may have bet on writers as they bet on actors, and win points by showing magnanimity as you show off your style. The audience will know the circumstances of the collaboration: the private spectacle and contest behind the public one. The collaborators should both be of a comparable age—Fletcher and the other one—but more important than age is that they should both be arriving at a propitious moment to whet professional desire. (The King's Men in 1613 had arrived at a professional watershed. They were about to lose, or had just lost, their chief playwright, a sovereign of sorts and very successful. Fletcher's old collaborator Beaumont was no longer collaborating for he had married and left the arena. Fletcher himself may have just married. That year

24. For a summary of the developing issues and positions, see Proudfoot, "Introduction" to *The Two Noble Kinsmen*, xiii-xix; the annotated bibliography in Erdman and Fogel, *Evidence for Authorship*, 486–94; G. Harold Metz, *Four Plays Ascribed to Shakespeare: An Annotated Bibliography* (New York: Garland, 1982), 135–81; and Hallett Smith, "Introduction" to *The Two Noble Kinsmen*, in *The Riverside Shakespeare*, ed. G. Blakemore Evans (Boston: Houghton Mifflin, 1974). For additional historical materials, see E. K. Chambers, *The Elizabethan Stage* (Oxford: Clarendon, 1923), 3:226–27; E. H. C. Oliphant, *The Plays of Beaumont and Fletcher* (New Haven: Yale University Press, 1927), 325–48; S. Schoenbaum, *Annals of English Drama 975–1700* (London: Methuen, 1964).

25. Bentley, *Profession of Dramatist*, 206, 201.

their theater was to burn down, and they would by the summer of 1614 have a new arena.)

Let there be some ground rules for the exercise of power. If there were usual procedures of collaboration (Bentley conjectures, without real evidence, that there were) let them be followed, but there will still be decisions to make, such as the choice of which acts each will write (usually thought to be a common means of division). Let the decision be made like a choice of arms, magnanimously, so that to choose first hints of one's weakness or lack of self-confidence. It is no special honor to go first. Let the weaker man have the positional or material advantage, at least the first and last acts, usually attributed for the most part to Fletcher's collaborator. Let your own writing spur on the other's. Let winning be everything, and nothing. Yet you must win; by making moves that the other won't match, by appropriating his moves, and even by writing him into an occasional corner. Let Shakespeareans attempt to explain inconsistent elements either as failures of design or as harmonious parts of an unobvious, organic unity—as if collaborative work is somehow on principle pacific and never dialogic; as if the paradigm for writing is editing; as if there were no place for, or no consequences of, professional envy, the emotion producing the chance conclusion of the play when a little "envious flint," envious of the horse dancing "to th' music / His own hooves made (for, as they say, from iron / Came music's origin)" (5.4.59–61), terrifies Arcite's horse, which throws the winner to his death. Let Fletcher win.

What prize? The 1634 title page of the play is a page of titles. "Written by the memorable Worthies of their time; Mr. *John Fletcher,* and Mr. *William Shakespeare Gent.*" One of its titles is *Gentleman,* applying, if it does, to Fletcher as well as Shakespeare, whose earlier personal ambition was a coat of arms. The other title is appropriate for military champions; the "Nine Worthies" were also contemporarily known as "The Nine Nobles." In a contest for fame, through a play that represents its own contest for fame around a "pyramid," one of the collaborators will lose title, fame, and, in the arena of the book, his name. His work is subsumed under the title of an artistic sovereign or master. In Italian Renaissance workshop paintings, novice work was treated this way; in fact, the signature of the master from some workshops actually confirms that the painting was not his but the work of assistants. In other cases, a master might sign, with his own signature, a student's work that particularly impressed him. What seems to us dishonest or cavalier merely operated in an unfamiliar system of honorable collaboration. We understand only with difficulty an era of artistic production in which the status of authorship was not as fixed as it now is, or was in contention, as is suggested by the circumstances of Elizabethan collaboration.

At about this time Fletcher becomes the new main playwright of the King's Men, replacing Shakespeare. He may have collaborated in the same year as *The Two Noble Kinsmen* on a play with Nathan Field and Philip Massinger.[26]

---

26. *Henslowe Papers, Being Documents Supplementary to Henslowe's Diary,* ed. Walter W. Greg (London: A. H. Bullen, 1907; rpt. New York: AMS Press, 1975), article 68, pp. 65–66.

Field, an actor-playwright, may have received Shakespeare's shares to the company, as Fletcher received his position. Massinger, by some scholars assigned the non-Fletcherian parts of the play, was buried, in a gesture of spectacular friendship, in a single grave with Fletcher.[27] The year 1613 was something of a watershed in the circumstances of Fletcher's dramatic career. After his collaborations of this and the preceding years, his usual practice changed to single authorship. Let Shakespeare, as artistic sovereign, be the judge of this masque of labor, this title match and tour de force of collaboration about collaboration. (But if Shakespeare was coauthor after all, let Fletcher be termed "coadjutor" in the term's other, power-differentiated sense, signifying the assistant to an aging and feeble bishop, an "assistance" in preparation for taking over the position.) Let Shakespeare judge between suitors, as Elizabeth did for Sidney's *Lady of May,* in which the judging sovereign is written into the spectacle, though the actual judgment left to her. Let the weaker collaborator honor the judge by displaying a familiar dense style and echoing some familiar moments of the master. Let the translucent play imply how hard it will be for a noble judge to decide between such emulous Philomels. If he has to decide between the styles of the future, let Shakespeare elect what some see as a cheap theatricality, over what some see as "the voice and music of the master."[28] If someone magnanimously swears the child is his, who would not believe him?

After all of this dreaming, let Shakespeare, for a moment reversing the direction of the cultural narrative in which he and his coworkers were all spectacularly inscribed, leave the powerful arena of artistic satisfaction and return home to three women.

Appendix: Shakespearean Conversation and
The Two Noble Kinsmen

The following is a brief discussion of a stylistic criterion that best distinguishes, I believe, the dialogue of the non-Fletcherian parts of *The Two Noble Kinsmen* from Shakespeare, thus arguing against Shakespeare's coauthorship. The criterion is the representation of natural conversation, a stylistic determinant not captured by any traditional stylistic tests of authorship, yet one crucial to the study of Shakespeare's language. A full discussion of Shakespeare's habit and skill at this can be found in my "Merry and Weary Conversation: Textual Uncertainty in *As You Like It,* II.iv.," *ELH* 46 (1979): 21–34. I must forego the possibility of proof here for several reasons: one can notice the differences in ability to represent conversation only in large stretches of text; procedures for identifying chains of speech acts would require an enormous interpretive apparatus; and in this case I am suggesting what is *not* there, an evidentiary situation entirely different from demonstrating what is there.

27. T. W. Baldwin, *The Organization and Personnel of the Shakespearean Company* (Princeton: Princeton University Press, 1927), 51.

28. Alfred Hart, "Shakespeare and the Vocabulary of *The Two Noble Kinsmen," Review of English Studies* 10 (1934): 274.

I can, however, give the reader a few guides to perform his or her own examination of the difference. First, one can recognize that one of the major skills Shakespeare developed was to represent the dialogic nature of conversation, including intentional or unintentional violations of straightforward communication such as topic changing, giving more or less information than is requested, breaking the established tone, answering questions with questions, and so on. In addition to showing how we do things to others' words in our speech, he becomes much more subtle at what are known as "indirect speech acts," in which an utterance takes a different form than its actual pragmatic force or point. In a direct speech act, for example, a question-form is used to ask a question ("What day is it today?"). In an indirect speech act, a question-form might be used for an entirely different point—to thank, to command, to request, and so on ("Can you pass the salt?" is a request that only looks like a question). To see Shakespeare's remarkable development at portraying the messy—though perhaps logical even in its messiness—sequence of real speech, one might compare the flat dialogue of the proposition scene of King Edward and Lady Grey in *3 Henry VI* (3.2) with the subtleties of the proposition scene of Angelo and Isabella in *Measure for Measure* (3.1). Since both scenes portray conversation at cross-purposes, the latter stands out in relief.

The non-Fletcherian parts of *The Two Noble Kinsmen*, while rich in a Shakespeare-style poetic diction and complex syntax, are almost entirely devoid of the misconstructions, inference-drawings, and indirect modes of conversation that occur in what is summed up in the idea of "uptake." Typically, the dialogue there is more limited to direct speech acts, in patterns of question/answer, assertion/agreement or disagreement, and topic/comment, requiring less sense of the context in order to convey complete meaning. Even the occasional interruption of dialogue is achieved mechanically, chiefly to convey information:

Pal. . . . that which rips my bosom
Almost to th' heart's—
    Arc.   Our uncle Creon.
    Pal.   He,
A most unbounded tyrant, whose successes
Makes heaven unfear'd . . .
                  (1.2.61–64).

A few brief instances from later Shakespeare plays may attune one to the skills Shakespeare had by that time developed, unevident in *The Two Noble Kinsmen*. (Fletcher, though otherwise stylistically quite distinct from Shakespeare, is actually much closer to Shakespeare in this.)

1. *Surry.* May it please your Grace—
    King.   No, sir, it does not please me.
I had thought I had had men of some understanding . . .
              (*Henry VIII*, 5.2.169–70)

The interruption is fully charged, as a deliberate refusal to accept a stock politeness, by taking the word *please* literally. The linguistic moment is fully dramatic, when an attempt to seize the floor and change the direction of conversation is abruptly warded off by the king, who willfully reads the conventional indirect speech act (a request to be heard) as if it were the direct one of its verbal form (a request to please).

2. *Anne.*   Pray do not deliver
What here y'have heard to her.
        Old L.   What do you think me? *Exeunt*
                        (*Henry VIII*, 2.3.106–7)

Shakespeare can even end a scene with a question, unlike a beginner at representing dialogue. But it is an indirect speech act—not really a question, but a promise not to tell. It carries with it a clear-cut tone, full implications of the spirit of the woman, and an index to their relationship. For a lesser writer the form of her response might simply be an agreement, however emphatically expressed, that she would not tell.

3. Subtle construction of oblique reference in conversation is represented in *Pericles* when Boult, who has just gotten customers for the virginal Marina's services, makes a very indirect request that he might try her out first, a request only developed as such in their shared, oblique language moves:

Boult. But, mistress, if I have bargain'd for the joint—
Bawd. Thou mayst cut a morsel off the spit.
Boult. I may so.
Bawd. Who should deny it?
                        (4.2.129–33)

By force of the delicacy of the context and evasion of responsibility, the process of request and permission doesn't even take on the speech act forms of request or permission. The bawd's final permission is masked as a question.

4. As the plot develops in *The Tempest* to kill Alonso, questions and answers are again obliquely used:

Antonio.   What a sleep were this
For your advancement! Do you understand me?
        Sebastian. Methinks I do.
                        (2.1.267–69)

The question here, superficially about understanding words, is actually a plea for consent to an assassination not spoken about as such. Sebastian's tentative reply is a partial denial, at that moment, of consent. We understand not that he is unclear about the point of Antonio's speech, but that he is hesitant to accept its clear proposal.

Readers are invited to compare these examples and others they can readily find, where there is such a striking residue of meaning outside the linguistic forms themselves, to the conversational sequences of the supposedly Shakespearean scenes in *The Two Noble Kinsmen*.

4 The Two Noble Kinsmen
Shakespeare and the Problem of Authority

Michael D. Bristol

"Shakespeare" occupies the center of contemporary, Anglo-American politics of literary culture, not only by virtue of his preeminent literary and cultural prestige, but also because of the degree to which he represents the canon of great literature for a wide public outside the context of academic literary scholarship. Within the perspective of normative institutional scholarship, however, it is evident that "Shakespeare" is a concept that does not bear much looking into. Expressions that take the form of "Shakespeare plus predicate" are in constant use among scholars of every ideological coloration. These expressions, which have the force of an ipse dixit, are deployed to reinforce a diverse range of assertions about collective life and culture. Although the spectrum of legitimate contention is apparently quite wide, it nevertheless excludes the fundamental question of "Shakespeare's" authority. In exactly what sense is Shakespeare to be regarded as the originator or begetter of the plays that bear his name? To pose this question is to demand some account of the historical practice of literary and theatrical production during the early modern period and of its social, legal, and technical ramifications. To proclaim, as many contemporary scholars do, that Shakespeare was a "man of the theater" is not an answer to this question, but instead represents the endless deferral of the problem. There is the further difficulty that Shakespeare's oeuvre retains its cultural force, or power to compel affiliation and conformity with some cluster of meaning, some totality of social, ethical, and moral imperatives.[1] This force is said to flow directly from the largely unexamined origin; from an artistic will that was "not of an age, but for all time." By means of this gesture, institutional scholarship excuses itself from giving any account of its own situation, or of its decisive role in sustaining and administering the authority to which we give the name of "Shakespeare."

In raising the issue of institutionalized scholarship, it is not my intention to treat it as a kind of carnival dummy to be ridiculed, thrashed, and run out of town so that the "real Shakespeare" may be revealed in all his pristine charismatic authority. The claim to be independent of the complex historical tradition of institutionalized scholarship, and to speak out of some kind of privileged, unmediated access to the original Shakespeare, is an expression of a fundamentalist and anti-intellectual attitude, a concern not with the creation

---

1. Edward Said, *Beginnings: Intention and Method* (New York: Basic, 1974), 83.

and dissemination of knowledge but with its administration and control.[2] In this discussion, I assume that the institutional "Shakespeare" is the one that really matters to us. To realize that "Shakespeare" actually corresponds to a historically contingent, institutionally sustained cultural artifact is not, however, to accept uncritically everything that has happened within that institution.[3] On the contrary, such a realization allows for interrogation of the persistent idealization of canonical authors. This idealization sanctions a "return to the text" as the decisive ethical move, conceding authority to "Shakespeare" and then moving directly to the question of what that authority has to say—directly to the generic "Shakespeare plus predicate."

In the discussion that follows I will argue that "Shakespeare" has come to represent canonical or lawful authority by virtue of the historical elaboration of an institutional tradition in which the publication of a First Folio was the decisive founding event. The broad, implicit claims of the First Folio have not been, indeed could never have been, questioned. To begin with, it established the principle of legitimate succession, though not necessarily the identity of the legitimate successors. This legitimate succession is, moreover, to be embodied in a text that will provide the exclusive channel or medium of transmission. Any transfer of authority, that is to say, interpretation, whether in the form of reading or performance, will be dominated by the ethical imperatives of preservation, restoration, and the return to lost origins. In addition, the First Folio establishes the principle of closure and offers the guarantee that it will put an end to the sporadic appearance of more plays by Shakespeare. Although there has been surprisingly little erosion of this claim since the appearance of the First Folio in 1623, *The Two Noble Kinsmen* is still regarded as almost-but-not-quite canonical, neither definitively included nor definitively excluded.

This play offers a particularly useful point of departure for consideration of "Shakespeare's" authority. In the first place, the problem of attribution and authenticity invites consideration of the basis on which institutionalized scholarship acknowledges literary paternity and therefore the cultural force of particular documents. Second, the narrative material itself can be read as a demonstration or reenactment of the origin and foundation of civil authority in which Theseus's unification of the scattered communities of Attica into the Athenian polis is the exemplary illustration. In the argument that follows, I maintain that in both aspects of the problem *The Two Noble Kinsmen* should be regarded as an ominous text. The appearance of one more play by Shakespeare suggests the possibility of disputed succession by blurring, if only slightly, the distinction between the canonical and the uncanonical. Even more disturbing, *The Two Noble Kinsmen* challenges the guarantee of closure, especially as this has come to be objectified in the doctrine of the Last Plays. This doctrine elaborates the idea of a definitive number of texts making up the

2. Richard Levin, *New Readings vs. Old Plays: Recent Trends in the Reinterpretation of English Renaissance Drama* (Chicago: University of Chicago Press, 1979).

3. Stanley Fish, "Profession Despise Thyself: Fear and Self-Loathing in Literary Studies," *Critical Inquiry* 10 (1983): 349–64.

canon into an idea of thematic resolution so that the Last Plays are read as the reconciliation of conflicting tendencies present in earlier works. *The Two Noble Kinsmen* constitutes a disruptive challenge to this doctrine in that it insinuates the reappearance of pervasive tragic violence of a kind supposedly dispelled or reconciled in the Last Plays.

I. Canonical Authority and the Problem of Apocrypha

The status of Shakespeare as a canonical author is well established and has not been in doubt for a considerable time. One of the fundamental reasons for this relatively uncontested status is that the First Folio of 1623 supplies the essential element for the subsequent recognition of any canonical authority by fixing that authority to a definite and limited number of individual books. Although the compilers of the First Folio are the founding fathers of institutionalized Shakespeare scholarship, their achievement was imperfect. The First Folio has never been regarded as the last word on the question of a Shakespeare text.[4] The canon as specified by the First Folio contains a fairly large number of anomalies, exceptional cases, and untypical examples—"early plays," "problem comedies," collaborations, and corruptions. In addition, many of the individual texts are problematic, derived from heterogeneous and not always reliable textual sources with differing relationships to what is assumed to be the author's own original composition. Nevertheless, the First Folio is a decisive event in canon formation in that it establishes a deuteronomic program as the ongoing basis for defining and elaborating "Shakespeare's" authority.[5]

To speak of a deuteronomic program in relation to the works of "Shakespeare" is to emphasize the secondariness of the literary material we honor and preserve under that name. This should not be construed as a suggestion that this material was really, or originally, written by some other person. Nor is it a case of proclaiming the "death of the author." The deuteronomic program, however, invents and retrospectively applies to various original writings by the individual Shakespeare a specific and historically limited model of literary authorship, specifically the model of individualized artistic production. The compilers of the First Folio thus seem to have followed or imitated the practice, eccentric and innovative at the time, of Ben Jonson in presenting theatrical scripts to the public in a finished, literary format. Jonson was at some pains to nominate himself an author, and in his encomium for his colleague he recruits Shakespeare to the same métier. What this amounts to is not the "death of the author" in a generic sense, but rather the birth of an author after the fact. Shakespeare's dramatic works, as originally published in the First Folio, are deuteronomic in respect to an earlier textual production that conformed to a quite different set

---

4. W. W. Greg, *The Shakespeare First Folio: Its Bibliographical and Textual History* (Oxford: Clarendon, 1955).

5. Gerald L. Bruns, "Canon and Power," *Critical Inquiry* 10 (1984): 462–80; Moshe Weinfeld, *Deuteronomy and the Deuteronomic School* (Oxford: Clarendon, 1972); Bruce Metzger, *An Introduction to the Apocrypha* (New York: Oxford University Press, 1957).

of working conditions, a radically different allocation of authority from that insinuated by the printing of collected works. "Shakespeare's" authority, which enters into our cultural history via this particular pathway of dissemination, can then be deployed to reinforce a particular division of labor within the institutions that sustain literary culture. In general the deuteronomic program sanctions the practice of assigning responsibility for its own work in producing consciousness to the nominal authority who is at once removed from direct accountability and at the same time firmly in the possession of the institution that administers culture in his name.

The publication of the First Folio should be seen as an early and a decisive victory for the deuteronomic program in which a full and unified conception of "The Man and His Works" virtually abolished all other local, fragmentary versions of Shakespeare. This event gives precedence to the written text at the expense of prophetic or charismatic authority.[6] The superior force of written or printed textuality favors the formation of a complex monopoly of knowledge that has the capacity to disseminate a uniform version of a particular canon over a wide geographical and social space.[7] This superiority of force gives rise to a distinctive ideological formation connected with all canon formation, namely the ethos of preservation. This outlook assumes that it is definitely better for the Shakespeare canon to exist than for it not to exist. It assumes further that the canon should be both large and exclusive. The more of Shakespeare we have, the better for us, provided only that no spurious or wrongfully attributed material is smuggled in. The First Folio thus does more than merely preserve the text of plays that might otherwise have been lost. It also provides the basis for a full and elaborate hierarchy of Shakespeare's oeuvre and for a coherent narrative overview of the canon as a whole. Differences within the canon are treated according to completely different analytic criteria and procedures than are differences between "Shakespearean" and "un-Shakespearean" materials.

The historical success of textuality, and of the powerful institutional apparatus that supports it, coincides with the virtual collapse of theater as a strong, independent center of cultural authority. In the case of the canonical, that is to say the deuteronomic, Shakespeare, the power of the text has been used against the theater, disabling its capacity to serve as the source and the origin of social and cultural institution making. This is, I take it, the real meaning of the virtually constant border disputes, skirmishes, and raids carried out between advocates of performance-oriented interpretation and the practitioners of more strictly literary and textual styles of criticism. The debate concerning text versus performance, like so many other professional disputes, is in fact a quarrel over precedence and the allocation of authority. One reason for the largely trivial character of this debate is that the question of authority is never openly addressed, nor is there any sense among the advocates of performance of where their own authority might come from.

6. Max Weber, *The Theory of Social and Economic Organization*, trans. E. M. Henderson and Talcott Parsons (New York: The Free Press, 1964).
7. Harold Innis, *The Bias of Communication* (Toronto: University of Toronto Press, 1951).

The First Folio thus accomplishes several purposes at once. It establishes priority for the conception of "The Man and His Works" as a unified totality. It effectively claims cultural authority and power for the text and diminishes the theater to the status of a subaltern, the dutiful agent of superior cultural authority. It substitutes the ethos of preservation for all radical or prophetic revisionism. In other words, the First Folio, even with its many imperfections, objectifies the principle of canonical authority and supplies the necessary conditions for its subsequent dissemination and administration.

Canon formation is never an entirely self-evident process, since the unity and coherence of the conception of "The Man and His Works" are open to serious philosophical and historical questioning.[8] In the case of "Shakespeare," the problem seems even more difficult. It is now accepted by some scholars that access to Shakespeare's original composition is impossible. More radically, it has been suggested that the plays first presented themselves only as a series of more or less ephemeral versions, or even that no finished original of any kind ever existed.[9] The situation is complicated by a number of individual preservations in quarto, some of which are "bad," of dubious authority. There is, however, a full deuteronomic compilation that purports to preserve and to represent the lost originals but that should also be thought of as standing in place of those lost originals. This substitution might appear to weaken the claim of the deuteronomic program to authoritative status, but in fact the force of the project is actually enhanced and strengthened by the effacement of the original, which can be reconstructed and nuanced in ways that favor the continuity of certain institutional and social forms and the discontinuity of others. One reason for this enhanced authority is, of course, the incremental value that the textual objects have acquired by virtue of their threatened loss and subsequent recuperation. This is further reinforced by the retrospective character of any deuteronomic program, which carries with it the implicit guarantee that everything merely ephemeral has been excluded from what is otherwise a finished totality. Finally, the editors or compilers do not write or compose in their own name but in the name of an authority already receding from contingent social reality. As Gerald Bruns has argued, the idea of a canon is a political rather than a literary one.[10] What is at stake in canon formation is nothing less than a struggle for power, in particular the culturally acknowledged power to deploy the force of collective tradition. This is in effect a religious power to control the redemptive media; in the case of an apparently secular critical field, the struggle is carried out in the name of "Shakespeare" rather than of "Moses" or "The Logos," but the project of retrospective canon formation has a similar cultural purpose in each case.

8. Michel Foucault, "What Is an Author?," in *Language, Counter-Memory, Practice*, ed. Donald F. Bouchard (Ithaca: Cornell University Press, 1977).

9. E. A. J. Honigman, *The Stability of Shakespeare's Text* (London: Arnold, 1965); Eleanor Prosser, *2 Henry IV: Shakespeare's Anonymous Editors* (Stanford: Stanford University Press, 1981); Stephen Urkowitz, *Shakespeare's Revision of King Lear* (Princeton: Princeton University Press, 1980).

10. Bruns, "Canon and Power," 478.

The existence of a larger, rather than a smaller, canon of Shakespeare plays makes it possible to extend the application of the concept "Shakespearean" without confusing the boundary between canonical plays by "Shakespeare" and all those plays known to be written by other authors. Viewed from a distance the canon appears to be stable and quiescent. From another perspective the entire project may appear quite ready to come unraveled. In addition to the first two quite unproblematic categories there are at least three others, each of which gives rise to its own kind of uneasiness. In addition to the early plays and the incidental corruptions, which do not materially threaten the ideal form of the finished and complete oeuvre, there are (1) canonical plays, parts of which are not by Shakespeare; (2) at least one apocryphal play in the complex sense of something hidden or held in reserve, supplementary to the canon but excluded from full and equal membership; (3) plays wrongfully attributed to Shakespeare, including most but not all of the plays added to the second impression of the Third Folio, such as *The Tragedy of Locrine* and *The London Prodigal*. Of these three additional and intermediate categories, the third is the most immediately and easily disposed of by the application of conventional philological and bibliographical methods so as to exclude in a final and decisive way all texts that wrongfully assert or hint at a Shakespearean origin.[11] As to the first category of known collaborations that are nevertheless canonical, these are absorbed by assigning them to a kind of permanent junior status in the hierarchy of the Shakespearean oeuvre. This eliminates virtually all the borderline cases and on the whole makes the canon in the sense that any canon requires broad agreement as to the number of texts it contains.[12] There is, however, one borderline case that cannot be resolved by the application of any combination of procedures.

The strange case of *The Two Noble Kinsmen* represents a genuine instance of an apocryphal text in the fullest sense of that complex term. To say that a text is apocryphal is not necessarily to say that it is spurious. On the contrary, the concept of *apocrypha* may be better understood as things hidden or held in reserve. The apocrypha are not simply illicit or uncanonical texts; if they were, they would not constitute a problem for the orderly dissemination of knowledge. As distinct from canonical texts, apocryphal writings are perhaps best thought of as close, but on the whole secret, affiliates of a particular canon, suitable for private, learned, or esoteric consideration, but not on the whole suitable for general, popular dissemination on the same basis as canonical writings.[13]

The title page of *The Two Noble Kinsmen* names Shakespeare and Fletcher as authors. Since it has not been possible by the application of philological or stylistic tests to convince everyone that this simply represents a forgery, there is

11. *The Shakespeare Apocrypha,* ed. C. F. Tucker Brooke (Oxford: Oxford University Press, 1908).

12. T. Henshaw, *The Writings: The Third Division of the Old Testament Canon* (London: George Allen and Unwin, 1963).

13. Bruns, "Canon and Power," 478.

a reluctantly sustained consensus that the attribution must be accepted.[14] Exclusion from the canon cannot follow from this determination, nor is collaboration itself grounds for denying this play full recognition within the canon. The main barrier to full canonical status is not the fact of collaboration, but the fact of collaboration combined with the failure to qualify for the original deuteronomic program. As to the question of why the compilers of the First Folio, and even of the Second Folio, did not include this play, not much is known. G. E. Bentley remarks only that it is puzzling.[15] It is possible that the play was excluded from the First Folio and thus from much fuller canonical status as the result of mere accident or circumstance. On the other hand, there may have been substantive programmatic reasons for the editors to withhold this play or to refuse to identify it with Shakespeare's oeuvre. The fact that neither chance nor deliberate conspiracy can be ruled out ought to suggest that the ethos of preservation cannot be taken as a sufficient account of this difficult problem. The criteria of inclusion and exclusion, the sense of identity and difference, are unsystematic, arbitrary, and incapable of being well specified. In other words the very necessary categories of "Shakespeare" and "non-Shakespeare" are neither as clear nor as valuable as the institution would seem to require.

The Two Noble Kinsmen approaches the canon from without, like an uninvited guest, a stranger with familiar features. It is assigned the status of a supplement, but, as with any supplement to a finished totality or canon, it constitutes a danger to that totality.[16] Since an apocryphal text may contain an esoteric or even heterodox teaching, it constitutes a threat to the relationship that prevails between a particular center of authority and the people whose intellectual and cultural lives are administered by that agency. An apocryphal text diverges from the center of authority to an alarming degree without offering to that authority sufficient reason for absolute exclusion or suppression.

The secular authority exercised in the name of "Shakespeare" does not have its origin in a singular, historically contingent individual, no matter how exceptional a subject he may have been. In a sense, the production of authority proceeds in the opposite direction. That is, "Shakespeare" has its source in the formation and re-formation of secular authority, which substantiates itself by objectifying, naming, and venerating some manifestation of the sacred. The politics of literary culture have the forms of a religion in the limited, materialist sense suggested by Durkheim and elaborated in the tradition of his sociology of religion.[17] The conventions of a social system may be a ramshackle and improvised construction of ordered principles, archaic practices, purely arbitrary preferences, and typographical errors. The function of religion is to

14. Greg, First Folio, 76ff.

15. G. E. Bentley, Shakespeare: A Biographical Handbook (New Haven: Yale University Press, 1961), 192.

16. Jacques Derrida, Of Grammatology, trans. Gayatri Chakravorty Spivak (Baltimore: Johns Hopkins University Press, 1974), 141–65; Leo Strauss, Persecution and the Art of Writing (Chicago: University of Chicago Press, 1950).

17. Emile Durkheim, The Elementary Forms of the Religious Life, trans. J. Swain (London: George Allen and Unwin, 1915).

objectify the most valuable and sustaining patterns of feeling within collective life and to cause them to be experienced as "the sacred" or "transcendental other." Numerous versions of "Shakespeare" exist; that is, numerous sensibilities seek to derive authority from this figuration of the sacred. *The Two Noble Kinsmen* is, however, equally troubling to all these versions of "Shakespeare" because it is by no means clear who or what would finally sanction or authorize a reading of a text with such an ambiguous allocation of authority. The apocryphal status of the text indefinitely suspends any possibility of reading as the return to origins. Alternatively, reading *The Two Noble Kinsmen* may indeed constitute a return to origins, but not necessarily to an origin with the genial and reassuring features of "Shakespeare" as his authority is resolved by the deuteronomic program and the doctrine of the last plays.

The Two Noble Kinsmen reveals too explicitly tendencies inherent all along in the canonical "Shakespeare," tendencies that are, however, disciplined by the affirmation of the reconciliatory power of imagination and erotic love. Intermittent disclosures of a pervasive underlying violence are referable, within the deuteronomic program as a whole, to the plenitude of imaginative sensibility provided by the last plays, and above all by *The Tempest*. What *The Two Noble Kinsmen* portends is that there is something more to be said, and that something more, in effect, cancels the reconciliatory hope. The text is thus a kind of scandal in that it denies priority to any form of sensibility in the formation and coherence of social life. It suggests instead that collective life is secured as a purely temporary expedient against baleful and malevolent energies, against the possibility of interminable social violence. Secular authority, personified in the character of Theseus, does indeed have its origin in religion, but its force depends on mutual terror and on adherence to superstitious procedure rather than on natural sociability and the hope for spiritual regeneration.

II. The Origin of Secular Authority in *The Two Noble Kinsmen*

The Two Noble Kinsmen does not lend itself to interpretive summaries in the form of "Shakespeare plus predicate." This would seem to preclude the possibility of a reading "of" the text where *of* is understood as stipulating both first and final authority for the text. To speak of the text in this context as "representative of the age" and to sanction reading on such authority is of very limited pertinence since such a way of speaking offers only to substitute the highly dubious conception of the age as a unified totality for the problematic "Shakespeare." The advantage of a historical reading is that it affords the possibility to weaken the claims of individualized authorship and to dissolve them back into the history of collective life. To speak of "the age" in general is a denial of history in the way that it perpetuates the stance of critical self-effacement and the implicit disclaimer of contemporary authority vis-à-vis canonical authority.

The analysis of *The Two Noble Kinsmen* that follows is deliberately antithetical to any canonically authorized reading of the text, and indeed it makes no claim to exclusive partnership with the text. The interpretation proposed is unbalanced in that it seeks to identify a heterodox teaching implicit in much of "Shakespeare's" canonical writing and emerging with stark and schematic clarity in the apocryphal text. The heterodoxy identified here refers, of course, to the institutional "Shakespeare" of contemporary literary scholarship. This reading is situated within the contemporary debate on the politics of literary culture; in particular, it relates "Shakespeare" as the exemplary figure of canonical authority to the discussion of the general nature and origins of authority as it has been argued in contemporary social theory.

The origin of secular authority is objectified in *The Two Noble Kinsmen* as a paradigmatic series of exemplary procedures that conserve stable authority by the recurrent acting out and resolution of violent crises. The play suggests that the experience of crisis is likely to recur and that the question of authority can never be regarded as settled once and for all. Crisis reoccurs with every instance of discontinuity and is especially dangerous whenever there is a problem of succession to be negotiated. Even when succession and the transfer of authority are confined to the sphere of literature, the process is precarious, likely to arouse rancor and spiteful rejection. Even more ominous, a new play derived from an old original is likely to arouse the ghost of its dead predecessor and to provoke his discontent and dissatisfaction:

If we let fall the nobleness of this,
And the first sound this child hear be a hiss,
How will it shake the bones of that good man,
And make him cry from underground, 'O, fan
From me the witless chaff of such a writer
That blasts my bays and my fam'd works makes lighter
Than Robin Hood!'
                                        (Pro. 15-21)

There is no smooth transfer of prior authority in the contemporary reanimation of venerable literary material. On the contrary, the whole enterprise is hazardous and depends entirely on the doubtful capacity of a new text to placate the spirits of the dead through the mediation of a generous responsiveness from the audience:

            To his bones sweet sleep!
Content to you! If this play do not keep
A little dull time from us, we perceive
Our losses fall so thick we must needs leave.
                                        (Pro. 29-32)

The performance must begin with this precautionary reminder to take appropriate measures to ward off bad luck. These superstitious gestures have a very real cogency in relation to the "new beginning" that takes place in the theater. The danger of invidious comparison and malevolent judgment—of the evil eye—is, from the point of view of theatrical performers, anything but imaginary.[18]

The story enacted is a schematic and highly stylized representation of crisis in the sphere of social and collective life. The mise-en-scène for this enactment is divided between two cities. On one side is Thebes, a community afflicted with the worst kinds of bad luck in the form of interminable civil strife and demoralization. On the other side is Athens, equally threatened by the possibility of endlessly recurring crises but capable of warding off perpetual and indiscriminate social violence by virtue of Theseus's fortunate ability to work through the ritual procedures that define and consolidate a stable and coherent allocation of authority. The play begins with the celebration of the marriage of Theseus, the Duke of Athens, and Hippolyta, a former queen of the Amazons. This marriage is the iconographic symbol of lawful and charitable subordination of women to men and thus figures forth an ideal of hierarchical order for all social relations. The establishment of an appropriate Pauline hierarchy by no means guarantees, however, a harmonious civil society. In fact, the opening scene depicts the very opposite. Before the marriage ceremonies can be concluded, and at the very moment that the birds of ill omen are banished, three Queens appear, dressed in black, bringing sorrow and discord into the center of an emerging harmony. The scene widens to include the highly significant conjunction of marriage and funeral, with the demand that funeral rites be fully concluded before wedding ceremonies can proceed.[19]

The juxtaposition of wedding and funeral occurs in a number of plays in Renaissance drama, perhaps most notably in *Hamlet* with its "mirth in funeral and dirge in marriage." It occurs in *The Tragedy of Locrine* as well, where the full schematic form is presented beginning with the division of an inheritance, followed by betrothal, death and funeral ceremonies, and finally the celebration of a marriage. The double ritual objectifies the complexity and the danger of temporal succession; every change in the social structure requires an elaborate reallocation of wealth and authority. As the examples of *Hamlet* and *Locrine* suggest, moreover, any rupture or breach in the observance, anything less than perfect adherence to correct ceremonial form, is likely to result in endless, gruesome social violence.

Marriage represents a reallocation of social status that intensifies certain chronic structural ambiguities in collective life. These ambiguities can be managed only by the deployment of both structural and antistructural devices in the form of conventional solemnities and perhaps equally conventional transgressions—the wedding feast and the charivari. Natalie Davis has suggested that *Hamlet* is "perhaps a charivari of the young against a grotesque and unseemly remarriage, a charivari where the effigy of the dead spouse returns, the vicious action is replayed."[20] The apparition of the three Queens in *The Two Noble*

18. Tobin Siebers, *The Mirror of Medusa* (Berkeley: University of California Press, 1983).

19. D. W. Robertson, *A Preface to Chaucer* (Princeton: Princeton University Press, 1962), 260–66.

20. Natalie Zemon Davis, "The Reasons of Misrule: Youth Groups and Charivaris in Sixteenth Century France," *Past and Present* 50 (1971): 75.

Kinsmen is yet another instance of this schematic social action, a black and ghastly charivari of the old against the young, whose marriage is apparently an unobjectionable, ideal, and exemplary union. What this example suggests, however, is that every marriage is in principle an objectionable social event. The charivari objectifies socially diffuse resentments against all marriages. From Theseus's point of view, the primary and overriding aim of all the nuptial ceremonies must be to ward off the threats embodied in the ill-omened procession so as to secure the benefits likely to flow from the new and powerful allocation of authority achieved through his marriage with Hippolyta.

Theseus at first seems to lack a necessary perspicacity in his reaction to the three Queens. He is evidently very much bent on consummating his marriage and therefore proposes first that the supplicants' request be deferred and second that it be delegated to a subordinate officer. Both of these expedients would, of course, be extremely unlucky choices. But the Queens persist, and, helped by the good advice of his friends, Theseus eventually grasps the situation. The first Queen makes the decisive appeal:

> O, when
> Her twinning cherries shall their sweetness fall
> Upon thy tasteful lips, what wilt thou think
> Of rotten kings or blubber'd queens, what care
> For what thou feel'st not, what thou feel'st being able
> To make Mars spurn his drum? O, if thou couch
> But one night with her, every hour in't will
> Take hostage of thee for a hundred, and
> Thou shalt remember nothing more than what
> That banquet bids thee to!
> (1.1.177–85)

This graphic description of Theseus's anticipated pleasure exposes to public scrutiny the intimate satisfactions enjoyed by man and wife. The audience for this—rotten kings and blubbered queens—will never again experience felicity of this kind. In order to defend against such a nemesis, a propitiatory action is required; in this play, it takes the form of military action against "unlucky Thebes." The success of this action constitutes the first step in the procedure of securing harmonious social life for the citizens of Athens. The continuity of that social peace and stability requires, however, a fuller and more elaborate ceremonial operation in which the two noble kinsmen, Arcite and Palamon, are destined to play the crucial role.

There have been several attempts in the interpretive literature on this play to discover differences between the two principal characters. These readings evidently assume that allocation of individuality would somehow make the play stronger, or more aesthetically satisfying. However, any attempt to differentiate between Arcite and Palamon would be to deny what I take to be the essential narrative and dramatic premise, namely, that the two cousins are exact sociological twins and that this exact social duplication is logically necessary to the depiction of social violence. The imprisonment of the two in Athens, the admiration they excite, their escape and recapture, and the climactic trial by combat are all stages in a large-scale social ritual that substantiates the authority embodied by Theseus and that sustains the hope of relatively peaceful collective life for Athens.

René Girard has argued that the existence of twins or duplicates creates a highly explosive problem of social classification: "Two individuals appear, where only one had been expected, and they share a single personality."[21] This anomalous duplication is dangerous as the sign or harbinger of sacrificial crisis, of interminable and indiscriminate violence brought about by the collapse of the fragile system of social differentiation. In *The Two Noble Kinsmen*, it is evident that Thebes is already at the brink of this sacrificial crisis and that the double example of "manly excellence" set by Palamon and Arcite has become a source of danger instead of an object of veneration:

> *Arc.*   I spake of Thebes,
> How dangerous, if we will keep our honours,
> It is for our residing; where very evil
> Hath a good color; where ev'ry seeming good's
> A certain evil; where not to be ev'n jump
> As they are, here were to be strangers, and
> Such things to be, mere monsters.
> (1.2.36–42)

This danger has its source partly in the envy directed against the prestige enjoyed by Palamon and Arcite and more generally in the collapse of social precedence.[22] But Palamon and Arcite are themselves part of the problem, despite their incontestable virtue, because their exact social equivalence makes it impossible to allocate precedence between them.

The capture and imprisonment of the two cousins by Theseus might constitute the same kind of danger for Athens, but the inevitable rivalry between Palamon and Arcite seems to have the opposite effect, even though the conflict between them gradually grows more intense as the action unfolds:

Any phenomenon linked to impure violence is capable of being inverted and rendered beneficent, but this can take place only within the immutable and rigorous framework of ritual practise. The purifying and pacifying aspects of violence take precedence over its destructive aspects. The apparition of twins, then, if properly handled, may in certain societies be seen to presage good events, not bad ones.[23]

21. René Girard, *Violence and the Sacred*, trans. Patrick Gregory (Baltimore: Johns Hopkins University Press, 1977), 56; see also Mary Douglas, *Purity and Danger: An Analysis of the Concepts of Pollution and Taboo* (London: Ark, 1984).

22. Jean-Pierre Dupuy, *Le signe et l'envie*, in *L'enfer des choses: René Girard et la logique de l'économie* (Paris: Seuil, 1979).

23. Girard, *Violence and the Sacred*, 58.

In *The Two Noble Kinsmen,* the potentially benign and purifying aspects of fraternal violence are not immediately apparent. In the first moments of their captivity Palamon and Arcite each continue to enjoy what amounts to a narcissistic contemplation of "manly excellence" reflected back from a double. The two cousins vow perpetual friendship—indeed, they utter what are virtually marriage vows. Just at that moment Palamon's loving gaze is diverted from Arcite to Emilia. A crucial rupture in the social fabric takes place. Palamon is struck dumb, and this mute fascination is interpreted by Emilia's question to her attendant.

> *Emil.* This garden has a world of pleasures in't.
> What flow'r is this?
> *Woman.* 'Tis called narcissus, madam.
>
> (2.2.118–19)

This exchange names the love experienced by Palamon as a self-regarding and ultimately self-destructive fascination. Since Palamon and Arcite are each the model of perfection for the other, it is inevitable that Arcite's desire will fix on exactly the same object. Indeed the action of the play is a highly schematic instance of what Girard has called "mimetic desire" in its most virulent and destructive form.[24] The exact parity of the two rivals leads to the bitterest and most intransigent violence. The "marriage" between the two cousins collapses immediately into jealousy, recrimination, and impotent verbal abuse. The perfect society of virtue and manly excellence reverts to the situation of "unlucky Thebes."

Since they are in prison, the cousins do not pose any immediate threat to Athenian society, but the social disease they represent soon begins to spread beyond the barriers designed to contain it. The condition of unlucky fascination spreads first to the Jailer's Daughter. This secondary plot completes the social and erotic pathology of the action. As more and more characters are drawn into the vortex of social discord, it becomes apparent that crises will arise as the consequence of "not enough difference" (two identical kinsmen afflicted with an unlucky fascination for the same person who is unable to find any basis for preferring one over the other) *or* of "not enough indifference" (the Jailer's Daughter maddened by unlucky fascination over a "difference in men" that is apparent only to her).

As the ritual action unfolds, it becomes clear that the contention and civil strife that appear with the crisis of differentiation cannot be resolved by administrative expedients. The arbitrary decree banishing Arcite and retaining Palamon in prison might be expected to effect a separation between the rival kinsmen; however, the duplicated individuals display an extraordinary energy and resourcefulness in finding each other out. The resolution of crisis cannot

---

24. René Girard, *Deceit, Desire, and the Novel,* trans. Yvonne Freccero (Baltimore: Johns Hopkins University Press, 1965), 1–52.

proceed from the application of some principle of social rationality, but only from careful adherence to a principle of ritual substitution. A carefully supervised overdose of the source of fascination expels and eliminates the contaminating and dangerous superfluity.

> *Doct.* All . . . shall become Palamon, for Palamon can sing, and Palamon is sweet, and ev'ry good thing. . . . Learn what maids have been her companions and play-feres, and let them repair to her with Palamon in their mouths, and appear with tokens, as if they suggested for him. It is a falsehood she is in, which is with falsehoods to be combated. (4.3.85–94)

The crisis brought about by "not enough indifference" may be resolved by the principle of erotic substitution, in which the mimetic double drives away the narcotizing influence of the evil fascinator. The crisis of "not enough difference" requires a stronger version of the same principle, trial by combat in which surplus individuality is violently suppressed. The problem posed by "one too many Thebans" is resolved by a procedure that allows for both exclusion and incorporation. There must be only one marriage and only one death, but there must be one of each. Because of this, Arcite's accident must be seen in the context of a ritual action as a final intensifying dose of bad luck driven off by the expedient of substitution after the fact.

In the world of *The Two Noble Kinsmen,* neither personal nor social misfortune comes about as the result of merely random and contingent mischance. Both are the consequence of malevolent regard. To avert the interminably threatening crisis of social violence it is not enough to issue decrees and to administer laws. The continuity of collective life requires a constant and diffuse alertness toward ill will and evil fascination. Authority has its origins in this alertness to ill will and in the alacrity and ingenuity of the social response against it. The inoculation against crisis does not have permanent effects. *The Two Noble Kinsmen,* as the exemplary demonstration of the origin of authority, is in effect circular. The final scene anticipates the simultaneous observance of a marriage and a funeral, that is, a return to the initial situation.

The anticipation of a new variant of the initial cluster of relationships situates this play within a wider world of collective life in which closure (endings or funerals) enjoys a promiscuous relation with continuity (new beginnings or marriages). Indeed, the Epilogue to the play announces itself as a beginning, promising "many a better, to prolong / Your old loves to us" (Epi. 16–17). This gesture suggests that authority is a form of social energy fundamentally tied to the concepts of initiative and differentiation; in these terms, the idea of established authority must be thought of as a contradiction in terms. As a social energy, authority must be a versatile capacity for the orderly articulation of difference. In the sphere of social experience, however, difference is not only an orderly articulation that permits a harmonious and productive division of sexual and social labor but also an invidious comparison. Authority comes into play precisely as a means to forestall the drift of orderly differentiation into invidious comparison and social or sexual rivalry. To establish such a principle, which is to situate it in relationship to a fixed and final origin, is to concede enormous cultural power to the inertia of archaic repression.

To make use of the generative formula "Shakespeare plus predicate" is to decide the question of authority in favor of the concept of individual origin and, more broadly, in favor of an implicit ideology of individualism. In this outlook, the individual is conceived as both ethically and ontologically prior to the social. Further, the individual becomes a kind of ideal image of collective life, the best form of social differentiation. This equating of individuality as social plenitude with the best form of orderly differentiation is an effort to imagine collective life without crowds, without productive activity, in short, without the imponderable difficulties of struggle and solidarity. The ideological bias in this cultural practice requires a view of canonical authority decisively embodied in the idea of a synoptic bringing together of diffuse tendencies; in short, of a Last Play. It requires, moreover, a Last Play that embodies the shift from politics to sensibility and holds out as an exclusive hope the idea of a politics recuperable by sensibility. *The Tempest* is thus the ideal candidate for nomination as Last Play in that it offers a powerful image readable as the essential "Shakespeare." As epilogue, supplement, and as a possibility for new beginnings, *The Two Noble Kinsmen* demands a critical reorientation toward the complexity of collective life, but without offering any guarantee that such reorientation will discover reconciliation, harmony, or natural sociability.

5 The Two Noble Kinsmen, the Friendship Tradition, and the Flight from Eros

Barry Weller

Like most Elizabethan depictions of symmetrical friendship, whether broken or preserved, *The Two Noble Kinsmen* owes something not only to its Chaucerian source but also to the Boccaccian tale of Tito and Gesippo from the tenth day of the *Decameron* (a tale that has, in turn, its own more ancient sources).[1] The question this tale confronts, as in a philosophical parable, is: if friendship is grounded on a similarity of character and tastes, strong enough to allow each friend to regard the other as an "other self," wouldn't it be logical for the desires of such friends to converge on a single erotic object, and what happens when they do? In the Boccaccian tale and its prototypes one friend surrenders his bride to the other, but this gift creates an asymmetry that, in the second movement of the tale, is presumably rectified when the recipient of the bride offers to die for the donor. The crises of death and sexual desire test the proposition that a friend is an "other self" under extreme conditions. In the variant narrative, exemplified by *The Two Gentlemen of Verona* and perhaps *Euphues*, friendship collapses, for one partner at least, under the first assault of eros. It is to this variant tradition that *The Two Noble Kinsmen* clearly belongs.

The earlier form of the story has also left its traces on this Shakespearean version of Chaucer. Talbot Donaldson comments, "Such differences as Chaucer wrote in or inherited from Boccaccio [in the *Teseida*] the dramatists wrote out. They did this largely, I suppose, to prevent our taking sides in the quarrel and thus being distracted from the more important issue of the sad destruction of their friendship; Shakespeare remembered the disastrous effect that his differentiation of Valentine and Proteus had on the issue of friendship in *The Two Gentlemen of Verona*."[2] Donaldson may overstate the lack of differentiation, at least in personal styles, between the two characters, perhaps because their dissimilarities are not those implied in Chaucer: in their encounters in the third act, Arcite seems the more gallant and generous, while Emilia testifies to a certain Byronic sulkiness in Palamon:

1. The most direct predecessors were tales from the *Disciplina Clericalis* of Petrus Alfonsi (ca. 1110) and from the *Gesta Romanorum* and the thirteenth-century *Romanz d'Athis et Prophilias* (alternatively called *L'Estoire d'Athènes*).
2. Talbot Donaldson, *Swan at the Well: Shakespeare Reading Chaucer* (New Haven: Yale University Press, 1985), 56.

93

He's swarth and meagre, of an eye as heavy
As if he had lost his mother; a still temper,
No stirring in him, no alacrity,
Of all this sprightly sharpness, not a smile.

(4.2.27–30)

Immediately afterward she declares her preference for Palamon's "sad" demeanor: "Palamon, thou art alone / And only beautiful" (4.2.37–38), and the love frenzy of the Jailor's Daughter offers even more powerful evidence of erotic magnetism in Palamon. It's hard to feel, nevertheless, that the cousins are strongly distinguished. As with other pawns of eros (the quartet of lovers in *A Midsummer Night's Dream,* for example), one is led to reflect that any grounds of choice between them (tall, short, dark, or fair) are arbitrary and accidental. Moreover, an erosion of individuality is one of the premises of the parable of friendship, as given classic form by Boccaccio and further elaborated by Sir Thomas Elyot in *The Book of the Governor.* Elyot's Titus and Gisippus share the moral affinity of Boccaccio's friends:

nature wrought in their hearts such a mutual affection, that their wills and appetites daily more and more so confederated themselves, that it seemed none other, then their names were declared, but that they had only their places, issuing (as I might say) out of the one body, and entering into the other.[3]

Not content with this overheated rhetoric, Elyot literalizes and physicalizes the similarity, making them doubles:

This Chremes happened to have also a son named Gisippus, who not only was equal to the said young Titus in years, but also in stature, proportion of body, favour, and colour of visage, countenance and speech. The two children were so like that without much difficulty it could not be discerned of their proper parents which was Titus from Gisippus, or Gisippus from Titus.[4]

In a sense Elyot goes too far even for his own purposes, undercutting the conception of friendship by turning it into mere narcissism.

A more significant, though related, legacy from the tradition of friendship narrative is the sustained focus of the friends on one another at the expense of the woman who presumably occasions a crisis in their friendship. *The Two Gentlemen of Verona* revealed the embarrassments of transferring such a plot to the stage because Silvia could not be regarded (like Sofronia in Boccaccio) as disposable property or as serving a cipher-like function of the plot. When Valentine offers Proteus "All that was mine in Silvia" (5.4.83), he leaves vague the exact nature of his rights in her, and Arcite and Palamon debate their respective claims to Emilia without expressed awareness of how tenuously either

3. Sir Thomas Elyot, *The Book of the Governor,* ed. S. E. Lehmberg (London: Dent, 1962), 136.
4. Ibid.

assertion of right is grounded. Examination of Valentine and Palamon is especially telling since both are putatively exemplary lovers: Valentine is faithful, if sometimes fatuous, and Palamon prays to Venus rather than to Mars (although his prayers to Venus put his vocation as lover into question); each is ultimately successful in winning his lady. They also share a male complacency about the extent to which "possession" of the lady exists independently of her will. Valentine is marginally less culpable; he founds his sense of possession on signs of reciprocated affection, but he assumes that her affections are alienable and disposable property to be assigned as he sees fit. Palamon is more nakedly imperialistic:

I, that first saw her; I, that took possession
First with mine eye of all those beauties in her
Reveal'd to mankind.
                    (2.2.167–69)

Palamon's assertion of rights based on priority sounds almost like a parody of primogeniture; perhaps that is why a patriarchal figure like Theseus ultimately seems to confirm this claim and to imply that the gods have upheld its justice (5.4.114–22).

While Silvia may not be a cipher in *The Two Gentlemen of Verona,* she remains a rather remote and shadowy figure, an ideal embodiment of feminine grace and virtue whose essence is most appropriately evoked interrogatively ("Who is Silvia? what is she / That all our swains commend her?" [4.2.39–40]). Emilia belongs to the same lineage. Donaldson argues that Shakespeare compensates for the pallid characterization of Palamon and Arcite by making Emilia "more fully developed and more interesting" than Chaucer's Emelye: "She has to receive fuller fleshing out in the play, for in the poem . . . she is hardly more than a poetic image, a lovely object without character or individuality who speaks never a word except in her prayer to Diana before the tournament."[5] It seems at least as plausible, however, to describe her, from a feminist perspective, as Jeanne Addison Roberts does, as "more a projection of a male dilemma than an interesting dramatic character."[6] As I have already suggested, and as Donaldson's own wording may imply, the reason she is more fully fleshed out than Emelye is more a generic necessity than a real change of perspective: drama resists her relegation to the background more strongly than narrative does.

Whether or not Emilia is dramatically individualized, the action largely isolates her from her suitors, and to the end of the play her primary allegiance is to Diana. Although she is capable of articulating a preference for one kinsman over the other (as in 4.2, a scene scholars prefer to attribute to Fletcher), her most frequently reiterated response is compassion and concern to prevent the death of at least one suitor, if not of both, rather than desire to have either as her

5. Donaldson, *Swan at the Well,* 60.
6. "Crises of Male Self-Definition in *The Two Noble Kinsmen,*" elsewhere in this volume.

husband. (To judge from this play and from *A Midsummer Night's Dream,* death and forced marriage constitute Theseus's customary solution to romantic triangles. This introduction of compulsion into the erotic arena both echoes his own courtship—"Hippolyta, I woo'd thee with my sword, / And won thy love doing thee injuries" [1.1.16–17]—and casts disconcerting shadows on the prospects of his union with Hippolyta.)

Emilia's fundamental aloofness emphasizes the extent to which, even after the friendship of the cousins has been apparently ruptured by the intrusion of sexual desire, the charged lines of force remain those between Palamon and Arcite rather than between the two kinsmen and Emilia. While it is assumed that their affections cannot survive, have indeed been turned inside out by their rivalry in love, it is on one another that their thoughts and even their most passionate words are still focused. In the first scene of the third act, Palamon invites, almost cajoles, Arcite to mortal combat:

> come before me then,
> A good sword in thy hand, and do but say
> That Emily is thine, I will forgive
> The trespass thou hast done me, yea, my life
> If then thou carry't, and brave souls in shades
> That have died manly, which will seek of me
> Some news from earth, they shall get none but this—
> That thou art brave and noble.
>
> (3.1.74–81)

In corresponding, if not more passionate, words, Arcite says, a few scenes later: "Defy me in these fair terms, and you show / More than a mistress to me" (3.6.25–26). Both these sections of the play may belong to Fletcher, but the erotic intensity with which well-matched and mutually admiring enemies greet one another would not be new to Shakespeare's imagination. This intensity finds, for example, extraordinarily naked expression in the language with which Aufidius greets Coriolanus:

> Let me twine
> Mine arms about that body, where against
> My grained ash an hundred times hath broke,
> And scarr'd the moon with splinters. Here I cleep
> The anvil of my sword, and do contest
> As hotly and as nobly with thy love
> As ever in ambitious strength I did
> Contend against thy valor. Know thou first,
> I lov'd the maid I married; never man
> Sigh'd truer breath; but that I see thee here,
> Thou noble thing, more dances my rapt heart
> Than when I first my wedded mistress saw
> Bestride my threshold.
>
> (*Coriolanus* 4.5.106–18)

Just as love or friendship can sometimes be a strategy for avoiding aggression—neutralizing the threat presented by another through identification and appropriation—so it can seem at such moments that the posture of aggression or the actuality of conflict is a means of deflecting inappropriately directed eros. While the language of Palamon and Arcite is less urgent and less sexy than that of Aufidius, they, contemplating a lifetime of shared imprisonment, relocate the erotic and social properties of the family within their friendship:

We are one another's wife, ever begetting
New births of love; we are father, friends, acquaintance;
We are, in one another, families:
I am your heir, and you are mine; this place
Is our inheritance.
                                        (2.2.80–84)

The Two Noble Kinsmen is, at least in part, about the means by which society disciplines and corrects such mutual self-sufficiency by seizing hold of such energies and incorporating them, often quite unerotically, for its own uses through the institution of marriage.

Even in its most classical presentation, friendship was seen to be potentially antisocial. In Aristotle's *Ethics,* the most philosophically authoritative source for the rhetoric of the friend as "other self," friendship is, like philosophy, introduced in the later books when the discussion begins to veer away from the more political virtues. Friendship and philosophy are in fact linked; the solution to the riddle of how the desires of friends can converge on the same object without conflict is that the object of their desire is to be ideal and infinite, in other words, philosophy (or, in the Augustinian transformation of this kind of friendship, God). Both friendship and contemplation, weaning men away from the problematic goal of public honor, draw them to the margins of society.

Of course the terms, or at least the rhetoric, of Aristotle's philosophical friendship were inevitably adopted for more mundane and carnal bonds, while the only other means of preserving true symmetry within the relationship—admitting each other as the object of the desire—remained socially inadmissible. If friendship alone could be understood as competitive with social bonds, friendship not qualified but strengthened by eros would be an even more significant threat to cohesion. In the final scene of the play, as the corpse of Arcite is carried off, Palamon exclaims:

O cousin,
That we should things desire which do cost us
The loss of our desire! that nought could buy
Dear love but loss of dear love!
                                        (5.4.109–12)

The gloss of these lines, to which the explicit level of the action invites us, is a lament that desiring Emilia should lead to the destruction of Arcite; the actual language points to the identity, rather than the difference, of "desire" and "dear love" and their objects. It requires less interpretation of this speech to produce the sense that Palamon is grieving because his love for Arcite has cost Arcite's life; his desire turned not to another object but against itself.

It is not merely the friendship of Palamon and Arcite that *The Two Noble Kinsmen* apparently defines as aberrant from, even hostile to, a well-ordered state founded on marriage. After Theseus leaves for his expedition against Thebes, Emilia and Hippolyta observe the grief of Pirithous for Theseus:

> *Emil.*   How his longing
> Follows his friend: since his depart, his sports,
> Though craving seriousness and skill, pass'd slightly
> His careless execution, where nor gain
> Made him regard, or loss consider, but
> Playing o'er business in his hand, another
> Directing in his head, his mind nurse equal
> To these so diff'ring twins.
>
> (1.3.26–33)

> *Hip.*   Their knot of love
> Tied, weav'd, entangled, with so true, so long,
> And with a finger of so deep a cunning,
> May be outworn, never undone. I think
> Theseus cannot be umpire to himself,
> Cleaving his conscience into twain and doing
> Each side like justice, which he loves best.
>
> (1.3.41–47)

The conversation continues edgily as Emilia, whether naively or deliberately, misunderstands her sister's final sentence and responds as though Hippolyta were speaking of a division of Theseus's affections between herself and Pirithous, rather than between himself and Pirithous:

> *Emil.*   Doubtless
> There is a best, and reason has no manners
> To say it is not you.
>
> (1.3.47–49)

Theseus and Pirithous, like Orestes and Pylades or David and Jonathan, are traditional exemplars of lofty and selfless friendship who are presumably adduced to strengthen the play's thematic emphasis. Nevertheless, the context in which their history is evoked makes it not merely a pattern but an alternative to marriage. Even more surprising are the following speeches in which Emilia remembers her childhood friendship with Flavina, who died at the age of eleven but whose memory is offered as evidence that "the true love 'tween maid and maid may be / More than in sex dividual" (1.3.81–82):

You talk of Pirithous' and Theseus' love:
Theirs has more ground, is more maturely season'd,
More buckled with strong judgment, and their needs
The one of th' other may be said to water
Their intertangled roots of love, but I
And she (I sigh and spoke of) were things innocent,
Lov'd for we did, and like the elements
That know not what nor why, yet do effect
Rare issues by their operance, our souls
Did so to one another. What she lik'd
Was then of me approv'd, what not, condemn'd
No more arraignment. The flow'r that I would pluck
And put between my breasts (O then but beginning
To swell about the blossom), she would long
Till she had such another, and commit it
To the like innocent cradle, where phoenix-like
They died in perfume. On my head no toy
But was her pattern, her affections (pretty,
Though happily careless wear) I followed
For my most serious decking. Had mine ear
Stol'n some new air, or at adventure humm'd one
From musical coinage, why, it was a note
Whereon her spirits would sojourn (rather dwell on)
And sing it in her slumbers.
                              (1.3.55–78)

Despite her previous sympathetic account of Theseus and Pirithous, Hippolyta responds rather crossly to this nostalgic rhapsody:

            Now alack, weak sister,
I must no more believe thee in this point
(Though in't I know thou dost believe thyself)
Than I will trust a sickly appetite.
                              (1.3.86–89)

Hippolyta concedes, "If I were ripe for your persuasion, you / Have said enough to shake me from the arm / Of the all-noble Theseus" (1.3.91–93), but she ends with a ringing assertion of the priority of marital affection over friendship, declaring she will enter the temple to pray for Theseus "with great assurance / That we, more than his Pirithous, possess / The high throne in his heart" (1.3.94–96).

As other critics have pointed out, this conclusion is a non sequitur, and in the fifty lines since she last spoke of Pirithous she has both accepted Emilia's revision of her own (that is, Hippolyta's) meaning and claimed victory in a previously unacknowledged competition. In rebuking Emilia's praise of single-sex friendship, she also seems to rebuke something in herself that Emilia's words have sympathetically evoked, and so marriage is presented less as an independently attractive choice than as a cure for something weak, sickly, and probably adolescent. This is much the tone that critics have taken not only toward Emilia but also toward Palamon and Arcite, insisting that all three are going through a stage: "When a resolution [to remain single] means resisting a stage of life on which nature insists, the life of sexual relations, there will be more than unexpected happenings to fight against it, there will be one's own desires."[7] It does Edwards's subtle reading of the play an injustice to quote this sentence out of context since he also recognizes that while "two ways of life have . . . been compared . . . the poetic weight is obviously with innocence and Flavina" and that the play is going "to show good grounds for that nostalgia for innocence."[8] Only Talbot Donaldson comments:

Although the play does indeed depict an unavoidable process of change, this is not necessarily growth; and though the movement is away from joy, it may not necessarily be away from innocence: it may simply be away from one experience to another that is less pleasant. . . . As for Emilia, Shakespeare (though not Fletcher) seems to suggest that her resistance to sexual love is mature and valid, and that the entanglement of marriage is not an inevitable prescription for all women's happiness.[9]

Even Donaldson does not extend this argument to Palamon and Arcite; partly because the poetry in which they celebrate their friendship is weaker and partly because they ostensibly succumb to the power of eros. On the other hand, as I have already suggested, once eros has set the cousins at odds, it appears to have done its work.

It becomes even more conspicuous how little attention is devoted to Emilia, as opposed to the rivalry, when the scenes involving the kinsmen are set beside those that dramatize the painful erotic obsession of the Jailer's Daughter. Everyone who has written about this play has expressed some degree of dismay at Palamon's shockingly inept and inappropriate praise of Venus:

                              I never practiced
Upon man's wife, nor would the libels read
Of liberal wits. I never at great feasts
Sought to betray a beauty, but have blush'd
At simp'ring sirs that did. I have been harsh
To large confessors, and have hotly ask'd them
If they had mothers; I had one, a woman,
And women 'twere they wrong'd. I knew a man
Of eighty winters—this I told them—who
A lass of fourteen brided. 'Twas thy power
To put life into dust: the aged cramp
Had screw'd his square foot round,

7. Philip Edwards, "On the Design of The Two Noble Kinsmen," Review of English Literature 5 (1964): 89-105, rpt. in The Two Noble Kinsmen, ed. Clifford Leech (New York: NAL, 1966), 255.
    8. Ibid., 253.
    9. Donaldson, Swan at the Well, 62-63.

The gout had knit his fingers into knots,
Torturing convulsions from his globy eyes
Had almost drawn their spheres, that what was life
In him seem'd torture. This anatomy
Had by his young fair fere a boy, and I
Believ'd it was his, for she swore it was,
And who would not believe her?
                                    (5.1.100–118)

Yet the critical consensus assigns these lines to Shakespeare, and if they were intended to convey a true lover's prayer, the ineptitude would not be Palamon's alone. His cousin, who addresses himself to Mars, is *a fortiori* even less concerned with desire. It is not clear that Palamon and Arcite, even at this stage of the play, know more about love—heterosexual love, at any rate—than Emilia, as she continues to cling to the altar of Diana. Marriage for all three becomes an exercise in what feminists have called "compulsory heterosexuality."[10]

Despite the affinities of the plot here with that of *The Two Gentlemen of Verona*, *The Two Noble Kinsmen* belongs to a set of plays different from those that dramatize the conflict between friendship and love; instead, it dramatizes the conflict between friendship and marriage, and in these terms its most obvious predecessor in the Shakespearean canon is *The Merchant of Venice*. There is even a sign of this connection in the motif of the unconsummated marriage. Portia refuses to allow Bassanio to "lie by Portia's side / With an unquiet soul" (3.2.305–6), and when the widowed queens fear that every hour of the marriage night will blunt the urgency of Theseus's resolution to avenge them, Hippolyta joins them in begging Theseus to "Prorogue this business we are going about, and hang / Your shield afore your heart" (1.1.196–97). (The delay of this particular marriage is a motif to be recognized and remembered from the opening lines of *A Midsummer Night's Dream*, where Hippolyta is again the more patient partner. It is possible to suspect in either case that the patience veils reluctance.) It is clear that Portia understands that she must supersede Antonio in Bassanio's affections before her marriage can be a true one; it is less clear how Hippolyta understands the Theban expedition as a prologue to marriage, but perhaps in espousing the cause of the widowed queens Theseus enacts a symbolic commitment to the marriage bond.

The modern view of *The Merchant of Venice* accords such centrality to the figure of Shylock that it may be necessary to sketch, at least briefly, how the contest between Portia and Antonio over Bassanio equally informs the play's basic structure. The play opens with parallel scenes in which Antonio and Portia confess an apparently groundless melancholy and world-weariness. The second scene makes it clear that the source of Portia's uneasiness is erotic and probably connected with Bassanio. In the first scene Antonio hastily rejects,

10. Cf. Adrienne Rich, "Compulsory Heterosexuality and Lesbian Existence," *Signs* 5.4 (Summer 1980): 631–60. Rich cites the use of this phrase at the Brussels Tribunal on Crimes against Women in 1976.

rather than refutes, the surmise that he is in love, and the parallelism of the scenes reinforces the suggestion of suppressed erotic feeling for Bassanio. When Salerio reports Antonio's grief at Bassanio's departure for Belmont, Solanio remarks, "I think he only loves the world for him" (2.8.50). Antonio would certainly call this affection for Bassanio friendship, and since it is in the name of friendship that he prefers to register its claims, it is probably irrelevant whether he recognizes it as something more. Antonio sends Bassanio off to marry Portia—that is, he underwrites the fortune-hunting suit—but he cannot so easily relinquish his claim to the first place in his kinsman's affections. When Shylock's bond comes due, Antonio wants Bassanio to witness his suffering on his behalf, and he embraces the occasion with a swooning intensity that suggests an otherwise unavailable consummation: "since in paying [the forfeit], it is impossible I should live, all debts are clear'd between you and I, if I might but see you at my death" (3.2.317–20). The indifference (and perhaps the generosity) of what follows is spurious: "Notwithstanding, use your pleasure; if your love do not persuade you to come, let not my letter" (3.2.320–22). The abrupt disavowal of pleading is more wheedling than the initial plea, and it demeans Bassanio in its implication of ingratitude. The note of passionate abandon is sounded once again in Antonio's "Pray God Bassanio come / To see me pay his debt, and then I care not!" (3.3.35–36). His combination of self-pity and self-exaltation reaches a nadir when he says:

I am a tainted wether of the flock,
Meetest for death. The weakest kind of fruit
Drops earliest to the ground, and so let me.
You cannot better be employed, Bassanio,
Than to live still and write mine epitaph.
(4.1.114–18)

It is within Bassanio that Antonio wants his epitaph engraved. Portia may be Bassanio's bride, but Antonio wishes to install himself in Bassanio's consciousness with a finality beside which the bond of marriage will seem trivial. Antonio tells Bassanio:

Commend me to your honorable wife,
Tell her the process of Antonio's end,
Say how I loved you, speak me fair in death;
And when the tale is told, bid her be judge
Whether Bassanio had not once a love.
(4.1.273–77)

Bassanio responds with the fervor Antonio desires:

Antonio, I am married to a wife
Which is as dear to me as life itself;
But life itself, my wife, and all the world,

Are not with me esteem'd above thy life.
I would lose all, ay, sacrifice them all
Here to this devil, to deliver you.
                        (4.1.282–87)

This declaration leaves Portia (disguised as the doctor of law, Balthasar) to remark, "Your wife would give you little thanks for that / If she were by to hear you make the offer" (4.1.288–89). The dead are formidable rivals to the living, and Portia cannot and will not allow such an intrusion into her marriage. Her active beneficence in saving Antonio's life removes the threat and counter-balances Antonio's passive willingness to suffer mutilation and death for Bassanio. In the final scenes she signals her complete victory by stage-managing the little drama of the rings, which, with their obvious sexual suggestion, emphasize the erotic bond between her and Bassanio. While Antonio retains the solitary dignity of an honored friend, he is conspicuously out of place, amid the conjugal couples and the densely amorous atmosphere of Belmont by night, and is orphaned by the happiness that he himself has made possible. Once again he offers his bond for Bassanio, this time pledging his soul rather than his body, with the implication that that marriage, too, is contractual and, more discon-certingly, that Portia has become a new version of Shylock.[11]

Nevertheless, in *The Merchant of Venice* the rival proponents of marriage and friendship are clearly visible. There is little question about either the nature of the conflict or the stakes. In *The Two Noble Kinsmen,* on the other hand, the conflict is not only internal but also occurs (except, perhaps, in the case of Emilia) below the level of conscious articulation. While the claims of marriage and friendship receive verbal expression, no single character steadfastly identi-fies her or his interests with either, so that, for example, in 1.3 Hippolyta can both praise the mutual devotion of Theseus and Pirithous and assert, somewhat arbitrarily, that she has now superseded Pirithous in Theseus's affections. Emi-lia, moreover, who is "bride-habited, / But maiden-hearted" (1.3.150–51), prays to Diana for either the "file and quality" of a militantly imagined virginity or a choice of husband that will leave her "guiltless of election" (1.3.161, 154). Friendship is apparently repudiated by the actions of Palamon and Arcite, but marriage is repeatedly disrupted, deferred, and finally accomplished only with

---

11. The reasons for regarding Antonio's sexual disposition as homosexual have been discussed by other critics, most notably W. H. Auden, who persuasively considers Shylock and Antonio as parallel figures, both excluded from full participation in Venetian society and its idealized mirror-image, Belmont. He also comments shrewdly on Shakespeare's alteration of his source: "Had he wished, Shakespeare could have followed the *Pecorone* story in which it is Ansaldo, not Gratiano, who marries the equivalent of Nerissa. Instead, he portrays Antonio as a melancholic who is incapable of loving a woman. He deliberately avoids the classical formula of the Perfect Friends by making the relationship unequal. When Salanio says of Antonio's feelings for Bassanio

I think he only loves the world for him

we believe it, but no one would say that Bassanio's affections are equally exclusive." "Brothers and Others," in *The Dyer's Hand* (New York: Random, 1963), 229.

a Claudian mixture of "mirth in funeral" and "dirge in marriage." The first scene brings a reminder of the "mortal loathsomeness" of decaying bodies into the midst of a wedding celebration, and one might reasonably expect this discord to be resolved by the end of the play. Instead, the final scene echoes the first, and if the corpse is more decorously treated than those of Thebes's fallen enemies, it is, this time, physically present. While the official rhetoric of the play may declare that we have witnessed, as Edwards says, the "movement from one stage to the next, the unavoidable process of growth,"[12] the message of its form is stasis, just as its Prologue imagines a bride who, on the morning after, "still retains / More of the maid to sight than husband's pains" (Pro. 8).

Even as the Prologue suggests that watching a performance of the play will be like a wedding, its ugly yet revealing language evokes defloration rather than consummation (assuming they can be distinguished) as the substance of this ritual observance. Despite the marriage of Emilia and Palamon, the expectations of most readers or auditors are probably unfulfilled (unconsummated) by this conclusion with its perfunctory mechanism and its message of self-canceling desire, neither of which corresponds to the Chaucerian prototype. *The Two Noble Kinsmen* may be no more antigeneric than other tragicomedies of the period, and its rebuff to comic form, or at least to a resolution based on marriage, is certainly less explicit than that of the much earlier *Love's Labour's Lost*. Nor is it the only Shakespearean play to end with marriages under the sign of compulsion; in *Measure for Measure*, for example, the legal rectifies the erotic in the marriage of Claudio and Julietta and wholly supersedes it in the marriages of Angelo and Mariana and of Lucio and Kate Keepdown, while the only voluntary marriage (or at least proposal) of the play, the Duke's to Isabella, is singularly devoid of romantic feeling. In *The Two Noble Kinsmen*, however, something happens beyond intermittent evocations of plays such as *The Two Gentlemen of Verona*, *The Merchant of Venice*, and *A Midsummer Night's Dream* that, while capable of questioning conventional social arrangements, still grant them at least a qualified affirmation and invest them with the glamour of a generally ungrudging lyricism. For it seems undeniable that, if a play like *A Midsummer Night's Dream* participates in the character of a wedding masque, a play such as *The Two Noble Kinsmen* is, in spirit at any rate, closer to an antimasque.

While the conflict between love and marriage may be transacted within the major characters, as already suggested, it is best seen as internalized, rather than merely internal. One of the antagonists is clearly the social authority of marriage and, at this historical moment, of patriarchal marriage in particular. Despite the inevitability of this institution as both the building block of the social order and the seal of adult sexuality, the mood of the play suggests a recoil before its appropriation of private feeling. Not only for Emilia, whose imagination is inhabited by the dead Flavina, but also, in different ways, for Hippolyta and for the two cousins, friendship represents a retreat from public imperatives and degradations. (This emotional withdrawal from the "common

12. Edwards, "Design of *The Two Noble Kinsmen*," 259.

stream" is the subject of the first scene between Palamon and Arcite, a scene that would otherwise be—as many critics have found it—extraneous.) Renewed contemporary interest in social history, furthermore, has made the ways in which marriage participates in and is informed by public and political spheres more evident than they might have been a generation ago. Recent scholarship, like that of Jonathan Goldberg and Coppélia Kahn,[13] has explored the implications of the patriarchal Renaissance family and particularly the intensification of its power in the early seventeenth century as recorded by Lawrence Stone.[14] Patriarchal power and its potentially deforming influence on the marital bond are felt throughout the Shakespearean canon, but it is at least possible that by 1613, a probable date for *The Two Noble Kinsmen,* it had assumed an especially repulsive form. The misogyny of James I, his ideological investment in patriarchy as a model for the state, and a sordid series of marital scandals among the aristocrats of his court all may have contributed to such a result.[15] It is not hard to imagine why a woman might hesitate to enter a legal condition that severely circumscribed her rights and virtually abolished her autonomy without a compensating rise in status; compared to the potential dangers of such a situation, the known restrictions of a paternal household might have seemed on the whole benevolent.

The official distribution of power within the household, furthermore, did not always make the arrangements of patriarchal marriage attractive to males. Although it is a slight weight to counterpoise to a long history of socially sanctioned abuses, one nearly contemporary voice may suggest the emotional costs of seventeenth-century marriage, even to a male:

For although God in the first ordaining of marriage taught us to what end he did it, in words expressly implying the apt and cheerful conversation of man with woman, to comfort and refresh him against the evil of solitary life, not mentioning the purpose of generation till afterwards, as being but a secondary end in dignity, though not in necessity: yet now, if any two be but once handed in the church, and have tasted in any sort the nuptial bed, let them find themselves never so mistaken in their dispositions through any error, concealment, or misadventure, that through their different tempers, thoughts and constitutions, they can neither be to one another a remedy against loneliness, nor live in any union or contentment all their days; yet they shall, so they be but found suitably weaponed to the least possibility of sensual enjoyment, be made, spite of antipathy, to fadge together, and combine as they may to their unspeakable wearisomeness, and despair of all sociable delight in the ordinance which God established to that very end.[16]

Throughout *The Doctrine and Discipline of Divorce,* Milton's plaintive artic-

13. Cf. Jonathan Goldberg, "State Secrets," in *James I and the Politics of Literature,* chap. 2 (Baltimore: Johns Hopkins University Press, 1983), 55-112; and Coppélia Kahn, *Man's Estate: Masculine Identity in Shakespeare* (Berkeley: University of California Press, 1981), 12-16.

14. Lawrence Stone, "The Reinforcement of Patriarchy," in *The Family, Sex and Marriage in England, 1500-1800* (New York: Harper, 1979), 109-46 is especially relevant.

15. Stone, *Family, Sex and Marriage,* 110; Goldberg, *Politics of Literature,* 85-86; and Stone, *The Crisis of the Aristocracy, 1558-1641* (Oxford: Oxford University Press, 1965), 665-67.

16. Preface to book 1 of *The Doctrine and Discipline of Divorce* in *Milton's Prose Writings* (London: Dent, 1958), 255.

ulation of the true end of matrimony implies, by its very insistence, how little disposed his contemporaries were to look for something in marriage beyond breeding, acquisition and transmission of property, and a fairly rudimentary sexual satisfaction. To admit, much less accommodate, some other and less carnal goal, such as companionship, would be to erode the principle of patriarchy so recently reinforced; the price of power was the loss, or inhibition, of intimacy.

In other Shakespearean texts an erotic world may be constructed as an alternative to the political and familial (as, for example, in *Romeo and Juliet,* where only after the lovers' deaths can their moon-silvered privacies be translated into public images, cast in the medium of commerce, gold), but in *The Two Noble Kinsmen,* as in *The Doctrine and Discipline of Divorce,* sexual desire is a betrayer. Milton protests against the tyranny "of an impetuous nerve" and the "venom of a lusty and over-abounding concoction":[17]

Who hath the power to struggle with an intelligible flame, not in Paradise to be resisted, become now more ardent by being failed of what in reason it looked for and even then most unquenched, when the importunity of a provender burning is well enough appeased; and yet the soul hath obtained nothing of what it justly desires.[18]

In *The Two Noble Kinsmen,* the fate of the Jailer's Daughter most clearly expresses the imperious brutality of desire, as she is worked into marriage with a surrogate Palamon (just as Palamon himself becomes, in effect, a surrogate Arcite for Emilia). While eros is both specific and clamorous in its demands, it appears easily deluded—as though to provide another gloss on the blindness of Cupid.

It is possible to feel that the interchangeability of one male for another is a comment on their slender endowment of individuality: the estranged cousins can seem twinned in nullity rather than in symmetrical virtues. More eloquent than the substitution of sexual partners, however, is the extent to which each major character encounters his or her fate in isolation. It is the prospect of loneliness within marriage that haunts Milton's tract, and, while the prayers in *The Two Noble Kinsmen* to the three different deities are modeled on *The Knight's Tale,* dramatic presentation makes even clearer the separateness and solitude with which Emilia, Arcite, and Palamon confront the future. Edwards describes the "growth into experience" in this play as "walking into the future as through a fog,"[19] but the extent to which that fog might evoke not only ignorance but also mutual isolation requires emphasis. Even more cheerful Shakespearean texts suggest the distance between the sexes by the strategies that must be employed to overcome it. Disguise and intrigue are the conditions for satisfactory romantic conjunctions; Viola and Orsino, or Rosalind and Orlando, can accomplish their courtships only in situations that one partner

17. Ibid., 263–64.
18. Ibid., 265.
19. Edwards, "Design of *The Two Noble Kinsmen,*" 259.

fails to recognize as such. Beatrice and Benedict may be brought together by hearsay and stratagem (not to mention the aggression through which they disguise their feelings from themselves and others), but it is the "straightforward" love match of Hero and Claudio that nearly produces disaster. Unfortunately, even without much investigation of the historical facts, one would suspect that the marriages of Hero and Claudio or of Emilia and Arcite, either sponsored or arranged by all the appropriate authorities, more closely resemble aristocratic marriages of the era than the playful and devious romances that occupy the center stage of Shakespearean comedy. It may have seemed, at some point, that the dreams of freedom, and of friendship within love, to which such comedy gave shape were no longer strong enough to resist, even imaginatively, the pressure of social realities.[20]

Ultimately, the revulsion from patriarchal marriage and the society of which it is the foundation also affects the presentation of friendship. Perhaps the treatment of marriage (and, more problematically, of eros as the power that delivers us to the uncertainties of union with a stranger) in *The Two Noble Kinsmen* would be less disconcerting if friendship itself seemed less of a recoil from experience. Like the reminiscence of a presexual and even pretemporal innocence in *The Winter's Tale* ("we knew not / The doctrine of illdoing, nor dream'd / That any did" [1.2.69–71]), longing for friendship in *The Two Noble Kinsmen* depends on negation, on an Edenic absence of conflict or dissonance.

Reticence about the essential character of friendship, or defining it by negation, need not be seen as a function of its weakness. In Emilia's case her rejection of self-consciousness may be seen as naive and rather touching:

I

And she (I sigh and spoke of) were things innocent,
Lov'd for we did, and like the elements
That know not what nor why, yet do effect
Rare issues by their operance . . . .

(1.3.59–63)

Yet a similar confession of verbal impotence (which Shakespeare may be deliberately echoing) can be found at the center of Montaigne's essay "De l'amitié," one of the Renaissance's most sophisticated and subtle accounts of friendship: "If you press me to tell why I loved him, I feel that this cannot be expressed, except by answering: Because it was he, because it was I."[21]

The moment before the friendship of Palamon and Arcite dissolves, or rather explodes, is one not of silence but of overabundant rhetoric:

20. For a discussion of the way in which marginal institutions, such as the Elizabethan theater, can articulate excluded or not yet realized social possibilities, see Louis Montrose, "The Purpose of Playing: Reflections on a Shakespearean Anthropology," *Helios* n.s. 7 (1980): 51–74.

21. "Of Friendship," in *The Complete Essays of Montaigne,* trans. Donald Frame (Stanford: Stanford University Press, 1965), 139.

We are an endless mine to one another;
We are one another's wife, ever begetting
New births of love; we are father, friends, acquaintance;
We are, in one another, families:
I am your heir, and you are mine . . . .

(2.2.79–83)

If eros offers the prospect of loneliness and self-alienation, such friendship seems to offer nothing more than a terrifyingly endless repetition of the self. The dream of intimacy turns into a nightmare of claustrophobia. The kinsmen escape from this impasse, but only into conflict. It is a conflict that more clearly exorcises the threat of excessive intimacy than it testifies to the redirection of their emotions. The true goal of their rivalry, as a flight from friendship, seems neither Emilia nor marriage but extinction of the self or of the other, and ultimately each wins some share of what he wants from this destructive compact.

6 Grinning at the Moon
Some Sadness in *The Two Noble Kinsmen*

Charles H. Frey

Nowhere does Shakespeare offer a title quite like *The Two Noble Kinsmen*. The Histories and Tragedies don't describe their protagonists: they name them, individuating the "life," the "part." The Comedies (I follow the Folio division of genres) allude sometimes to season and weather—Twelfth Night, Winter, Summer, Tempest—but more often to casual and somewhat dismissive views of their own actions miniaturized into tags and proverbs—errors, taming, love lost, a night's dream, ado about nothing, as you like, what you will, all's well, and measure for measure. There's no other comic title remotely like *The History of Troilus and Cressida*. Where proper names enter into the comic list—Verona, Venice, Windsor—the protagonists also enter, but only in descriptive phrase, comic style, not with historical specificity—Gentlemen, Merchant, Wives. Gentlemen and Wives, indeed, receive qualifying epithets, but each time only one: the two gentlemen, the merry wives. Our play could have been titled "The Two Kinsmen of Thebes" or "The Noble Kinsmen of Thebes." Is the adopted title with its unique double epithets simply fortuitous? Is there a hint of "too noble kinsmen"? Or does the title reach more deeply into the play to ask whether a truly shared nobility demands an impossible identity; not a kinship but a twinship of immaterial essence, "single nature's double name," or a kind of married chastity?

I. The Opening

"New plays and maidenheads are near akin" (Pro. 1): there's kinship for you! A title-subverting kinship, a deeper theme of the play, and a promise, it soon appears, of truly noble "married chastity." How in this fallen world could nobleness better survive the making of kin than in the kinship of art's foreconceit, or foreplay, and innocent love?

When I read the first line, I think prospectively: yes, new plays and maidenheads are kin because both are fresh, innocent, vulnerable, and untried. I wonder just how physically to take "maidenheads." Might the term be accommodated to "maidenhoods," an idea as tentative and bodiless as a new and unperformed play? The kinship, I find, arises mysteriously in and out of the physical performance: "Much follow'd both, for both much money gi'n" (Pro. 2). The play attracts its following in the theater, in performance, and earns its

109

money there. The maidenheads would be much followed, indeed most followed, before performance, and much money might be given for them in anticipation of performance, but the Prologue conditions both following and payment of money, it would seem, upon performance itself: "Much follow'd both, for both much money gi'n, / If they stand sound and well . . ." (Pro. 2–3). The rich verb "stand" is where all the relational actions of establishing kinship, following, and giving money come to their proof in a tense climax of combined stasis and engenderment. The new play stands sound and well as the actors stand forth to the sounds of the play and as the play stands or remains sound, of tested value in performance. But how does the maidenhead stand sound and well? Before and during lovemaking, it may stand sound and well for a time against the male member's "stand," as gage of true virginity. But can it physically stand sound and well afterward? Wouldn't that stretch one's belief and cast suspicion on the virginity? As if partly answering this uneasiness, the Prologue immediately goes on to dephysicalize both play and maidenhead:

> and a good play
> (Whose modest scenes blush on his marriage-day,
> And shake to lose his honor) is like her
> That after holy tie and first night's stir,
> Yet still is modesty, and still retains
> More of the maid to sight than husband's pains.
> (Pro. 3–8)

New play and maidenhead become kin in a kind of Marian intercourse. Surely editors are wrong to gloss "his" solely as "its" and "honor" solely as female "virginity," thus disallowing for the new play an additionally masculine presence who stands for the first, or wedding, night and whose bride-scenes blush and shake for fear of compromising male honor (as well as, perhaps, bridal honor). Indeed, "husband" connects to the male playwrights and ultimately to Chaucer, the play's "noble breeder." The new play is both male and female—feeling potent "pains" of creation but hiding them from sight, keeping the story line pure, "constant to eternity." The playwrights must be careful never to "let fall the nobleness of this" new play (or Chaucer's tale?) as product or offspring of performance. "This child" must be protected from any bastardizing hiss contributed by the audience, which seems both to participate in and to observe, or judge, the generative act of performance.

The project of creating a play boasting a noble maiden purity that can survive performance aims not only to protect the pure, nonbastard nobleness of the play-child but also to honor the nobleness of the grandfather, the patriarch who listens from underground and whom the playwrights would lull back to sleep. As the "good play" would "shake to lose his honor," so the lost honor would "shake the bones of that good man" Chaucer, the "noble breeder" of the story line. The play is a maidenhead and a would-be participant in something approaching procreant virginity, but a larger aim is not to let fall the nobleness of ancestry, not to disturb holy ghosts (and, beyond them, it turns out, the highest powers of the cosmos) with the infecting stains of our sinful mortality. From the outset, then, *The Two Noble Kinsmen* complicates the issue of "nobility" in kinship beyond nobility of social status or clan identity. The Prologue identifies first a lateral kinship, or twinship, of nobleness in creative function. Then that kinship vertically produces offspring. As perfect as lateral nobility may be, fears and concessions question any certitude of passing on nobility: "more of the maid *to sight*"; "This is the fear we bring" (Pro. 8, 21).

As the play proper begins, the Prologue's first verbal image of maidenhead becomes visually embodied onstage: "Enter HYMEN with a torch burning." This male torchbearer may symbolize both the glory and the consuming destiny of maidenhead/hood, but the virginal procession and the song of the Boy point, again as in the Prologue, toward the wish for an almost unnaturally or supernaturally chastened generativity in nature. The sharp spines are gone from the roses. The maiden pinks have but faint odor, and the daisies are odorless. Oxlip and marigold encompass cradle and deathbed as if the threats of middle vigor were elided just as the discordant cuckoo is banished. The sweet children of nature appear here in a blessed but desensualized aspect. It cannot be a very happy song. By virtue of sin's declared absence, the consciousness of threat is much too present.

The three Theban Queens bring in the very "discord" of unchastened nature that the song would banish, and they know it. Yet their project is to remove gross "mortal loathsomeness" from the infected air, and all three stake their claims for respect on our common desire to cleanse the generative cycle from bodily "stench," to protect the gentleness of our ancestors and selves:

1. Queen. For pity's sake and true gentility's,
Hear and respect me.
2. Queen. For your mother's sake,
And as you wish your womb may thrive with fair ones,
Hear and respect me.
3. Queen. Now for the love of him whom Jove hath mark'd
The honor of your bed, and for the sake
Of clear virginity, be advocate
For us and our distresses! This good deed
Shall raze you out o' th' book of trespasses
All you are set down there.

(1.2.25–34)

To honor the nobleness of Chaucer and to guarantee that noble breeder's sweet ancestral sleep required binding the play to a procreant virginity. The Queens argue that respect for their husbands' bones, for ancestral ashes, underlies respect for the purity of motherhood, of generative kinship. The third Queen suggests, in particular, that Emilia is to be linked paradoxically both with a husband "and for the sake / Of clear virginity" in such a way that she may escape listing in the "book of trespasses." Once again, the mind of the "wrighter" turns toward the chance of sinless procreation, and the prospect of the drama opens out far beyond merely social nobility.

In the processional song, the crow and boding raven, pals of the slanderous cuckoo, had been banished from the bridehouse. The three Queens, who say they come from "the fowle feilds of Thebs" (as the Quarto puts it), reintroduce those birds of slander and foreboding as birds of vulturous disfigurements:

> We are three queens, whose sovereigns fell before
> The wrath of cruel Creon; who endured
> The beaks of ravens, talents of the kites,
> And pecks of crows in the foul fields of Thebes.
> He will not suffer us to burn their bones,
> To urn their ashes, nor to take th' offense
> Of mortal loathsomeness from the blest eye
> Of holy Phoebus, but infects the winds
> With stench of our slain lords. O, pity, Duke,
> Thou purger of the earth, draw thy fear'd sword
> That does good turns to th' world; give us the bones
> Of our dead kings, that we may chapel them . . . .
>   (1.1.39–50)

The loathsome look of unfresh mortality and the smell of it offend the pure eyes of the sun and nostrils of the wind. Those mortals concerned with purging birth of all ignoble hiss have still to contend with purging death of deeper stains. Love's children keep their freshness but a moment. Theseus may enforce a ritual cleansing of those who exit from the earth, but to solve the inmost wrench of our mortality, he would have to become a quite literal "purger of the earth."

Theseus, who speaks on his marriage day in a play itself personified as acting "on his marriage-day" (Pro. 4), drives the memory of the first Queen back to a time when he met her husband-to-be by Mars's altar "the day / That he should marry you" (1.1.59–60). This proleptic reminiscence introduces one view of the dynamics governing a suitor who prays, as Arcite will, at the altar of Mars. The devotee of Mars won the first Queen, but what did he win? The knowledge that "a man may weep upon his wedding-day" (*Henry VIII,* Pro. 32)? Though she then rivaled a goddess (Juno) in noble beauty and bounty, her "wheaten wreath" (textualizing the "wheaten chaplet" seen in the bridal procession) was destined to be "threshed" and "blasted" (as Chaucer fears the "chaff" that "blasts my bays"?). Though she then tamed the god or demigod Hercules, she was not by that excused from the ravages of consuming, devouring time. No suitor, no matter how martial, can win in the war on time. The Queens, however, want Theseus's war power as "soldier" to bury offensive mortality. He suggests that they pray to the goddess of war, Bellona, and they turn, appropriately, to his bride, the "dreaded Amazonian." The interior debate turns in this way to ask if some feminine principle/principal, a war-goddess or Amazon, may combine the powers of mercy and manhood to "undertake" and lay to rest this last funereal exploit.

The second Queen views Hippolyta as bested in physical combat against the male only to win the wider war of wills. Poising sternness with pity and owning Theseus's love as well as strength, Hippolyta may bring a cool shadow of Theseus's sword to the aid of the Queens. Then, in an incantation followed by suddenly grotesque, horrific images, the Queen drives toward an angry, climactic imperative:

Speak't in a woman's key—like such a woman
As any of us three; weep ere you fail;
Lend us a knee;
But touch the ground for us no longer time
Than a dove's motion when the head's pluck'd off;
Tell him, if he i' th' blood-siz'd field lay swoll'n,
Showing the sun his teeth, grinning at the moon,
What you would do.
(1.1.94–101)

If we discount the possibility that it's not the dove's "head" but rather "hood" or "lead" plucked off, we face the image of Hippolyta kneeling only so long as it takes the dove to die; as the dove falls, Hippolyta is to rise. Having risen, she's to picture aloud Theseus lying dead on the ground, bloated in the bloody field of battle, yet seeming not quite dead, still showing his teeth and grinning horribly. The day and the night receive alike the same unchanging smile. Is the corpse translated into a deathly stillness, almost gaily beyond the reach of living care? Does it wilfully insult "the blest eye / Of holy Phoebus"? Does it laugh at the moon's lost power to personify desire? Plucking off the dove's head provides, associatively, the blood for the following line, and Shakespeare here seems engrossed in the physicality of death. But then the transmuting strangeness, the dismissive and diminutive image of "grinning at the moon," takes over and represents, even as it depicts, an inability to feel or, if not an inability to feel, a knowledge of death's import so sure, so cool, so glinting, so agedly and ruefully wise and spiteful that a sadness of unmotivating disgust here enters the play, never to leave it.

The reader or spectator goes on, of course, to "enjoy" the rest of the play, but from this moment forward, I would say, the cards are faceup on the table. In Shakespeare's elder vision, the gods groan under the mastery of the affections (1.1.231). The nobility of kinship that would be "dearer in love than blood" (1.2.1) proves unachievable. The world's insane. We hear of women who boil their babies in their own tears; of "sickness in will / O'er-wrastling strength in reason" (1.4.44); of "the world 'tis but a gaudy shadow" (2.2.103); of "I must love, and will, / And for that love must and dare kill" (3.6.261); of "Narcissus was a sad boy, but a heavenly" (4.2.32); of "sometime we go to barley-break, we of the blessed" (4.3.30); of Mars "whose breath blows down / The teeming

Ceres' foison" (5.1.52); of Venus "whose chase is this world, / And we in herds thy game" (5.1.131); of "on the sinister side the heart lies" (5.3.76); of "Is this winning?" (5.3.138); of "O you heavenly charmers, / What things you make of us!" (5.4.131).

Yet Shakespeare and perhaps another wrote it. Why? For the "market" mentioned in the Epilogue? Or for the "honest purpose" mentioned there to "any way" content the audience? What I find in the opening of the play is what I find in the play entire: a shrewd and sad skepticism about the capacity of men and women to create lives or art of true nobility. "For I am sham'd by that which I bring forth" (Sonnet 72). Not that it matters, for we will always take an interest, if only in the details of our own degradation.

II. Development

Once the play has defined nobility as a tragic emblem that dies, like knighthood, with the bearer, then the play is free to view the characters' attempts to harness nobility to procreant purposes as fundamentally shaming or comic. What should we see as the central motivator of the play's action? The drive in Theseus to marry, or to reinstitute marriage? This drive, it turns out, threatens not only to be blocked by "cruel Creon" and his stoppage of death's exit but also threatens to be drained, swerved, or detoured from its aim by a profusion of lateral nobilities, competing aims, and ideals: Theseus's relation with Pirithous, Hippolyta's with Emilia, and Palamon's with Arcite.

> If you grant not
> My sister her petition, in that force,
> With that celerity and nature, which
> She makes it in, from henceforth, I'll not dare
> To ask you any thing, nor be so hardy
> Ever to take a husband.
>
> (1.1.200–205)

Emilia's threat opens up one vista upon the social analysis in the play. What is she saying? (1) "If my sister cannot succeed in asking this from you, then I won't ask anything from you, nor will I marry." (2) "If my sister can't make you 'captive' (1.1.81) in this respect, then I shouldn't marry." (3) "If you won't help bury the dead, then I won't make new life." And, possibly, by implication (4) "If you do bury the dead, I will marry (risk birth)." In light of Emilia's speech, the central action of the play could be seen as her making good on her implied promise to base her marriage on Theseus's agreement to purge Thebes.

In *A Midsummer Night's Dream,* Theseus says: "Hippolyta, I woo'd thee with my sword" (1.1.16). In *The Two Noble Kinsmen,* however, the Second Theban Queen's address to Hippolyta portrays Hippolyta as independently aggressive, slayer of the "scythe-tusk'd boar" and "near to make the male / To thy sex captive" (1.1.79). Hippolyta is seen as threatening to overflow a natural "bound" (1.1.84), and Theseus's job is to "uphold creation" (1.1.82). The story tells of a threat to the procreative, generative cycle through some misrelation of the sexes. Theseus's successful defense against, or conquering of, Hippolyta, to be complete, should lead to marriage and procreation—both of which are plainly anticipated in the processional song. But two obstacles block reintegration of male and female sexuality and reestablishment of the full procreative cycle: (1) as the Theban Queens reveal, the generative cycle is blocked at the exit, as it were, by Creon's profane denial of burial; (2) Theseus may have only partially conquered the Amazonian/Lesbian principle in that he brought back with Hippolyta her unconquered sister. The erasure of Amazonianism is incomplete.

The two hindrances to Theseus's function—Theban undeath and Amazonian unbirth—are removed in one act and in one place; Theseus extracts from Thebes both the completion of death (ritual burial of the slain kings) and the inception of life (Palamon as future husband of Emilia). From this perspective, it looks as if Emilia was saying, "If you, Theseus, will bury the dead in the earth, submerge death in the source of life, I will submerge my fruitless virginity in life." So, Theseus finds (unwittingly) Emilia's husband in Thebes; in the city of death, lives life.

Conceived in this way, the story treats what is embodied in Theseus as the human energy toward vertical kinship. Beyond that, Theseus as "purger of the earth" seems connected with a vision of ritually purified life cycles as envisioned in the processional song of Nature's chaste flower children and in the ritual burial that "does good turns to th' world" (1.1.49). But the images of pure or noble breeding all tend to compromise heterosexuality. The spineless rose, the new play as both male and female, the maid still virginal after her wedding night, Chaucer the "noble breeder" breeding the story out of himself, and the play as "this child" of nobility produced by Chaucer and the playwright(s) breeding it, all suggest a kind of parthenogenetic ideal. In the body of the play, the erotic drive toward vertical kinship continually finds obstruction in the form of preexisting lateral kinships where nobleness most easily resides and would persist free from taint.

To marry a wife, Theseus must marry off her sister. The principle of obstruction to energy in the action is a sly obtruding of doubles that continually deflect the central aim. Instead of finding one suitor for his bride's sister, Theseus finds a perfectly matched pair of suitors who already subsume nobility of kinship in their relation, just as Theseus himself is guilty of a compromising lateral friendship with Pirithous and Emilia is guilty of nostalgia over her lateral friendship with Flavina. Almost everywhere in the play, the drive toward vertical kinship is thwarted or questioned by preexisting lateral attachments.

Shakespeare invents and gives extended attention (1.3.26–97) to the love between Theseus and Pirithous, a love that only doubtfully gives place to Theseus's love for Hippolyta. The text suggests that nobleness of male desire lies in its glorification of will in the holder's lifetime: Pirithous and Theseus "have / Fought out together where death's self was lodged; / Yet Fate hath brought them off" (1.3.39). In this way the procreative drive is ever threatened by the male drive for a war on tragic, individual death, so that Theseus's project to purge and renew the life cycle is fundamentally flawed from the start because of his love for Pirithous. That love, moreover, seems to reflect an attempt at self-division, mirroring, or self-duplication more personal and more fully idiosyncratic than the extension of self through progeny. Pirithous and Theseus share a propensity for spiritually nurturant doublings: "his mind nurse equal / To these so diff'ring twins" (1.3.32–33); "Cleaving his conscience into twain and doing / Each side like justice, which he loves best" (1.3.46–47).

In depicting the friendship of Emilia and Flavina, Shakespeare turns from the perhaps masculinist language of difference and cleaving to hints of a spiritual creativity that might provide life beyond death. Whereas Theseus and Pirithous fought off "death's self," Emilia and Flavina effect "rare issues" by the operance of their souls. Emilia's flowering breasts compensated for or became the new life of the literally plucked blossoms:

> The flow'r that I would pluck
> And put between my breasts (O then but beginning
> To swell about the blossom), she would long
> Till she had such another, and commit it
> To the like innocent cradle, where phoenix-like
> They died in perfume.
>
> (1.3.66–71)

Do the images of cradle and phoenix hint at a (male?) view of strangely regenerative power in such feminine love? Or is the emphasis here more strongly on the wistful and pathetic inability of the two girls to make their love physically regenerative?

In prison, Palamon and Arcite give their own version of the progenitive affection envisioned by Emilia in her relation with Flavina. Arcite at first laments, "No figures of ourselves shall we ev'r see" (2.2.33), but soon he corrects this doubt: "We are one another's wife, ever begetting / New births of love" (2.2.80–81). Shakespeare always seems to look for a "birth" out of same-sex love, a birth of noblest spirituality. Shakespeare doubts, moreover, whether such births are possible when one of the same-sex lovers turns to a heterosexual attachment. Emilia opines, "the true love 'tween maid and maid may be / More than in sex dividual" (1.3.81–82), and she is "sure" (1.3.85) she will never love a man.

How could Palamon or Arcite fall into heterosexual love without compromising the nobility of the kinship between them? By both loving the same woman? Only, it would seem, so long as such dual loves remained unconsummated. The nobility is in part a metaphysical compression of two souls into one space, object, or aim. Arcite hints at an ignobling solution when, in reply to Palamon's "you must not love her," he says:

I will not, as you do—to worship her
As she is heavenly and a blessed goddess;

I love her as a woman, to enjoy her.
So both may love.

(2.2.162–65)

But Palamon denies the possibility of any such division in their loved object and hence in their purposes. He accuses Arcite of lowering his social status—of becoming a "fellow" baser than a cutpurse—for not recognizing Palamon's claim of prior sight. Arcite asks how Palamon could deal "so unlike a noble kinsman, / To love alone?" (2.2.190–91). They are in this way teaching each other the nature, or implications, of their claims to nobility as a union of their psyches. Perfect nobility of kinship would require complete identity of loved object and simultaneity of love's inception. Nobility is thus the enemy of difference.

By implication, if Theseus and Pirithous had enjoyed greater nobility of friendship, they would have rivaled for Hippolyta. We may assume that Pirithous, not a duke, is of lower social status. But the two kinsmen, sons of sisters of the Theban king, cannot easily differentiate themselves socially. Palamon seizes on the smallest division in their inceptions of desire for the same love object as grounds for lowering the status of Arcite. As the plot works out, both of the kinsmen in a sense win Emilia, but Arcite deserves to lose because he thought to love equally and failed to honor either the necessity for only one sexual partner to perform one instant of procreant love or the natural (ignoble) desire of males (no matter how nobly twinned to lateral kin) to distinguish self from friend through identification of one's own offspring, allowing patrilineal kinship identification. That is, if Palamon wants to author his children definitively, he cannot nobly share Emilia with Arcite; of course this is also Theseus's view as he advises Emilia to take one of them for her "husband": "They cannot both enjoy you" (3.6.275). In a different society they might both enjoy Emilia, but a deep subtext of the story grounds on the assumption of monogamy. The assumption of monogamy appears grounded, furthermore, on the assumption that the desire to know oneself the father of specific children inevitably contradicts one's desire to identify with friends or lateral kin no matter how identically noble.

III. Moving Through

The first act of the play appears to conclude with the burial of the Theban dead and the way opened for consummation of Theseus's intent toward marriage. There has already been advanced, proleptically, the noble kinship of Emilia's potential suitors, who would prefer to "keep in abstinence" (1.2.6) from lusty "crimes of nature," and, additionally, the declared intention of Emilia never to love a man in deference to the perfection of her love for Flavina. This threat of a high-leveling, ennobling abstinence against the meeting/mating of "sex divid-ual" reveals a need in the society for distinction and differentiation. That, despite the finality of the Queens' funeral rites, such distinguishing force remains current in the world of the play appears from the Queens' insistent separation of death's meeting place, the "one sure end" (1.5.13), from life's "thousand differing ways" to this end: "This world's a city full of straying streets." Such imagery closely follows Theseus's catalog of subrational provocations in life to reach beyond the equable standards of "what man to man may do" (1.4.39):

> . . . I have known frights, fury, friends' behests,
> Love's provocations, zeal, a mistress' task,
> Desire of liberty, a fever, madness,
> Hath set a mark which nature could not reach to
> Without some imposition, sickness in will
> O'er-wrastling strength in reason.
>
> (1.4.40–46)

To save Palamon and Arcite from dying (and alike from living in noble barrenness) requires recognition of the mark they have set that nature could not attain unless aided by some "sickness in will." "Death's the market-place" (1.5.16), says the Third Queen to end act 1, but death is approached only through the "straying" streets of life.

> *3. Queen*. . . . And death's the market-place, where each one meets.
> Act II, Scene I.
> *Enter* Jailer *and* Wooer.
> *Jailer*. I may depart with little, while I live. . . . Marry, what I have (be it what it will) I will assure upon my daughter at the day of my death.

Immediately upon the Queens' departures, the Jailer and Wooer enter, bargaining in the marketplace of the Jailer's will over the marriage portion of his daughter. She becomes an embodiment of "differing," "straying" life in the play, a bridal force of sickness in will who magnifies through her love for Palamon differences in status and gender on which the story implicitly conditions generation. Entering the prison, the play opens simultaneously, and for the first time, to two generations (father/daughter) and to nonnoble characters and setting. The Jailer's Daughter, moreover, declares not only "the difference of men" (2.1.54) but also a first difference between Palamon and Arcite: "No, sir, no, that's Palamon. Arcite is the lower of the twain" (2.1.49). In her "holiday" appreciation of the kinsmen, she seems to initiate the elevation of Palamon into Venus's devotee, to initiate the two kinsmen into acolytes of Love and War.

The Jailer's Daughter first appears bearing clean, fresh vegetative growth, rushes, "strewings," her own wheaten offering for the kinsmen's chamber where she soon imagines herself "comforted" (2.1.44). The prison becomes an image of the constraint or bondage the world imposes on inert nobility, insisting on catalytic contamination that can bring life out of the house of death. Shakespeare loves the pregnant prison where a Julietta (*Measure for Measure*) or Hermione (*Winter's Tale*) enters under threat of death but at the same time with child, only to be miraculously delivered. When the Jailer's Daughter frees Palamon in the mad hope to gain his love (2.4.29–33), she emulates Helena in *A Midsummer Night's Dream* and, to a lesser extent, Julia in *The Two Gentlemen of Verona,* Viola in *Twelfth Night,* and Helena in *All's Well,* each of whom offers aid to her beloved on his path to her rival. But the lovers of comic heroines are always deflected back to those heroines, whereas the Jailer's Daughter wins Palamon only in delusional denial of the Wooer's substitution.

As the action moves toward the self-subverting center of the play, the scenes in which the Jailer's Daughter declares her ever more irrational desire for Palamon alternate with scenes in which Palamon and Arcite struggle to establish some sense of order and exclusivity in their claims to Emilia. On the one hand, love's a madness. "Thus much for law or kindred!" (2.62.33) says the Jailer's Daughter, who proceeds to "venture" (2.62.33) further and further into the wood of anarchic, willful and physical desire: "O for a prick now, like a nightingale, / To put my breast against!" (3.4.25); "Sirrah tinker, / Stop no more holes but what you should" (3.5.83); "Raise me a devil now . . ." (3.5.85), and so on. On the other hand, Palamon and Arcite fuss over how to allot Emilia in the style of "a true gentleman" and "a good knight," working toward ceremonial combat "brave and noble," upholding honor—"you shall not die thus beastly," "Well, sir, I'll pledge you," and so on (3.3). Nobility comes to seem more a matter of ideals in social ordering remote from the origins of desire.

Far from being an interpolated irrelevance, the morris dance is arguably the dynamic center of the play. By the time we come to it, the daft Jailer's Daughter is leading the troupe. The dancers include lascivious Chambermaid and Servingman and an ape with "long tail and eke long tool" (3.5.132). Pirithous rewards the Schoolmaster after the dance with "something / To paint your pole withal," and the Schoolmaster prays in turn that Hippolyta and Emilia may eat the testicles of the long-standing stag. Such exuberant coarseness rather undoes the fine Shakespearean fret, in the opening and closing acts, over the loss of nobility in heterosexual unions. Beneath nobility of kinship, and quite independent of its aims, lies the sheer, blind, mad drive for sex itself:

They come from all parts of the dukedom to him.
I'll warrant ye he had not so few last night
As twenty to dispatch. He'll tickle't up
In two hours, if his hand be in.
                    (4.1.136–39)

And now direct your course to th' wood, where Palamon
Lies longing for me. For the tackling
Let me alone.
                    (4.1.144–46)

After we pass with the Jailer's Daughter through the sex-wrecked center of the play, we are asked to see Emilia in a compromised, confusing light. She looks upon Arcite and muses:

> If wise Nature,
> With all her best endowments, all those beauties
> She sows into the births of noble bodies,
> Were here a mortal woman, and had in her
> The coy denials of young maids, yet doubtless
> She would run mad for this man. . . .
> . . . I am sotted,
> Utterly lost. My virgin's faith has fled me.
> (4.2.8–46)

We come out of the play through the mordant and rechastening prayers at the altars to Mars, Venus, and Diana, where Love and War are mocked to futility and where the Difference that is Desire becomes horrific. But once the jail where love is kept has been opened by the Jailer's Daughter, there can be no going back. Of Emilia and the Jailer's Daughter alike, it may be said: they want to tame all want, to gentle our condition. Yet so to pass on desire is to enter the shadow of sad wisdom, to grimace at the moon, to keep close a knowledge of the lover's common pain. I believe those playwrights, gender-tired as they may have been, saw and agreed upon as much:

> *Daughter.*   We'll to bed then.
> *Wooer.* Ev'n when you will.   [*Kisses her.*]
> *Daughter.*   O, sir, you would fain be nibbling.
> *Wooer.* Why do you rub my kiss off?
> *Daughter*   'Tis a sweet one,
> And will perfume me finely against the wedding.
> (5.2.84)

The kiss consumes and perfumes. The lovers think to bed, then wed. To catch a kiss, to keep a kiss: only in the giddiness of mad imagination. Only in the truth of dreams. Only love could be that wise.

7 "A mad woman? We are made, boys!"
The Jailer's Daughter in *The Two Noble Kinsmen*

𝕴(♦)𝕳(♦)𝕴

Susan Green

Scholarly interest in *The Two Noble Kinsmen* has taken its energy from the ascription of dual authorship to the "memorable Worthies" John Fletcher and William Shakespeare on the title page of the 1634 quarto. The 350 years since that publication have produced commentary centering mainly on questions of authorship.[1] That commentary has not generated a conversation easy to follow or to join. Its productions of elaborate metrical and linguistic tests, supposedly designed to investigate the question of authorship, aim to settle with certainty the question of who wrote the play, or who wrote which portions of it. For general readers and audiences, however, a part of the authorship controversy more consequential than stylometric testings has been that over the authorship (and hence the significance) of the role of the Jailer's Daughter. Taken up not only into the morris dance, which finds such dizzying use for her in the play, but also into the turns and returns of the "authorship question," the Jailer's Daughter has become the pivot, the stakes, the crux of the entire question.

Her role in the critical conversation produced through the play mirrors her role in the drama as it unfolds; by noting connections between the status of the Jailer's Daughter within the play and her status in the critical commentary surrounding it, we can see how questions of authorship become, in this drama, questions of gender and generativity. Male artistic collaboration, celebrated in earlier Shakespearean comedies, is here shown to be so deeply at odds with Nature that the play itself comes to question an aesthetic requiring women to be characterized as Nature's own. Just as Theseus contrives a deadly contest when confronting two men who love one woman, so also critics, when confronting a play by two authors, have wanted to settle the issue of authorship once and for all, as if the play could not offer up its experience until lines of generative / artistic responsibility were firmly established. Within both these sets of interpretative relations, Theseus's bewilderment over two wooers and critics' bewilderment over two authors, the Jailer's Daughter moves frenetically, slightly off center, but always, I shall argue, a crucial locus of the play's illusioning power.

Henry Weber's 1812 edition of *The Works of Beaumont and Fletcher* offered the first assignment of particular scenes to each of the two dramatists. Fletcher

---

1. Paul Bertram, *Shakespeare and "The Two Noble Kinsmen"* (New Brunswick: Rutgers University Press, 1965), summarizes this history.

121

was given the scenes that carry the underplot of the Jailer's Daughter. Paul Bertram, whose 1965 study gives the most complete history of scholarly activity surrounding the play (however controversial his conclusions may be), argues that Weber's "division appears to have been simply to assign to Shakespeare those scenes in Acts I, III, and V whose sustained rhetoric and ceremonious character make a strong immediate impression, and to assign to Fletcher most of the scenes in which the underplot of the Jailer's Daughter is worked out or in which low-comedy dialogue predominates."[2] Subsequent nineteenth-century editors and commentators—William Spedding in 1833, Samuel Hickson in 1847—argue for a similar attribution, offering refinements that pull the story of the Jailer's Daughter further and further out of the fabric of the play and then stitch her to Fletcher's apprentice talents. As if the play were a broken-backed thing to begin with, the attributers of authorship apply pressure where they think to find the play's weakest point—the mad female of the piece—and forge a critical apparatus made to intensify class divisions. Lower-class characters go with Fletcher, the lesser dramatist; Shakespeare is preserved for the formal, "sane" realm of male authority.

When twentieth-century critics began to discuss *The Two Noble Kinsmen* in more conceptual, thematic terms, raising issues that might speak more directly to the experience of readers or audiences of the play, the Jailer's Daughter remained a sticking place. Clifford Leech could not wrest her from the old authorship problem but was finally able to offer interpretative consideration of her role: "If general opinion is right in assigning the opening of 2.1 to Shakespeare, it was he who introduced the Jailer's Daughter. But the use made of her is characteristically Fletcher's."[3] He sees her descent into madness as "comic" and links her to Emilia in that "neither girl has choice, neither girl has, ultimately it seems, the power to differentiate."[4] M. C. Bradbrook, in 1971, concurred: "The Jacobean audience would have hastened to see what most readers look on as its chief weakness—the Jailer's mad daughter, a parody of Ophelia, in her unrequited love for Palamon."[5] These critics concede, however, that her role in performance differs from the role scholars have supposed from their closeted studies. In reference to the two productions he had heard of, Leech says: "It is evident that something happened to the Jailer's Daughter's scenes when they got on the stage."[6] Bradbrook's speculation is even more tantalizing, though disturbingly remote from any claims she might make about her own experience of the play: "It is said that in performance the Jailer's Daughter turns out to be the star part."[7] That Bradbrook is referring to Leech's admittedly secondhand report, as quoted above, only adds to the atmosphere of incestuous

2. Ibid., 18.
3. Clifford Leech, Introduction to *The Two Noble Kinsmen* (New York: NAL, 1966), xxxii.
4. Ibid., xxxii.
5. M. C. Bradbrook, "Shakespeare and His Collaborators," in *Shakespeare 1971: Proceedings of the World Shakespeare Congress—Vancouver, August 1971*, ed. Clifford Leech and J. M. R. Margeson (Toronto: University of Toronto Press, 1972), 29.
6. Leech, Introduction, xxxvi.
7. Bradbrook, "Shakespeare and His Collaborators," 29.

generativity that becomes such a potent wish and anxiety of the play itself and that has received a kind of fulfillment in the scholarly activity surrounding it as evidenced here.

Certainly a role with power to galvanize an audience deserves more attention than it has been given by critics who use it merely as a wedge to divide authorship responsibilities for the play and to find the Master's hand. My own examination of the play also requires the use of the Jailer's Daughter, but for this study I will think of the role as pointing to a collaborative achievement of the authors. Authorship, then, will not require assigning particular scenes to particular men but will manifest itself as an inscription across the entire surface of the play. I take the terms for this analysis from the play's prologue.

> New plays and maidenheads are near akin—
> Much follow'd both, for both much money gi'n,
> If they stand sound and well; and a good play
> (Whose modest scenes blush on his marriage-day,
> And shake to lose his honor) is like her
> That after holy tie and first night's stir,
> Yet still is modesty, and still retains
> More of the maid to sight than husband's pains.
> (Pro. 1-8)

The play seems first like pricey virgin skin tested on "first night's stir," material proof "sounded" through "husband's pains." It then achieves an innocence reconstructed through a scopophilic epistemology producing "a maid to sight"—innocence despite, or perhaps because of, secret ravishment. The Prologue's prayer (Pro. 9) that the play may be a "modest" maid suggests that the playwright/husband's mastery will provide a screen of innocence surrounding the postnuptial bride through which one may know the husband's work. The materiality of the sound maidenhead becomes transformed into an inscription across her body so that semiotically she signifies both her husband's mastery and the now "naturalized" generativity of their procreant sexuality. Disorienting shifts in gender reference throughout the prologue, however, throw doubt on both the purity of innocence thus constructed and the artistic cum sexual processes that may bring it into the world. By line 4, the pronoun *his* in the parenthetical "(Whose modest scenes blush on his marriage-day, / And shake to lose his honor)" masculinizes the play and turns the question of its success into a question of male honor, but a male honor now under the pressure of a homoerotic creative potency.

By line 16, the play is a newly dropped child, progeny of "noble breeding" between playwright(s) and Chaucer whose chastising voice reaches from the grave and prompts the prologue's baldly stated admission: "This is the fear we bring" (Pro. 21). This fear can be felt as an artistic crisis located specifically in an anxiety surrounding gender and generativity and in contradictions between maidenhood's innocence and poet's potency. When the Prologue anxiously places its hopes on a rivalrous masculine creativity expressed in reference to Chaucer—"It were an endless thing, / And too ambitious, to aspire to him"— we return to the Prologue's deepest contradiction. Male bonding to produce art seems able to create an eternity of narrative productivity, but art produced by men requires Woman to be fictionalized as Nature's own—materially linked through her body to "natural," reproductive, creative energy. Throughout this Prologue, however, shifting sexual imagery in comparisons of plays with men and maids may respond to concepts of sexual difference so unstable that human generative capacity seems nothing at all like Nature's or is strangely at odds with it. The Prologue points to a resolution of this anxiety in an aesthetic in which maiden innocence becomes residual proof of masterly creativity through an equation where loss of maidenhead, in the first instance, brings forth a new arena of symbolic mastery—the creation of a "modest maid" or of a play that will seem fresh and new at every performance.

Thus, gender, figured through the construction of innocence on the body of Woman—the locus of the maidenhead—becomes the play's supreme fiction. We can sense, everywhere in the play, a sorrow over gender when we feel the desire of the narrative to find nobility in male collaboration at odds with the desires of characters (Theseus, in particular) set against such homoerotic wishes. As if Nature were deeply coded against us, the play produces a knowledge about gender construction for which there seems to be no solace. Palamon's final insight, on seeing Arcite carried from the stage, responds to this most basic loss: "O cousin, / That we should things desire which do cost us/ The loss of our desire!" (5.3.109–11).

The Jailer's Daughter, in her mad love for Palamon, functions as the play's most potent figure of desire, the site of the narrative's deepest struggle in constructing both maidenly innocence and a successful play through the vehicle of the maidenhead. In this last of the "Shakespeare" plays, the role of the daughter shifts from her mediating and curative functions in the late romances to her position as the figure who herself must be "cured." Consider that in *The Two Noble Kinsmen* the story of a father, his daughter, and her wooer is significantly subordinated to the story of the kinsmen and that, therefore, the play may be responding to a deep wish to find generative capacity in the kinsmen's noble friendship.[8] The complex relations between these two stories, the two interlocking triangles (Arcite-Emilia-Palamon and Wooer-Daughter-Palamon), focus the crisis of creativity most acutely—a crisis made explicit through contrasting "playwright" figures in the drama, Theseus and the Jailer's Daughter. Both draw others into their imaginative processes, each controlling in his or her own way the two stories of the play and the characters who perform in them their overtly projective fantasies. The desire of the Jailer's Daughter for Palamon, however, pushes the drama deeper and deeper into its own losses—losses felt most acutely by Theseus, whose eroticism calls for bounds, containment,

8. The subplot of the Jailer's Daughter does not appear in Chaucer's version of the story.

and mediation with the gods and whose manipulations most thwart the desires of others.

Twice in the play Theseus staggers from the requests of women. The Jailer's Friend reports in 4.1 the action of the previous scene where Duke Theseus, in response to Emilia's pleading, set conditions for a final contest between Arcite and Palamon instead of acting on his first impulse and killing them both on the spot:

> for Hippolyta,
> And fair-ey'd Emily, upon their knees
> Begg'd with such handsome pity, that the Duke
> Methought stood staggering whether he should follow
> His rash oath, or the sweet compassion
> Of those two ladies.
>
> (4.1.7-12)

A stage direction in the first scene points explicitly to Theseus's first troubling moment. In line 77, he "Turns away" after agreeing to help the three Queens bury their slain kings left to rot on the fields outside Thebes. His first speech in reply to them earlier in the scene suggests what trouble their presence causes him. Where they have asked for help in burying the kings, he offers "vengeance and revenge for 'em" (1.1.58) and immediately relates the decay of women's bodies to their allegiance with men, remembering the First Queen on her wedding day when her "wheaten wreath / Was then nor thresh'd nor blasted" (1.1.64). In taking up manly responsibility for preserving/restoring a bride's innocence, Theseus seems overcome by the task, ending his speech with the oceanic exclamation: "O grief and time, / Fearful consumers, you will all devour!" (1.1.69-70). In language and experience, Theseus seeks the sensation of expanse for the pleasure his constraints will bring.

That *you,* in this speech, may refer to the queens (perhaps all women) as well as to *grief* and *time* is substantiated by Theseus's further responses when the Queens press him to abandon his wedding ceremony and instantly take up their cause. The wedding to him is "a service . . . / Greater than any war; it more imports me," he says, "Than all the actions that I have foregone, / Or futurely can cope" (1.1.174). It is "This grand act of our life, this daring deed / Of fate in wedlock" (1.1.164). Theseus's imagination moves toward constraint, boundary, contest, and ceremony. His wooing of Hippolyta was a contest of warrior strength. She was, in the words of the Second Queen, "shrunk . . . into / The bound (she) wast o'erflowing" (1.1.83). "Leave not out a jot / O' th' sacred ceremony" (1.1.130) he instructs as he hastens to marry before fulfilling his promise to help the Queens. But they are unsatisfied and press him to forego his marriage rites in favor of their burial rites.

The Queens' uncanny knowledge of Theseus's imaginative requirements influences the language they use. The Third Queen is, in fact, a bit embarrassed at the excesses needed to prompt Theseus's response. In seeking Emilia's support, she finds her metaphors awkward:

> He that will all the treasure know o' th' earth
> Must know the centre too; he that will fish
> For my least minnow, let him lead his line
> To catch one at my heart. O, pardon me,
> Extremity, that sharpens sundry wits,
> Makes me a fool.
>
> (1.1.114–19)

Emilia's response points to a problem of language the Queens encounter in their exchanges with Theseus. Her comment, "Who cannot feel nor see the rain, being in't, / Knows neither wet nor dry" (1.1.120–21), imagines a reduction of sensation so acute as to erase language's ability to discriminate "natural" phenomena. In redirecting Theseus's attention from his marriage rites, the Queens' language pushes connections between marriage and death so that Theseus can feel implicated in their dilemma. In getting him to feel the linkage between his marriage and his own death, they transfer his erotic interest in his bride to an interest in language itself, letting their elaborate metaphors sensualize him to their ends. "What care / For what thou feel'st not?" the First Queen asks him (1.1.180). As it turns out, eroticizing Theseus in the direction of loss is not that difficult: the Queens are more than equal to the task.

To begin with, Theseus's wedding procession opens with a remarkably funereal song that includes "marigolds on death-beds blowing" (1.1.11). The song's final evocation forbidding the "crow, the sland'rous cuckoo," the "boding raven," and other ominous birds from the "bridehouse perch" seems only to prompt their emergence in the form of the Queens themselves, dressed in black with stained veils. Their first words speak of the "beaks of ravens" and "pecks of crows" that even then devour the bodies of their dead kings.

Emilia's shrewd analysis of language in its capacity to elide difference, suggesting that one needs a language of *wet* and *dry* in order to "feel" and "see" the rain, aids the Queens, whose language must play on differences between death and marriage in such a way as to heighten Theseus's anxiety that they are, in fact, identities. He will feel their connection even as the language speaks of their separation. His wedding day, thus far, has prompted him to grave wonderings about his responsibility for women's decay and about the efficacy of patrilinearity when kings lie dead in fields, where, in fact, the Second Queen imaginatively places his own body alongside the three others, "swoll'n, / Showing the sun his teeth, grinning at the moon" (1.1.99–100). This was the trick: to locate Theseus within an excessively sensual language that draws him further and further from his immediate desires—his apparent wish to be married—while at the same time satisfying his need for the sensation of bounded excess by using metaphors that seem to "contain" his experience. The First Queen, under the pressure of this aesthetic, eventually produces a startling image, in the form of a question, that combines elements the scene has elaborated thus far: erotic experience with a woman covering the "truth" of a man's destiny; kings rotting while language swells into the fullness of both sensual arousal and the bloatedness of deteriorating flesh:

> O, when
> Her twinning cherries shall their sweetness fall
> Upon thy tasteful lips, what wilt thou think
> Of rotten kings or blubber'd queens?
> (1.1.177–80)

Substituting the sensuousness of language for a real experience with a bride can appeal to a sensibility whose anxieties about responsibilities to bridehood only point to death.

It is Emilia's final threat never to take a husband if Theseus will not help the Queens, though, that seems to trigger his abandonment of his bride. In leaving Hippolyta, he has Emilia's negative promise insuring he will have another bride to tend to, another scene for exercising mastery, another "new night's stir," in the words of the Prologue, through which to prove a patrilineal surmounting of death. He spends the remainder of the play setting up conditions, contests, and ceremonies that will allow him to share his "daring deed of fate in wedlock" with another—either Arcite or Palamon—a singular man, one of a pair. Further, Theseus has the Queens' praise and promise that he may be above the gods, more masterful than they who do not "make affections bend" (1.1.229).

Before he leaves for Thebes, Theseus explicitly instructs Pirithous to continue with the wedding celebration, even though no one has been married. This empty celebration underlies, in a sense, the entire play. We never learn when Theseus and Hippolyta do marry—when he is able to "dispatch / This grand act of our life" (1.1.163–64). The play goes from one celebration to another—from the ersatz wedding feast to the debauched victory party in Thebes to the final May Day celebration, which is so much under Theseus's control and by which time he and Hippolyta are, it seems, married—and it doesn't seem to matter when the real celebrations begin or what exactly is being celebrated. A language for understanding such differences seems abandoned in the first scene with Emilia's sense that Theseus can't tell the difference between *wet* and *dry*.

In taking up the Third Queen's rather bungled fish image—which was, perhaps, too self-directed, too inviting of Theseus to find his solution to a bride's decay in knowing her "centre" or "least minnow"—the First Queen, after Emilia's sly analysis, which has only made Theseus turn more resolutely to his marriage ceremony, creates an image pointed exactly at Theseus's desires vis-à-vis language. She says to him, "But, O Jove, your actions, / Soon as they move, as asprays do the fish, / Subdue before they touch" (1.1.137–39). Excessive language works for Theseus because it offers the sensation of bounded expanse and because it, like his actions, can "subdue before [it] touch[es]." Such a taming is only the prelude to death—fish turn over as if dead, subdued at the mere sight of the osprey. A celebration before a wedding, a fresh bride promised before the first is married—Theseus's remarkable capacity to deflect experience before he even touches it makes the contradictions of his final speech in the scene both poignant and frightening: "As we are men / Thus we should do, being sensually subdu'd / We lose our human title" (1.1.232–34). Has he or has he not just been "sensually subdu'd"? Would he know the difference?

The play offers another version of language in its relationship to sensuality in the figure of the Jailer's Daughter. She seems to embody the difference Theseus lacks. "Lord, the diff'rence of men!" (2.1.53), she says, in a phrase that becomes her driving motto. Where Theseus's imagination manufactures difference out of a displacement of sensual experience into language through the vehicles of contest, ritual, and enforced celebration, her imagination prompts her to become that difference, to come between seeming identities, as she suggests in her first scene when she wishes she could be the "divided sigh" that sometimes comes between the imprisoned Arcite and Palamon (2.1.40–41).

She enters the play to marvel at a sight we can take to be the very image of Theseus's imagination: two contented prisoners locked up forever, where "the prison itself is proud of 'em; and they have all the world in their chamber" (2.1.24–25). She looks and comments as if she had never contemplated such a thing before. She knows what it is, however, and appreciates the art of it: "Tis pity they are in prison, and 'twere pity they should be out" (2.1.22). The sight of the imprisoned pair flattens the verse, in comparison to the Queens' baroque language in the first scene; but the Daughter's prose hesitates and wonders while her thought works to encompass the import of the image she sees:

. . . for they are noble suff'rers. I marvel how they would have look'd had they been victors, that with such a constant nobility enforce a freedom out of bondage, making misery their mirth, and affliction a toy to jest at. (2.1.31–35)

She grasps the terms of this art. The idea of an "enforcement" of freedom in bondage surely speaks to the creative imperatives driving Theseus. She refers to Theseus and the spirit of willing confinement that surrounds his imagination in a mock competitive way: "It seems to me they have no more sense of their captivity than I of ruling Athens" (2.1.37–38). Her attraction to Palamon, who at the end of the scene receives her whole attention (she only sees "a part" of Arcite), draws her deeper and deeper into the meaning of imprisonment. Gradually, under the force of the experience of this art, she produces her own in answer to it. In the world of this play, however, her difference means madness.

She becomes mad slowly and in a context of the natural world where night falls, wolves howl, and hunger and lack of sleep can make a mind "mop'd." Her influence on the language of the play can be felt by comparing the status of fishing in scene 1 and in the Wooer's description of finding her by a lakeside singing of Palamon. Whereas the Queens construct a fishing image rhetorically powerful enough to catch Theseus in their language, the Wooer is actually fishing when he hears the Daughter singing. He lays aside his "angle / To his own skill" (4.1.59–60) to seek her and ends up pulling her from the lake:

> As I late was angling
> In the great lake that lies behind the palace,
> From the far shore, thick set with reeds and sedges,
> As patiently I was attending sport,
> I heard a voice, a shrill one; and attentive
> I gave my ear, when I might well perceive
> 'Twas one that sung, and by the smallness of it,
> A boy or woman.
>
> (4.1.52–59)

That the homoeroticism of the boy actor should emerge in the verse at this point, where we may be imagining the Jailer's Daughter in her most heterosexual guise, responds to the profound unease over gender I sense in the play. This is, nevertheless, her setting—a nonpastoral, natural environment. An idea of experience coming to one almost inseparable from the conditions of the elements of nature is pointedly expressed in the Jailer's Daughter's own speeches. She sees a shipwreck, imagines one, draws others into antic imitation of another, then journeys inward on her own voyage "to th' end o' th' world" (5.2.72) in progressive enhancement of experience into imaginative enactment and onward to madness.

In 3.4, having decided that Palamon is dead, the Jailer's Daughter wanders onstage and, in the coldness of a starlit night, locates herself by sighting the sea. Her imagination quickens as she watches a ship veer toward a rock lying underwater (how does she know it's there?). As it goes down, she matches with her words the rhythm and intensity of the event she observes (or imagines occurring?):

> And there's a rock lies watching under water;
> Now, now, it beats upon it—now, now now!
> There's a leak sprung, a sound one. How they cry!
> Open her before the wind! you'll lose all else.
> Up with a course or two, and tack about, boys!
> Good night, good night, y' are gone. I am very hungry.
>
> (3.4.6–11)

It is characteristic of her experience of the world that the idea of death—here, in the beat of one line—quickly turns her attention to her own sentient being. In her preceding soliloquy, she concludes Palamon must be dead and empties herself of that knowledge in the same half-line turn:

> I'll set it down
> He's torn to pieces. They howl'd many together,
> And then they fed on him. So much for that,
> Be bold to ring the bell.
>
> (3.1.17–20)

When her imagination turns fantastical, it retains its grounding in a natural environment. After she sees the shipwreck, she calls for a frog to tell her the "news from all parts o' th' world" so she can sail in a cockleshell ship to have her fortune told by the King of Pigmies (3.4.11–15). Her insistence that a natural environment informs her knowledge of the world makes the fantastical elements of her imagination—her "horse," for example, that can dance, read, and write—seem more "real" than similar elements in the main plot. By comparison, Emilia's horse, whose mad ride seems profoundly connected to a madness in the narrative the characters inhabit (but which stands for connections we can never fathom), seems utterly fantastical, disturbingly disconnected to a natural world we can inhabit with some comfort.

Such is the power of the Jailer's Daughter's imagination that she can draw others into it, giving them the illusion that in acting out her fantasies, she will be restored to their world where dowered maidens marry within their class and where sexuality does not explode into excessive conceptions of a universe of sexed relations. In 4.1, she demonstrates her madness to her father, her wooer, and their friends. The scene ends when she calls for them to set sail for the woods where Palamon, she says, waits for her. In what surely must be a galvanizing theatrical moment, her skeptical, perhaps frightened audience gives over to her, answering her madness with their own portrayal of a ship's crew set dead for a wood.

In the next scene, she has sailed on alone. With a piece of silver on the tip of her tongue (suggesting that her language, new-coined for death, would buy her a place in the underworld where she will pick nosegays for Palamon and contemplate the wretched in Hell whose sexual deceptions and excesses lie just beyond the "barley-break"), she comes to link death and sexuality in ways that may remind us of Theseus in their frightening unity. In being true to Palamon, however, she is also being true to something in her own language—some difference she has come to embody. Her insistence on her heterosexual passion (in a play where homoeroticism seems doomed to be channeled into orthodox union) ought to be at one with the desire of the narrative; but, of course, it is not. In 3.2, her night's suffering drives her to make herself the stakes in the play of difference that moves across language, sexuality, and the natural world: "O state of nature, fail together in me, / Since thy best props are warp'd!" (3.2.31–32). When nature does fail her, her language achieves a purity and directness of which Theseus can only dream.

Twice the Jailer's Daughter mentions her maidenhead. Once, in the exuberance of her resolve to "enjoy" Palamon, she associates herself with other impassioned women by accepting the commonality of her sexual response. In describing the course of her affections for Palamon she says:

> Next, I pitied him;
> And so would any young wench o' my conscience
> That ever dream'd, or vow'd her maidenhead
> To a handsome man.
>   (2.4.11–14)

Later, after her Wooer rescues her from drowning, she knows she must be "cured": "For I must lose my maidenhead by cocklight, / 'Twill never thrive else" (4.1.112–14). What will not thrive? Her sexuality? Nature's "props?" The play itself? The forces working within her implode in this vague reference as she accepts her "cure." In terms of the world of this play, Theseus, from his great distance, has brought another maidenhead under his sway. She becomes, now, too much like the other wenches who, in her imagination, are all with child by Palamon and whose children's destiny she articulates with a strange prescience:

> There are at least two hundred now with child by him—
> There must be four. Yet I keep close for all this,
> Close as a cockle. And all these must be boys,
> He has the trick on't; and at ten years old
> They must be all gelt for musicians,
> And sing the wars of Theseus.
>
> (4.1.129–33)

The tortured sexual references of the Prologue may be the furthest thing from our minds when we see the last of the Jailer's Daughter, but the connections are strong. Surely, we must be witnessing one of the most tender and most breathtaking scenes in Shakespearean writing when the Jailer's Daughter goes off with her Wooer, who poses as Palamon, and we listen to her fright at the prospect of her "first night's stir":

> *Daugh.* And then we'll sleep together?
> *Doct.*   Take her offer.
> *Wooer.* Yes, marry, will we.
> *Daugh.*   But you shall not hurt me.
> *Wooer.* I will not, sweet.
> *Daugh.*   If you do, love, I'll cry. *Exeunt.*
>
> (5.2.109–14)

It would be possible to list many more references to mastery and innocence that the play weaves into its language: the Jailer's Daughter's call for the master in her re-creation of the ship scene (4.2.145–55); her taunting greeting of her masters when she asks, "How far is't now to th' end o' th' world, my masters?" (5.2.73); the Queens' promise of "mast'ry" to Theseus at the end of the first scene (1.1.231); the Jailer's description of his Daughter "as if she were a fool, / an innocent" (4.1.40–41); Palamon's offer of money for her dowry upon hearing she has been "restor'd" by saying "and to piece her portion / Tender her this." (5.3.31–32); and many more. In discussing the relationship of mastery to innocence as suggested by the Prologue, however, I would prefer to understand that relation not as a conflict of alternative ways of viewing the world—from Theseus's point of view and from the Jailer's Daughter's—but rather as an interdependence. An imagination like Theseus's requires a figure like the Jailer's Daughter—something in reserve, something hopeful, some preserve of eccentricity and passion distant and remote but totally responsive to Theseus's desire for symbolic mastery. The potency of the Shakespeare/Fletcher collaboration in knowing this need reaches deeply into the fissures of Chaucer's story until it finds the "maidenhead"—the play itself, singing the achievements of Theseus.

8 Crises of Male Self-Definition in *The Two Noble Kinsmen*

Jeanne Addison Roberts

The appearance of an Amazon in the scenario of a classical or Renaissance tale is an infallible clue to an area of male anxiety, a signal of threatened erosion to a systematically constructed patriarchal world view.[1] As a virginal or only rarely sexual (and then exclusively for procreation) female, the Amazon is impervious to male charms; living without men, she fights them as their equals or superiors; as horsewoman, archer, and hunter, she impinges on and sometimes invades male domains, threatening even such strongholds of civilized (patriarchal) sanctity as Athens itself.[2] For the Greeks she was an intriguing and terrifying male nightmare. For the Elizabethans, the Amazonian image was revivified by the real presence of a queen whose formidable virginal power conjured up but never completely coincided with memories of the classical myth. Although it surely hovered in the background, the identification of Elizabeth with the Amazon was rarely overt, and some distinction seems to have evolved between Amazons and warrior women.[3] Elizabeth was in any case regarded as exceptional. Most Elizabethan Amazons, like their

1. Extensive discussions of the significance of Amazons in classical Greece may be found in Page duBois, *Centaurs and Amazons: Women and the Pre-History of the Great Chain of Being* (Ann Arbor: University of Michigan Press, 1982), and William Blake Tyrrell, *Amazons: A Study in Athenian Mythmaking* (Baltimore: Johns Hopkins University Press, 1984). For a survey and discussion of Amazons in Elizabethan literature, see C. T. Wright, "The Amazons in Elizabethan Literature," *Studies in Philology* 37 (1940): 433–56, and Simon Shepherd, *Amazons and Warrior Women* (Brighton, Sussex: Harvester, 1981).

2. Many descriptions of Amazons were available to Elizabethans. The account of the Amazon attack on Athens is recorded in Thomas North, trans., *[Plutarch's] Lives of the Noble Grecians and Romans* (London, 1579). A full narration of Theseus's war with the Amazons is to be found in Giovanni Boccaccio, *Teseida delle Nozze d'Emilia*, trans. Bernadette Marie McCoy as *The Book of Theseus* (New York: Medieval Text Association, 1974), 1 (further references to *The Book of Theseus* are to this edition and will be made parenthetically in the text). Boccaccio also furnishes a gloss (p. 48) describing Amazons as women dedicated to war, who have killed their males and cut off their right breasts to facilitate the shooting of bows. He adds (p. 21) that, though liberated, they are unable to remain free.

3. The distinction is epitomized by Radigund and Britomart in Edmund Spenser's *The Faerie Queene* (in *Poetical Works*, ed. J. C. Smith and E. de Selincourt [London: Oxford University Press, 1948], book 5, canto 7). Although Britomart brutally destroys Radigund, it is notable that she too disappears from the story after this feat. Winifred Schleiner, "*Divina virago:* Queen Elizabeth as an Amazon," *Studies in Philology* 75 (1978): 163–80, outlines the limited identification of Elizabeth with Amazons; Louis Adrian Montrose, "Shaping Fantasies: Figurations of Gender and Power in Elizabethan Culture," *Representations II* (1983): 61–94, traces the extreme ambiguity of Elizabethan male feelings toward their sovereign.

classical antecedents, were designed either to be seduced and subdued or to be destroyed.[4]

The Middle Ages may have had fewer problems with Amazonian women, accepting them as mythical constructs from alien antiquity. Boccaccio in book 1 of the *Teseida* lingers with apparent pleasure over his descriptions of the Amazons and their fortress, but the certainty of the impending subjugation of the females by Theseus prevents titillation from escalating into alarm. For Chaucer in *The Knight's Tale,* the Amazonian threat seems safely contained from the start.[5] As the tale begins, Theseus, with "his wysdom and his chilvalrie," has already "conquered al the regne of Femenye" and "weddede the queene Ypolita" (865-68); although her sister Emelye loves "huntynge and venerye" and prefers "to walken in the wodes wilde, / And noght to ben a wyf and be with childe" (2308-10), Ypolita is docile and conventional in accepting her marital fate. Chaucer never elaborates on the Amazonian past of the two sisters. Similarly, in *A Midsummer Night's Dream,* Hippolyta's past, glimpsed perhaps in her description of the moon as a "silver bow / New bent in heaven" (1.1.9-10), elicits only the momentarily troubling reference by Theseus to his wooing her with his sword and winning her love by doing her injuries (1.1.16-17). It might be argued that the quarrel between Oberon and Titania with its passing remembrance of Oberon's flirtation with the "bouncing Amazon" (2.1.20) and of Titania's having incited Theseus to "break his faith" with the Amazonian Antiopa (2.1.80)—a quarrel that has precipitated major confusions and reversals in the natural order of seasons—is in fact a covert manifestation of the convulsive effects of a union contracted in defiance of cultural expectations; but, if so, the subtext is securely buried under the relatively smooth surface of the festive comedy.[6]

In *The Two Noble Kinsmen,*[7] however, the threat to male definition posed by

4. Penthesilea, celebrated in Ben Jonson's *The Masque of Queens* (London, 1609) is the most famous example of the Amazon killed in battle. Her valor is described at some length in William Caxton, trans. *The Recuile of the Histories of Troie* by Raoul Le Fevre (London, 1553), 3.25-29. Thomas Heywood, *The Exemplary Lives and Memorable Acts of Nine of the Most Worthy Women of the World* (London, 1640), describes examples from both categories: Penthesilea in *Exemplary Lives* is the woman killed, and a digression in his *Troia Britanica* (London, 1609), 307-77, deals with a typical seduction. Beaumont and Fletcher's *The Sea Voyage* recounts a similar conquest of Amazons. *The Masque of Queens* vividly illustrates the uneasy balance of anxiety and titillation in the representation of extraordinary women. In a masque celebrating the virtues of Queen Anne, Jonson devotes considerably more than half of his attention to the monstrous figures of witches.

5. Geoffrey Chaucer, *The Knight's Tale,* in *Complete Works,* ed. F. N. Robinson (Boston: Houghton Mifflin, 1933). Further references to *The Knight's Tale* are to this edition and will be made parenthetically in the text by line number.

6. Plutarch notes the confusion of Hippolyta and Antiopa in his sources. Shakespeare in *A Midsummer Night's Dream* clearly chooses to regard them as separate women. If Theseus/Oberon and Hippolyta/Titania were played by the same actors, obviously any reverberation between their roles would be reinforced.

7. Although I am inclined to accept the assignment of the play to Shakespeare and Fletcher, I have chosen not to deal here with the authorship question. The play seems to me coherent enough to justify discussing it as an artistic unit representative of its age. I have focused primarily on the main plot not because I reject the subplot but because a thorough analysis of it would take me beyond the scope of this paper.

Hippolyta before her subjugation to Theseus is clearly spelled out by the second
widowed Queen, who addresses her descriptively:

> Honored Hippolyta,
> Most dreaded Amazonian, that hast slain
> The scythe-tusk'd boar; that with thy arm, as strong
> As it is white, wast near to make the male
> To thy sex captive, but that this thy lord,
> Born to uphold creation in that honor
> First Nature styl'd it in, shrunk thee into
> The bound thou wast o'erflowing, at once subduing
> Thy force and thy affection . . . .
>   (1.1.77-85)

There are, furthermore, repeated reminders of the barbaric background of the
Scythian Queen. Proposing that Hippolyta kneel to enlist Theseus's aid in
recovering their husbands' bodies, the Second Queen offers, presumably as a
palliative appropriate to her addressee, a grotesquely violent comparison: "But
touch the ground for us no longer time / Than a dove's motion when the head's
pluck'd off" (1.1.97-98). Even more shocking to conventional expectations of
women is Hippolyta's savage account of the effect of her war experiences:

> We have been soldiers, and we cannot weep
> When our friends don their helms, or put to sea,
> Or tell of babes broach'd on the lance, or women
> That have sod their infants in (and after eat them)
> The brine they wept at killing 'em.
>   (1.3.18-22)

In addition to Theseus's bride, the presence of her sister Emilia, absent in *A
Midsummer Night's Dream,* here compounds the unsettling effect of the alien
women. Clearly disturbed by Emilia's resolution never to "Love any that's
called man," the newly "civilized" Hippolyta says:

> If I were ripe for your persuasion, you
> Have said enough to shake me from the arm
> Of the all-noble Theseus, for whose fortunes
> I will now in and kneel . . .
>   (1.3.91-94)

Primacy in the affections of Theseus is to be Hippolyta's compensation for her
capitulation, and she finds this preeminence called into question by Emilia's
reminder of the "knot of love" between Theseus and Pirithous. In a non sequitur
that suggests the urgency of her need to believe in her reward, she quickly
resolves to reject her earlier uncertainty about "which he loves best" and asserts,
without further evidence, her "great assurance / That we, more than his

Pirithous, possess / The high throne in his heart" (1.3.94–96). From this point on Hippolyta dwindles into a conventional wife, conforming to male expectation; but Emilia remains a problem.

A story told about both Thales and Socrates implies that the Hellenes defined themselves as human Greek males, conceiving the rest of the world in terms of otherness: a human was a creature not animal, not barbarian, not female, and not divine.[8] Such a definition provided a stable center to Greek culture (as it probably has to most cultures), but contrasting Others lurked dangerously around this central core. The threatening erosion of the boundaries of human definition is signaled by the ubiquity of such peripheral hybrids as satyrs and centaurs; by the man-animal metamorphic shapes of Teiresias, Callisto, and many others; by partially assimilated aliens such as Medea; and by such semi-divine heroes as Hercules and Achilles. Amazons rank with hermaphrodites as forms of male-female hybrid. According to legend, they usurped such male prerogatives as horseback riding, fighting, and the rejection of orderly monogamous marriage. Usually associated with distant outposts like Scythia, they qualified as "nonhuman" aliens as well as "nonhuman" women. In Greek legend and literature Amazons appear at moments of cultural crisis—always on the wrong side. Hippolyta/Antiope is implicated in an invasion of Athens and subdued by Theseus in a short-lived marriage that eventuated in the catastrophic destruction of their son Hippolytus.[9] Penthesilea surfaces fighting along with a centaur, the "dreadful Sagittary," for the Trojans. She is killed by Achilles, who, ironically, falls in love with her as soon as she is safely dead and no longer threatening.

Both Boccaccio and Chaucer seem to have been able to adapt the story of Theseus and Hippolyta by using the two characters as received legendary figures with recognizable values and suppressing disturbing overtones. Boccaccio says he wants to celebrate the "toils endured for Mars" (12.10.84–86), and Chaucer seems to want to demonstrate the admirable but limited philosophy available to the highest pagan society. According to V. A. Kolve, Theseus was to the Middle Ages "a man seeking consciously to embody the highest chivalric ideals of his civilization."[10] In *The Knight's Tale* Hippolyta is so much the gracious, docile aristocratic lady as hardly to evoke any memory of her origins. Most of Chaucer's characters have relatively stable, almost allegorical significance, and Kolve has worked out a precise and consistent Christian interpretation of the tale.[11] Allegory, like ritual, serves to repeat and reinforce accepted cultural norms.

Allegory, like ritual, was also breaking down in the England of Shakespeare and Fletcher. The hierarchy of male/female attributes had become blurred, and

8. Diogenes Laertius, *Lives of Eminent Philosophers,* trans. R. D. Hicks (London: Loeb Classical Library, 1925), 1:33. See also duBois, *Centaurs and Amazons,* for an extended discussion.

9. North, trans., *[Plutarch's] Lives,* 14–15.

10. V. A. Kolve, *Chaucer and the Imagery of Narrative* (Stanford: Stanford University Press, 1984), 101. D'Orsay W. Pearson, "'Unkinde' Theseus: A Study in Renaissance Mythography," *English Literary Renaissance* 4 (1974): 276–98, notes the many negative aspects of Theseus's career as described in Seneca's *Hippolytus* and Plutarch's *Lives,* arguing that by 1590 the image of the noble Theseus had begun to tarnish.

11. Kolve, *Chaucer and Imagery,* 156–57.

the struggles between Venus and Mars, and Venus and Diana, were shadowed with ambiguities. Allegorical affinities certainly remain in *The Two Noble Kinsmen,* but they are shifting, inconsistent, and disturbing rather than reassuring. In this climate the Amazonian presence comes to life again as a signifier of marginal territory in the definition of the "human."

The first dilemma of Theseus is set up with dazzling clarity at the beginning of the play with the conjunction of unconsummated marriage and impending funeral. His crisis is a peculiarly male one: Theseus is torn between Venus and Mars. His heart is with Mars. Chaucer makes his loyalty more overt than does Shakespeare—describing his white banner emblazoned with "The rede statue of Mars, with spere and targe" (975)—but the play also repeatedly emphasizes the King's devotion to battle and to the service of his "master Mars" (5.4.106). In order to subdue Hippolyta and produce death-defying progeny, however, Theseus must marry. His extraordinary description of marriage as "This grand act of our life, this daring deed / Of fate in wedlock" (1.1.163–64) and his insistence that "This is a service, whereto I am going, / Greater than any war; it more imports me / Than all the actions that I have foregone, / Or futurely can cope" (1.1.171–74) show his sense of the magnitude of the act and suggest some reluctance. His willingness to be diverted from his purpose by the grieving Queens is rewarded by their promise that his deed will earn him a deity equal to or even greater than that of Mars (1.1.227–28). The god of war is inevitably linked with death, and the discordant reminders of the grim reaper multiply with the appearance of the widowed Queens at the marriage festival.[12] Their black veils, their memories of the stench and "mortal loathsomeness" of the rotting corpses of their lords (1.1.45–47), their imagined vision of Theseus's own corpse lying "i' th' blood-siz'd field . . . swoll'n / Showing the sun his teeth, grinning at the moon," and their rapid imagistic alternation between the marriage bed and the death bed of "rotten kings" (1.1.139–40, 175–82) effectively cancel out the elevated ceremonial mood of the initial Hymeneal procession. Theseus, going off to fight Creon as proof of his "humanity" and affirming that "As we are men / Thus should we do, being sensually subdu'd / We lose our human title" (1.1.232–34), leaves his nuptials.

Immediately following these words of Theseus, we are presented with Palamon and Arcite, similarly concerned that "Widows' cries / . . . have not / Due audience of the gods" (1.2.79–81). They describe the perils of peace—the forgotten soldier and the dissolute city "where every evil / Hath a good color; where ev'ry seeming good's / A certain evil" (2.1.38–40) and where men are monsters. Lamenting Mars's "scorn'd altar," Palamon wishes that Juno would stir up trouble enough to start a new war. Their response to their revulsion from the corruption of Creon is to plan to leave his court, until they are reprieved in fact by a new war. At this point Palamon and Arcite are scarcely distinguishable. If anything, Palamon is more concerned than Arcite with Mars and his soldiers, and more determined to be "forehorse in the team" or none. As the

12. Chaucer's description of the temple of Mars (1981–2040) makes the association of death with the god detailed and explicit.

children of two sisters, Palamon and Arcite are essentially undifferentiated adolescents fearful of sullying their "gloss of youth" with "crimes of nature" (1.2.3–5). They are enamored of war and eager to escape the unknown perils (probably venereal) of the peaceful city. They are younger versions of Theseus and Pirithous, who have "Fought out together where death's self was lodg'd" and woven a "knot of love" that, it seems, "May be outworn, never undone" (1.3.40–44).

Viewing their hearse-drawn bodies, Theseus reveals that he has instantly recognized Palamon and Arcite as kindred spirits when he saw them in battle like "a pair of lions smear'd with prey," adding "I fix'd my note / Constantly on them; for they were a mark / Worth a god's view" (1.4.18–21), and concluding, "their lives concern us / Much more than Thebes is worth" (1.4.32–33). He fears them and would rather have them dead than free. However, he adds, "But forty thousand fold we had rather have 'em / Prisoners to us than death" (1.4.36–37). Fearing and cherishing them, he confines them to prison, and from this point on Palamon and Arcite act out almost emblematically the Venus-Mars struggle in Theseus's mind and in the male progress toward adulthood.

Together in a narcissistic prison, Palamon and Arcite think wistfully of war and women. Palamon remembers the two of them in battle, "like twins of honor" enjoying the feeling of their "fiery horses / Like proud seas under" them (2.2.18–20); and Arcite yearns self-absorbingly for "The sweet embraces of a loving wife" (2.2.30) who might furnish him with a kind of immortality by providing him with a replica of himself to memorialize him in victorious combat. The two find consolation, however, in regarding their prison as a "holy sanctuary" to keep them from the "corruption of worse men" and the menace of seductive women (2.2.71–72). They resolve, with ludicrously shortsighted assurance, to be content to be "one another's wife" and heir (2.2.80–83). Immediately there appears the figure of Emilia, plucking, appropriately enough, the Narcissus flower and remarking of its namesake, "That was a fair boy certain, but a fool / To love himself" (2.2.119–21). Like Actaeon's confrontation with Diana, the vision of Emilia results in a second male crisis, a fragmentation of the identity of her viewers that dominates the rest of the play. It is a curious but psychologically acute fact that in Renaissance mythologizing the sight of the naked virgin goddess Diana transforms the male viewer into a victim of Venus, pursued and ultimately torn apart by the hounds of desire.[13] Other-directed passion fractures the narcissistic self-absorption of Palamon and Arcite; and in transferring their affection from each other to Emilia they recapitulate Theseus's earlier progression from Pirithous to Hippolyta. As in the case of Theseus, their newfound recognition of Venus remains weak and ineffectual; they are torn in this crisis between conflicting goals.

In a patriarchy, the male cherishes the female's virginity, which certifies her as his inviolate possession; but he also depends on her fecundity for the propaga-

13. See especially *Twelfth Night* 1.1.17–22.

tion of his species.[14] Divided between Diana and Venus, he resents and depends on the presence of other males. Theseus has faced one side of this problem, accepting belatedly, in a bow to Venus, the responsibilities of marriage; but he imprisons his younger "rivals" who may challenge his proprietary interest in his sister-in-law. Male rivalry (the arena of Mars) is at least as powerful as heterosexual lust (the arena of Venus) in this play. The fractured friendship of Palamon and Arcite reflects both the Mars-Venus and the Venus-Diana conflict. The kinsmen's instant Venus-induced enmity propels them toward martial conflict, while their contrasting attitudes toward the lady reveal the Diana/Venus dilemma posed by women. Palamon perceives Emilia as a goddess to be worshiped (Chaucer says as Venus, but the play's lack of specificity makes the symbolically more apt connotation of Diana available), whereas Arcite sees her "as a woman, to enjoy" (1.2.163–64). In both cases, however, their passion begins and remains a distant infatuation; and we suspect its roots are firmly fixed in the violent male rivalry suggested by Palamon's threat to nail Arcite to the window and Arcite's reciprocal vow, "I'll throw my body out, / And leap the garden, when I see her next, / And pitch between her arms *to anger thee*" (2.2.215–17, italics mine).

In a neatly constructed allegory we might expect the fragmented psyches of Palamon and Arcite, reflections of Theseus's own divided mind, to define themselves as they will appear at the end—as servants respectively of the goddess of love and the god of war. To some extent this does occur, but the distinction is never absolute or clear-cut, and the situation is complicated by the Diana/Venus polarization. Male self-definition is not simple in this play. Although the knights are not fully rounded characters, neither are they merely emblems. Theseus, perhaps betraying his own predilection for Mars, frees Arcite to return to Thebes,[15] and the languishing Palamon immediately fantasizes his rival's reappearance as a victorious warrior. Arcite, on the other hand, imagines Palamon winning Emilia through seductive speech because "he has a tongue will tame tempests, / And make the wild rocks wanton" (2.3.16–17). Palamon is subsequently freed from prison by love, and the amorous devotion of the Jailer's Daughter secures for Palamon a more central position than Arcite's in the unfolding of the drama. Of the two knights Palamon is the gentler, the sadder, the more passive. After desire has seized him, he reveals a bizarre imagination

14. Tyrrell, in *Amazons: A Study,* explains the significance of the classical Amazon as an expression of the patriarch's fear of what his daughter, whom he wants to preserve intact as his own possession, may become if he does not secure for her a husband, thereby giving up his control of her for the sake of progeny.

15. It is true that Theseus does this at the instigation of Pirithous, but it still reveals a greater willingness to free the spirit of Mars than to free that of Venus. Paula S. Berggren, "'For what we lack, / We laugh': Incompletion and *The Two Noble Kinsmen*," *Modern Language Studies* 14:4(Fall 1984): 3–17, suggests that Arcite seems to be the wrong victim and that his end shows that the gods punish unfairly. Gods have, of course, always seemed unfair in tragedy. Arcite belongs, I believe, in the company of Hippolytus, Pentheus, and Shakespeare's Adonis (Seneca locates Hippolytus's death wound, like Adonis's, in the groin), all of whom have slighted passionate gods— Venus or Dionysius. Arcite has, quite literally, "backed" the wrong horse.

that repeatedly identifies him with the feminine. He wants to be a blooming apricot tree that will fling wanton arms into Emilia's window and bring her fruits to make her even more divine than she already seems to him (2.2.234–39). He fancies that if free he would do such deeds that "This blushing virgin, should take manhood to her / And seek to ravish me" (2.2.258–60). Whereas Arcite's tournament companion looks like a "heated lion" and has eyes that show fire within, Palamon's follower has "a face far sweeter," colored with "The livery of the warlike maid . . . / . . . for yet no beard has blest him" (4.2.81–82, 95, 105–7). It has been remarked that Palamon's puzzling prayer to Venus sounds more as if it should be addressed to Diana.[16] Indeed, in the polarization between Venus and Diana, Palamon seems almost as close to the latter as to the former.

Arcite is on the whole more active, more aggressive, and more masculine. He prides himself on being "a man's son" (2.2.182) and compares his wooing to a battle charge (2.2.195). He takes the initiative in disguising himself and seizes the opportunity to win running and wrestling matches so brilliantly that Theseus says he has not seen "Since Hercules, a man of tougher sinews" (2.5.2). He glories in the challenge of riding a rough horse so that he won't "Freeze in [his] saddle" (2.5.48). Theseus is so taken with Arcite that he advises Emilia to make him her master (2.5.62–64) and proposes prophetically that the jealous gods will want him to "die a bachelor, lest his race / Should show i' th' world too godlike" (5.3.117–18). Indeed, as the feats of Mars are inextricably linked with death, Arcite's victory in the tournament proves to be sterile.

It is notable that from the moment of their separation and fragmentation, the young men are constantly referred to (like Petrarch's Laura) as *parts*.[17] Arcite worries about Palamon's tongue; we hear of Arcite's sinews; the Jailer's Daughter fancies that Palamon has been torn to pieces by wolves; Emilia thinks of Arcite's face, eye, figure, and brow (grotesquely comparing it in smoothness to Pelops's shoulder),[18] and of Palamon's eyes, face, body, and brow, concluding of her suitors, "Were they metamorphis'd / Both into one . . . there were no woman / Worth so compos'd a man" (5.3.84–86).

If the first male conflict in the play epitomized by Theseus and played out by Palamon and Arcite is between Venus and Mars, the second conflict, projected chiefly onto the females, is between Venus and Diana. The women of the play represent the standard Renaissance stereotypes—maid, wife, and widow. The widows vanish early, and Hippolyta, as wife, gets relatively short shrift—her wedding is upstaged by the war with Thebes, and her resolution to believe herself dearer to Theseus than Pirithous is mustered with suspicious alacrity and carried out with an arbitrary decision to repress doubts. Pirithous doesn't

16. See Hallett Smith, "Introduction" to *The Two Noble Kinsmen* in *The Riverside Shakespeare,* ed. G. B. Evans (Boston: Houghton Mifflin, 1974), 1641.

17. See Nancy J. Vickers, "Diana Described: Scattered Woman and Scattered Rhyme," *Critical Inquiry* 8 (1981): 265–79, for a discussion of the fragmentation of Laura in Petrarch's sonnets.

18. John Milton, "Elegia Prima," in *Complete Poems and Major Prose,* ed. Merritt Y. Hughes (New York: Odyssey, 1957), 9, line 57, makes a similar comparison, with a similarly unsettling effect.

help matters when he begs Theseus to show mercy, conjuring him anticlimactically "By all our friendship, sir, all our dangers, / By all you love most—wars, and this sweet lady—" (3.6.202-3).

The Amazonian Emilia comes closer to being a simple allegorical figure than any of the men. Like Hippolyta she remains curiously static, seeming more a projection of a male problem than an interesting dramatic character. Although her portrait is not as uncomplicated as that of Chaucer's Emelye, who never expresses any erotic interest in either of her suitors and prefers right up to the end of the tale to remain a maid, Emilia is throughout most of the play clearly the servant of Diana. Somewhat ironically, in view of her subsequent dismissal of Narcissus as a fool for loving himself, she proclaims her own narcissistic attachment to her childhood alter ego Flavina, asserting that she will never love any man as she has loved her friend (1.3.84-86). In gathering flowers, although she chooses the equivocal rose, which will later become for her the emblem of Diana's concession to Venus, as well as the univocal narcissus, her desire is to preserve the flowers' springlike beauty with the art of embroidery rather than to enjoy their living presence.

Emilia repeatedly identifies with *women*, defining herself as "a natural sister of our sex" (1.1.125), invoking "The powers of all women" (3.6.194), and thinking of others in terms of their mothers. On seeing Arcite she supposes his handsome face inherited from his mother, and she asks Theseus's mercy on the two knights because of "The goodly mothers that have groan'd" for them (3.6.245). She tries to choose between them for the sake of "their weeping mothers" (4.2.4) and thinks of them as their mothers' joy (4.2.63). This concern with maternal feelings may suggest Diana's embodiment as Lucina (specifically included by Chaucer in his description of Diana's temple), but more important to Emilia is the virginal aspect of the goddess. Like Diana, patron of Amazons, Emilia hunts, and she apparently keeps a stable since she is able to provide Arcite with a brace of horses fit for kings (2.6.19-21). She thinks of herself as a "female knight" (5.1.140). Initially, she embodies one facet of the female threat to male-dominated society—the unavailable woman protected by female solidarity. The image, however, projected through a male lens, begins to blur—the unattainable female cannot be allowed to exist. Unlike Emelye, Emilia grows increasingly interested in her two suitors. Although most often she finds them interchangeable, she confesses in one speech that she is "sotted, / Utterly lost" and that her "virgin's faith hath fled" her (4.2.45-46). Her prayer to Diana is not, like Emelye's, just a request to remain a maid but includes the alternative of being won by the suitor who loves her most. As Palamon moves closer to Diana, Emilia moves closer to Venus; but, whatever passion she may feel, she shows no joy on Arcite's victory and speaks not at all to Palamon after she is awarded to him by default. The final transaction is still between Palamon and Arcite.

The true exemplar of Venus in the play is the Jailer's Daughter. It is she who sees, pities, and loves Palamon in spite of the equal charms of Arcite, who knows that she "would fain enjoy him" (2.4.30), who frees him from his prison of arrested development, pursues him into "Dian's wood," and, finally, subdued by her father and the Wooer, agrees to marry Palamon's double. Her venereal freedom and boldness are welcomed happily by the rustics as part of the May Day saturnalia, but in the sober postfestive view of the Jailer and the Wooer such excess is alarming, or "mad." As the Amazonian frigidity of Emilia has been warmed by desire, so the equally menacing specter of voracious feminine appetite must be curbed. At the advice of the doctor, her father confines her to a small room with a dim light in order to dupe her into a suitable marriage that will control her "extravagant vagary." For these males, she embodies the fantasy of unbridled female sexuality—a sexuality that is a necessary evil, but one that demands the "bridaling" enacted in wedlock.

At the end of the play, Diana and Venus find a compromise acceptable to the males in the union of Palamon and Emilia and that of the Jailer's Daughter and her surrogate Palamon. Fertility is both restricted and provided for. Mars is not so easily dealt with because his deadly shadow looms darkly over all. As the action has begun with mirth and funeral, so it concludes. Although both Theseus and the younger generation have yielded to the power of Venus, Theseus continues to claim Mars as his master and to focus attention on Arcite's funeral (5.4.106). The refrain of the widowed Queens hangs hauntingly in the memory: "This world's a city full of straying streets, / And death's the market-place, where each one meets" (1.5.15-16). A measure of the distance between Chaucer and the Renaissance is suggested by the modification of this image. In Chaucer the world is a "thurghfare" from which wandering pilgrims are released by death (2847). In the drama, death is the heart of the mystery.

As I have suggested earlier, both Palamon and Arcite can be seen as spiritual offspring of Theseus. He admires both and fears both, wishing to keep both imprisoned under his control. Later the two fight each other in Theseus's armor (3.6.54), but we sense that Arcite is closer to Theseus's own self-image. Theseus releases him freely, without ransom, while at the same time confining Palamon even more strictly than before. Arcite is more successful as a warrior than a lover. Even though he has been in close proximity to Emilia as her servant, while Palamon has never met her, Arcite has not won her unequivocal love. His fate is oddly premonitory of that of Hippolytus, the unborn son of Theseus and Hippolyta, who is similarly destroyed by his own horses, frightened by a monster sent by Poseidon at the behest of Aphrodite. In both cases death is the result of failure to come to terms with the goddess of love.

The figure of the horse runs like a leitmotif through the play. Palamon and Arcite remember with pleasure their fiery steeds under them in battle (2.2.18); Arcite prides himself on his horsemanship; the two of them recall the good bright bay (3.6.76-77) that Arcite rode in the war against the three kings; and Arcite boasts of the brace of fine horses given him by Emilia. In the subplot, horses are a source of frequently coarse humor. The countrymen speak of tickling work out of "the jades' tails" after their day of maying. The mad Jailer's Daughter sings of a lover who will give her "a white cut . . . to ride" (3.4.22) and later declares that Palamon has given her an extraordinary horse, which can dance, read, and write and is beloved by the Duke's mare (5.2.45-65). A human hobby horse, along with the Bavian, is a usual part of the morris dance. These mergings of man and animal, like the presence of the Amazons, suggest the erosion of conventional "human" boundaries in the world of the play.

Skillful horsemanship is an image of success in war and of the individual's ability to control passion by reason; it is also frequently an image of matrimony—with "female" passion controlled by "male" reason. In each case the rider is conventionally presumed to be male, although the mounted Diana is tolerated as image of the hunt. The horse-rider figure thus links Diana, Mars (the equestrian warrior), and Venus (the promoter of amorous conjunctions). Generally speaking, a woman in the saddle, like an unbridled horse, is profoundly disturbing. It is surely no accident that, in the play, Arcite is killed by Emilia's horse. In Chaucer's tale, Arcite is fatally wounded, while parading under the eye of Emilia. He is thrown on his head by his horse, which has been frightened by an infernal fury sent by Pluto at Saturn's request to placate Venus. The drama, perhaps elaborating on the brief description in the *Teseida,* introduces an extraordinary modification (the merest shadow of Saturn remains in a simile). Arcite is injured because, in spite of almost superhuman efforts, he cannot control Emilia's horse. The description is grotesquely detailed and almost explicitly sexual (5.4.70–83). The horse, excited by a spark from its own hoof and enraged by the spur, whines like a pig and thrashes wildly in the effort to unseat his rider. When, in spite of all, Arcite still keeps his steed between his legs, the horse upends the rider and falls backward, crushing him. The "natural" order has been overturned. Arcite, the professed servant of Mars, has been confused by Venus and defeated by Diana. Proud of his equestrian skill in battle, he succumbs to his failure to subdue the unruly spirit embodied in the horse of his Amazonian mistress. Whether the instigator is Venus or Diana is not so clear as in Chaucer. In effect the two have joined against Mars. Disruptive female forces have temporarily unsettled patriarchal order.[19]

Theseus may have succeeded in wooing Hippolyta with his sword and winning her love by doing her injuries, but the Amazonian Emilia remains beyond Mars's power. The gentler, sadder Palamon, who has eschewed horses when fighting in the forest (3.6.59; this may have been dictated by stage convenience), and who adhered, albeit somewhat reluctantly, to Venus, and who has perhaps been secretly favored by Emilia (she wore his picture near her heart [5.3.73–76]) will inherit her. This final crisis resolves, at least for the moment, the problem of Theseus and his society. The beloved rivals merge in a way that neutralizes the menace of male aggression and yet secures potency for posterity. Theseus himself retains the power of Mars. Patriarchy has been shored up; the threatening Amazon will be safely married off; and the new generation will have Theseus's blessing, if not an enthusiastic one. All this has been played out not in terms of subtle character distinctions but emblematically. However, as the simpler allegorical figures of Boccaccio and Chaucer have blurred and even merged, the

19. Natalie Zemon Davis, "Women on Top," in *Society and Culture in Early Modern France* (Stanford: Stanford University Press, 1975), 124–51. Davis discusses provocatively whether folk images of "women on top" serve to reinforce or undermine the established order.

struggle to clarify male identity is heightened. We see that male boundaries threatened by the inroads of both females and their surrogate horses have been temporarily shored up. Social definitions survive, but the embattled beachhead remains insecure and unstable.

The sense of instability is reinforced by the unconventional generic form of the play. Although the Stationers' Register identifies it as a tragicomedy, the play does not conform to the definition set out by Fletcher in his preface to *The Faithful Shepherdess*.[20] The play's very structure reflects the erosion of boundaries. Palamon and Arcite are repeatedly brought near death and reprieved; yet the progress toward a festive culmination in marriage and the triumph of a new generation is continually frustrated by the realization that one of the lovers must be eliminated in order to effect such a conclusion. Instead of wanting, like the audience of comedy, to hurry the action toward consummation, here the audience's desire is similar to that aroused by tragedy—the desire to retard the relentless progress of the plot.

The end is a disturbing compromise. It allows for neither catharsis nor satisfying social reintegration. Diana and Venus have been brought to an uneasy truce: the dual female threats of virginity and lasciviousness have been tamed by matrimony. Similarly, Mars and Venus are both in some sense victorious: following Arcite's victory, death claims center stage, but it is the death of the follower of the death-dealing Mars. The victory of Venus through Palamon does at least promise new generations, though Mars, as embodied in Theseus, still remains a controlling presence. The comic and the tragic have been momentarily balanced rather than resolved. The Duke's conclusion is exceedingly apt: "For what we lack / We laugh, for what we have are sorry" (5.4.132–33).

In attempting to encompass new realities, tragicomedy, like allegory, has moved beyond the bounds of received definitions into a confusing maze like the "city full of straying streets." The struggle to possess the Amazonian Emilia, to confine the female eroticism of the Jailer's Daughter, and to reconcile the conflicting male impulses of Palamon and Arcite both mirrors and reenacts the effort of art to build an orderly vision of the universe on the shifting sands of Stuart England. The play's "order" inevitably represents a male vision, although the artist's empathy with many sorts of humanity may sometimes seem to transcend the boundaries of his gender. We are only now beginning to discover what might be the outlines of a female world view. An important step is understanding the workings of patriarchal worlds, and for this purpose *The Two Noble Kinsmen* is a profoundly illuminating text.

20. John Fletcher, *The Faithful Shepherdess* (London, 1610): "A tragicomedy is not so called in respect of mirth and killing, but in respect it wants deaths, which is enough to make it no tragedy, yet brings some near it, which is enough to make it no comedy." The preface is omitted in the second, revised edition of 1629, which may suggest that the definition no longer seemed relevant or adequate.

9 *The Two Noble Kinsmen* as Bourgeois Drama

Richard Abrams

The work of an age of chivalric nostalgia and mercantile ambition, *The Two Noble Kinsmen* constantly grinds the one against the other. Presenting himself to Theseus, Arcite avows that he hopes "To purchase name, and do my ablest service / To such a well-found wonder as thy worth" (2.5.26–27). Noble titles are not literally for sale in Theseus's court, as they were in James's England.[1] But Arcite's metaphor captures the spirit of a world in which name must now be "bought," can no longer be won through disinterested service. The cohesiveness of *The Two Noble Kinsmen*'s mercantile images, occurring in scenes attributed both to Shakespeare and to Fletcher, signals a wider artistic unity; though I shall not pursue an argument for unity here, I hope by example to encourage study of the play as a seamless web able to stand up to the scrutiny to which Shakespeare's undivided works are routinely subjected. Beginning with the Prologue's complaint of the difficulty of marketing Chaucer's *Knight's Tale* to a modern audience, I relocate the spirit of bourgeois London in the world of the dramatis personae. Like the Prologue, the kinsmen aspire to noble ideals of antiquity, but their pursuit of commercialized versions of love and honor reveals an underlying coarseness. Indeed, the final couplet of act 1 suggests the centrality of commerce to human society and the consequent futility of lofty aspiration: "This world's a city full of straying streets, / And death's the market-place, where each one meets" (1.5.15–16). Tracing the mediations of the marketplace in the lives of the principal characters I turn afterward to a discussion of dramatic structure, reading the interplay of loss and gain in the main plot and subplot as an authorial excursion in that favorite bourgeois form, the balance sheet.

I

A study of *The Two Noble Kinsmen* as bourgeois drama may properly begin with the Prologue's admission of a pecuniary motive. Conjuring a contempo-

---

1. The controversy surrounding this royal practice heated up again at the time of *The Two Noble Kinsmen*'s first performance. Although in 1610 King James apologized to Parliament for creating knights "by the hundreds," in the winter of 1612–1613 it was reported that Princess Elizabeth's followers, on the occasion of her marriage, "'make portsale of knighthoods and kepe as yt were open market to all commers for 150 li a man.'. . . A fortnight later, however, these hopes were dashed, for James refused to oblige and so 'mard the market, or rather raised the price to an extraordinarie rate'. In February it was said to be impossible to get a knighthood even for £300 or £400 and frustrated status seekers hurried off to Ireland where one could still be obtained . . . for between £100 and £150. In November of the same year the king was still reported to be 'very daintie of that dignitie, minding to raise the market and bring yt to 500 li for a knighthoode.'" Lawrence Stone, *Crisis of the Aristocracy* (Oxford: Oxford University Press, 1965), 79–80.

rary London hostile to heroic endeavor, this impresario-figure sets the tone of the action that follows. Though the play's title promises men performing noble deeds, the first lines compare the play to a marketable maiden, plunging us into a world of trade:

New plays and maidenheads are near akin—
Much follow'd both, for both much money gi'n,
If they stand sound and well . . . .
                                              (Pro. 1–3)

Crassly commercial, these lines offer a candor significantly lacking in Theseus's later auction of Emilia's favors. But soon, the Prologue mends his speech; his simile of a bought woman mutates toward married respectability (Pro. 4–8) as he admits a motive coequal with profit. Because the play's story derives from an honored ancestor, "Chaucer (of all admir'd)" (Pro. 13), an unsuccessful adaptation may cause *The Knight's Tale*'s "noble breeder" (Pro. 10) to turn in his grave, menacing his latest heirs:

If we let fall the nobleness of this [Chaucer's tale],
And the first sound this child [the play] hear be a hiss,
How will it shake the bones of that good man [Chaucer]
And make him cry from under ground . . . .
                                              (Pro. 15–18)

"This is the fear we bring," the Prologue stresses (Pro. 21), to allay which, he invites the audience to participate in a rite of propitiation, assimilating the noble breeder to the sociable middle classes. Already co-opted by the phrase "that good man"—at once a euphemism placating an irascible spirit and a bourgeois formula of respect—Chaucer may enjoy "sweet sleep" (Pro. 29), lulled by the hum of business as usual, if the audience will play its part.

That part consists of recognizing that,

                          it were an endless thing,
And too ambitious, to aspire to him [Chaucer],
Weak as we are, and almost breathless swim
In this deep water. Do but you hold out
Your helping hands, and we shall tack about
And something do to save us.
                                              (Pro. 22–27)

By reaching forth their hands as if to save a drowning swimmer or propel with winds of applause a becalmed ship, the spectators step out of their initial scripted roles of customers, becoming fully active in the drama's production. No longer the play-following leisure class of the opening lines, they become a group of honest tradesfolk mirroring the hardworking actors. In short, improving upon a cash nexus ("much money gi'n"), the Prologue suggests a friendly barter arrangement: our time for your time, our labor for yours. By collaborating in the play's production, the spectators may achieve "Content" (Pro. 30) beyond that gained by passive viewing, for in working with their imaginations they relieve the boredom of "A little dull time" (Pro. 31)—that "period of slack trade"² in which shopkeepers wait idly for business. Though the play affords "Scenes . . . below [Chaucer's] art," the audience may glean pleasures "Worth two hours' travail" or the players will bear the cost, their losses fall so thick [they] must needs leave" the profession of acting (Pro. 28–29, 32).³

So saying, the Prologue departs, and the scene shifts to an Athens as yet untainted by modern commercial values. Three widowed Queens of Thebes disrupt Theseus's and Hippolyta's wedding—decorously, to be sure, though presently amid reminiscences of the Prologue (bridal, burial, deep water in the Queens' flood of tears), the formality of the scene breaks down; the spirit of workaday London intrudes on noble antiquity. Applauding a crying queen's soliloquy, Emilia echoes the Prologue's comparison of marketable plays and maidenheads, facetiously offering to "buy" her interlocutor (1.1.121–24). This in turn opens a door to further commercial usage such as the metaphor of "business" for both warfare and marriage (1.1.162, 196), and, in echo of the Prologue's fear of lost labor, the Queens' threat of "bootless toil" if Theseus delays battle (1.1.153). Finally, when Hippolyta "lend[s]" the supplicant Queens her marital "fee" of her spouse's services (1.1.198), even Theseus succumbs to the language of bourgeois enterprise. Losing chivalric definition in the very act of declaring martial service, the noble duke speaks like a harried businessman settling his domestic affairs (1.1.215–17, 220, 225) as he departs for Thebes to "make . . . work with Creon" (1.1.150).

Thebes also suggests the Prologue's London; its citizens affected in gait, voice, and appearance (1.2.44–58) recall the free-spending, fashion-following audience of the Prologue's first lines;⁴ and even the kinsmen, critical of such comportment, display a kind of materialism. Arcite's first speech, echoing the Prologue's anxiety of falling short of a heroic standard, couples the metaphor of swimming in "deep water" (Pro. 25) with the notion of an entrepreneurial setback. Concerned that he and Palamon will "let fall the nobleness" of their princely breeding if they remain in corrupt Thebes (Pro. 15), he counsels leaving at the earliest opportunity:

> for not to swim
> I' th' aid o' th' current were almost to sink,

2. The gloss of G. R. Proudfoot, ed., *The Two Noble Kinsmen* (Lincoln: University of Nebraska Press, 1970).

3. Is there a reminiscence in the travail/travel pun of Chaucer's Canterbury pilgrimage? Note "hear" rather than "see" (Pro. 27) and "tale" (Epi. 12).

4. The act of following is significant. Echoing Pro. 2 ("Much follow'd both"), Arcite declares his reluctance to "follow / The common stream" (1.2.9-10), and Palamon declines "to follow him / Follows his tailor, haply so long until / The follow'd make pursuit [pursues legal remedies]" (1.2.50-52); yet in the scene's last line the kinsmen resolve to "follow / The becking of [their] chance" (1.2.115-16). Later, the idea of following becomes central to the play's treatment of emulous love.

At least to frustrate striving, and to follow
The common stream, 'twould bring us to an eddy
Where we should turn or drown; if labor through,
Our gain but life and weakness.

(1.2.7–12)

As the Prologue feared a profitless venture and Theseus bootless toil, so Arcite fears ill-paid "labor"—a fear exemplified by the plight of the unemployed soldier "who did propound / To his bold ends honor and golden ingots, / Which though he won, he had not" (1.2.16–18).[5] Of course the kinsmen, as aristocrats, fight for honor rather than ingots; yet they conceive this ideal materialistically.[6] When Theseus approaches "to seal / The promise of his wrath" (1.2.92–93)— metaphorically, to conclude a commercial transaction—Arcite the anxious investor frowns at the bad business of "Third[ing one's] worth" by fighting in an unjust cause (1.2.96), and Palamon concurs:

Let's to the King, who were he
A quarter carrier of that honor which
His enemy come in, the blood we venture
Should be as for our health, which were not spent,
Rather laid out for purchase.

(1.2.107–11)

Mercenary in spirit, the kinsmen resent being cheated of their due. Risking their lifeblood, they prefer a fair return on their capital outlay.

At first they seem to gain it; in battle the kinsmen purchase honor so palpable that its trappings are measurable by a material yardstick: Theseus orders the expenditure of Athens's "richest balms" in their recovery (1.4.31). But the duke's coin is counterfeit. Because Theseus regards his captives as a treasure "Worth a God's view"—"(millions of rates) / Exceed[ing] others" (1.4.21, 29–30)—and locks them away in prison where he alone can view their worthiness, his gesture savors more of investment and hoarding than of true reward. Though Arcite rationalizes that the kinsmen's cell is a rich "inheritance" (2.2.84), this rationalization is short-lived. Theseus's expenditure on their behalf, yet subsequent

5. Thus, Arcite's and Palamon's first speeches anticipate each other's fates. Palamon will win through to "life and weakness," a "gain" of dull survival; Arcite will win but have not the prize for which he fights. Palamon's "honor and golden ingots" recalls the Prologue's twofold anxiety to maintain Chaucer's "nobleness" and succeed commercially; his wish that Juno renew her anger "To get the soldier work" (1.2.23) recalls the Prologue's concern about heavy losses driving the players from the acting profession. Finally, the action of 1.2 presents Arcite's "frustrate striving," his struggle to return to the question of leaving Thebes (see 1.2.26–31, 34–35), as Palamon grumbles about the soldier's vain labor (1.2.33–34; cf. 1.1.153–54; 3.6.79).

6. For honor as remuneration, see William Segar, *Honor Military, and Civill* (London, 1602): "The principall markes whereat every mans endeuor in this life aimeth, are either Profit, or Honour; Th'one proper to vulgar people, and men of inferior Fortune; the other due to persons of better birth, and generous disposition. For as the former by paines and parsimony do onely labour to become rich; so th'other by Military skil, or knowledge in Civill government, aspire to Honor, and humane glory." Cited in Charles Barber, "The Theme of Honour's Tongue," *Gothenburg Studies in English* 58 (1985): 7.

hiding of his prisoners from the world, robs the kinsmen of that noble remuneration, honor, for which they fought. Hidden discontent emerges when, gazing out their prison window, they glimpse Emilia, whom they dream of possessing in much the way that Theseus has seized on them.

II

"Dear," the first word spoken in the play by either kinsman, suggests the connection of love and commerce. "Dear Palamon," Arcite salutes his cousin, "dearer in love than blood" (1.2.1). If the commercial antecedents of this usage easily escape notice, they are unmistakable when woman, conceived as chattel, becomes the object of desire. In prison Arcite employs a telling parallelism: "Were we at liberty, / A wife might part us lawfully, or business" (2.2.88–89); and when immediately thereafter a prospective wife indeed parts the kinsmen, their rivalry takes the form of a business dispute for ownership of Emilia. The use value of the feudal order implicit in Arcite's initial salutation gives way to bourgeois exchange value; dearness becomes a reflection of market price:

> Emily,
> To buy you I have lost what's dearest to me
> Save what is bought, and yet I purchase cheaply,
> As I do rate your value.
>   (5.3.111–14)[7]

Frank in his covetousness, Arcite establishes a paradigm of bourgeois desire that then emerges more subtly in the disingenuous Palamon.

Claiming title to Emilia while in prison, Arcite on his release displays entrepreneurial zeal. Determined to "make . . . / Or end [his] fortunes" in Athens, he encounters, as a mirror of his ambition, the enterprising rustics, from whose "venture" to gain Theseus's patronage he forges his own (2.3.21–22, 70).[8] Proclaiming his ability to outrace the wind that curls the

---

7. The locus classicus for the two senses of "dear" is Portia's notorious pun, "Since you are dear bought, I will love you dear" (*Merchant of Venice*, 3.2.313). Typically, Palamon's usage is more discreet than Arcite's. He intimates that he will "tender" Arcite's life, not tenderly, but as the currency to advance his own suit (5.1.25). Shakespeare occasionally puns on the two senses of "tender" (*Richard II*, 2.3.41–42) or plays legal "tender" off against sentimental "dear" (*Hamlet*, 4.3.41). Raymond Southall, *Literature and the Rise of Capitalism* (London: Lawrence & Wishart, 1973), chap. 2, studies the impact of the rivalry of exchange and use values on Renaissance love literature. For value-relativism in Shakespeare, see W. R. Elton, "Shakespeare's Ulysses and the Problem of Value," *Shakespeare Studies* 2 (1967): 95–111; Burton Hatlen, "Feudal and Bourgeois Concepts of Value in *The Merchant of Venice*," in *Shakespeare: Contemporary Critical Approaches*, ed. Henry Garvin (Lewisburg, Pa.: Bucknell University Press, 1980), 91–105. More generally, see Sandra K. Fischer, "Drama in a Mercantilist World," *Mid-Hudson Language Studies* 6 (1983): 29–39; Sandra K. Fischer, *Econolingua: A Glossary of Coins and Economic Language in Renaissance Drama* (Newark: University of Delaware Press, 1985), 18–20.

8. The rustics' longer scene teems with the language of commerce, echoing the Prologue and anticipating Theseus's entrepreneurial efforts in staging the tournament as a "noble work" (5.1.6). Thus, the Prologue's preproduction jitters are matched by the schoolmaster's when a girl dancer

"wealthy" fields of grain, he proposes to climb the social ladder, "ventur[ing]" in some "poor" disguise and winning royal "prefer[ment]" (2.3.76–79). Then, after his athletic success, he basks in the language of contracts and remuneration his victory has inspired. His dazzling triumph puts all Athens in debt, and as his "due" he gains an introduction to Emilia (2.5.30, 37). But he wants more: like Spenser's Guyon tempted by Mammon's daughter Philotime, "the love of honor," he desires not only a wife rich in beauty but the status deriving from possession of a commodity in short supply. Amplifying his wish "To purchase name," he tells Theseus, "For only in thy court, of all the world, / Dwells fair-ey'd honor" (2.5.26–29). This female personification glances slyly at "fair-ey'd Emily" dwelling at Theseus's court (4.1.8) but also candidly expresses a deeper desire. For if Arcite seeks honor (victory in the May games) as an entrée to Emilia, he hopes reciprocally, by winning Emilia, to gain further honor. Like Demetrius of *A Midsummer Night's Dream* who thrives by winning not Hermia's love but Egeus's, Arcite courts the fair-eyed regard of Theseus, capable of awarding him Emilia's hand, and expects, by impressing the great duke, to win the wider respect of chivalric society.[9]

Arcite's desire to purchase name by prestigious sexual acquisition emerges still more clearly in his next scene. Giddy with success, he praises his Athenian benefactors for their policy of generosity—beyond enriching him, they "pay" dearly the "rite / They owe bloom'd May"—and pledges fealty to a Pecunia-like "Lady Fortune" who sets a "jewel" in his path (3.1.2–16). Arcite again strives less for intimate possession of a beautiful woman than for the honor deriving from conspicuous ownership. Even at his most lyrical, a nostalgia for the competitive male world of sporting occasions appears in his use of the comparative form of the adjective and in his mannerism of topping his own utterances:

> O queen Emilia,
> Fresher than May, sweeter
> Than her gold buttons on the bough, or all
> Th' enamell'd knacks o' th' mead or garden! yea
> (We challenge too) the bank of any nymph,
> That makes the stream seem flowers! thou, O jewel
> O' th' wood, o' th' world . . . .
>   (3.1.4–10)

---

fails to honor her contract ("break[s]," 3.5.47; cf. 3.3.45, and the entry in Fischer, *Econolingua*, 45). The schoolmaster is certain that all have "washed a tile," "labored vainly," that their "business" has become "a nullity," that "the credit of [their] town" is lost (3.5.40–41, 54, 56). When the Daughter discharges the missing girl's role, their credit is redeemed; they are "made again," fixed for life (3.5.74; cf. 76, 102, 158; also Arcite at 2.3.21).

9. The effect of Arcite's prowess on Theseus is evident in Theseus's advice to Emilia, "you have a servant, / That if I were a woman, would be master" (2.5.62–63)—a sexual transformation that would render Theseus synonymous with the female personification "fair-ey'd honor." Arcite's triumph in so moving Theseus represents a reversal of Palamon's fantasy at 2.2.257–59. In keeping with Arcite's quasi-sexual appeal to Theseus, Emilia views him as Ganymede at 4.2.15; see my "Gender Confusion and Sexual Politics in *The Two Noble Kinsmen,*" *Themes in Drama: Drama, Sex and Politics* 7 (Cambridge: Cambridge University Press, 1985), 69–76.

Emilia is not just fresh and sweet but fresh*er* than this, sweet*er* than that; spoiling for challenges, Arcite conjures a host of rival beauties against whom to champion her claim. Similarly, exulting in the first fruits of his venture, he returns in imagination to the field of honor. Emilia has given him a brace of horses: "two such steeds might well / Be by a pair of kings back'd, in a field / That their crowns' titles tried" (3.1.20–22). Her gift, worthy of royalty, will win him universal admiration; more than that, because his fantasy of kings contesting titles transparently figures his rivalry with Palamon, Emilia's gift, affording him the edge in battle, seems to announce that she has chosen him her favorite. In this sense, Arcite's ownership derives savor from Palamon's lack. Though he is still but a "poor man" with respect to his ambitions (3.1.12), his progress differentiates him from "Poor cousin Palamon, poor prisoner" (3.1.23), and he desires only to publish their difference that Palamon's envy may crown his triumph.

Here Palamon enters to challenge both Arcite's claim to Emilia and the correlation of wealth and worth that claim supports. If Arcite credits his success to fortune and *virtù,* Palamon parades his poverty as the mark of moral scrupulosity. So poor that he is not even the "owner of a sword" (3.1.33), he begs Arcite to "Quit" him of his chains, "give" him a weapon, and "lend" him the "charity" of a meal (3.1.72–74). Arcite gladly assents, foregoing his advantage in order to restage his own rise to prosperity, this time by *virtù* alone. Amid legalisms (3.1.90, 112–15, 121–23) the kinsmen part, agreeing to a later meeting at which to settle what has become in Arcite's mind an inheritance dispute, determining "to whom the birthright of this beauty / Truly pertains" (3.6.31–32).

Arcite's frequent resort to commercial metaphor seems to proclaim Palamon the unworthier suitor, one who wishes neither to gain honor by sexual conquest nor to excite envy. Many passages show Palamon to advantage. On initially beholding Emilia, the aspiring Arcite judges her a "rare" beauty worth possessing, while Palamon gushes, "Might not a man well lose himself and love her" (2.2.153–55). Later, Palamon elaborates this selflessness into a formal posture, reversing Arcite's metaphor of inheritance ("the birthright of this beauty") in telling of "bequeath[ing to Emilia his] soul" (3.6.148). Though Palamon guards his tongue against acquisitive implications, however, he is equally as covetous as Arcite, as his pattern of defensive assertions gradually makes apparent. In prison Palamon represents his interest in Emilia as custodial. Boasting of taking "possession / First with mine eye of all those beauties / In her reveal'd to mankind" (2.2.169–71), he implies that on the day Arcite proves worthy, he is prepared to walk away, ceding all claim (2.2.204). But in the same scene the truth of his desire emerges in metaphors of violated property rights (2.2.213–14), leading to his eventual blurted claim of "mine she is—" (3.1.118).[10] Finally,

10. At 3.6.55, Arcite admits to petty theft in another context, setting up an interesting associative pattern. In the Prologue, "that good man" Chaucer fears an incriminating linkage with the thief Robin Hood (Pro. 17, 21); correspondingly, Arcite, who is at least a petty thief (Palamon believes his theft more serious), gains final vindication as "a right good man" (5.4.97). Cf. too the recurrence of "chaff" (Pro. 19) in adjectival form, coupled with "thief," at 3.1.41.

though, it is less what Palamon says than his silence that convicts him. Assenting to Theseus's tournament arrangements, which permit him to obtain Emilia under cover of protecting her from a worse claimant, he stands revealed as Arcite's fellow traveler, profiting from the very ethos he denounces. Although the kinsmen pride themselves on mutual dissimilarity, their readiness to receive Emilia as an exchange object at Theseus's hands discloses them to be variations on a single cruel theme.

Yet if Palamon fails to provide a foil to Arcite, that function is fulfilled by Emilia herself, who in her first speech rejects exchange value in favor of a more compassionate reckoning of human worth. The third Theban queen has been disparaging her own oratorical skills, but Emilia assures her:

> If that you were
> The ground-piece of some painter, I would buy you
> T'instruct me 'gainst a capital grief indeed—
> Such heart-pierc'd demonstration! but alas,
> Being a natural sister of our sex,
> Your sorrow beats so ardently upon me,
> That it shall make a counter-reflect 'gainst
> My brother's heart, and warm it to some pity,
> Though it were made of stone.
>   (1.1.121-29)

Characterizing the queen as a precious artifact, Emilia quickly repudiates this depersonalizing representation, transferring the status of object to the stony heart of Theseus. Her vehemence is surprising, yet explicable as a proleptic defense against the male practice of commodifying women in evidence throughout the drama. For instance, in her next scene, Pirithous flatters her as a "precious maid," one of the heavens' "best-temper'd pieces" (1.3.8-10), prompting Emilia to venture a less objectifying account of her own beauty. Recounting a childhood intimacy, she describes her friend Flavina and herself as works of living art, not for the consumption of the marketplace but for mutual emulation and delight. Echoing the Prologue, this distinction between a vendible, well-tempered artwork and living art appreciable only by intimate involvement underpins a further distinction between the kinsmen's acquisitive desire for Emilia and her generous affection for them.[11] "[T]wo fair gauds of equal sweetness," Emilia's suitors at first merely tickle her "child[ish] fancy" (4.2.52-53). But later, when the tournament approaches, her feelings deepen. Though to them she is a "prize" (5.1.42; cf. 5.3.16-17, 31-32), they to her are "precious," possessed of a "richness / And costliness of spirit" (5.1.155, 5.3.96-97), which not even their proprietary arrogance can vitiate. Transcending distress for her

---

11. The call for the audience's "helping hands" in realizing "Scenes . . . below [Chaucer's] art" (Pro. 26, 28) further suggests, as a linking text with the Flavina soliloquy, Emilia's collaborative role as audience to the Third Queen, "stead[ing]" her in what the Queen deems an inadequate performance.

own plight, she suffers both with the "poor" loser of the tournament and with the winner, whose loss in his friend's death, she humbly acknowledges, her own "value's shortness" can never repay (5.3.104, 88).

Emilia's foreboding of a pyrrhic victory in which "whosoever wins / Loses a noble cousin" (4.2.155–56), experiencing grief beyond her power to compensate, proves correct. Intending gallantry, the triumphant Arcite balances Palamon's life against Emilia's hand and avows that he "purchase[s] cheaply" as he "rate[s her] value" (5.3.113–14). But the acuity of Emilia's rhetorical question, "Is this winning?" (5.3.138), appears in Arcite's dejected failure to reiterate his endorsement and in Palamon's later questioning of his own amatory enterprise:

> O cousin,
> That we should things desire, which do cost us
> The loss of our desire! that nought could buy
> Dear love, but loss of dear love!
>
> (5.4.109–12)

Though dear love for dear love is fair exchange, to lose one's desire in the bargain puts the cost too high. Long denying his own covetousness, Palamon finally acknowledges his attempt to "buy / Dear love." His enterprise has been akin to Arcite's, and, like Arcite's, ends in loss.

III

But if Arcite loses life, he gains honor; and as the play expresses in an economic computation the grief of Palamon, whose loss outweighs the gain of victory, so it inquires whether Arcite ultimately profits from his mortal exchange. Announcing the tournament, Theseus promises the contestants symmetrical rewards: "who wins I'll settle here; / Who loses, yet I'll weep upon his bier" (3.6.307–08). One must die; yet Theseus's balanced construction obscures the cost of defeat by promising the vanquished a wealth of tears. This noble fiction of double victory, which Theseus will maintain to the end (5.3.131–33), is belied, however, by the humane wisdom of the characters of a lower social order, who view life as uniquely precious. Anticipating the tournament, one subplot character, the Jailer's Second Friend, acknowledges that Theseus's arrangements "are honorable: / How good they'll prove, I know not" (4.1.30–31). Another, the Doctor treating the Jailer's Daughter for madness, counsels her father, "Nev'r cast your child away for honesty" (5.2.21), obliquely commenting on the kinsmen's folly in casting life away for honor. Such solicitude sets the Daughter on the path to health. But finally she heals herself through a retrenchment in desire which provides the play's chief critique of mad love. Overextended in her pursuit of the noble Palamon, she accepts in his place the humble Wooer—a substitution of the "good" for the "honorable," which throws in relief Palamon's and Arcite's madness in courting death as the one fit indemnification against the loss of Emilia.

Considerations of social status dominate the subplot from the beginning. Introduced by her father's and Wooer's talk of dowry, the Daughter laments her class difference from the kinsmen, whose "constant nobility" affords them "no more sense of their captivity than I of ruling Athens" (2.1.33–38).[12] As feelings of inferiority arise within her, she curses her lowly station:

Why should I love this gentleman? 'Tis odds
He never will affect me. I am base,
My father the mean keeper of his prison,
And he a prince.

(2.4.1–4)

Craving the glamour of association with a gentleman too dear for her possessing, the Daughter, fallen both from sexual and social innocence, hopes to raise her status by "venturing" boldly.[13] Her act of freeing Palamon backfires, however; failing to win his love, she recognizes herself worse off than ever before (3.2.20–25). In response, "her brain coins" (4.3.40). Cognizant of the social cost of poverty (as in her observation that even in hell "you must bring a piece of silver on the tip of your tongue, or no ferry" [4.3.19–21]), she repays herself in fantasy for the pleasures of which she feels materially deprived. Recasting herself in a life of privilege, she dreams of finding an enchanted frog, sailing off on a cargo ship, and meeting a Pygmy king (3.4.12–16).

The larger significance of the Daughter's coinage of compensatory pleasures is suggested by a passage of the Prologue examined earlier, which may be useful to have in front of us again. If the players' desire to emulate Chaucer reverberates in the kinsmen's aspiration to retain their honor in ignoble Thebes, then the Prologue's proposal of an alternative project suggests the Daughter's adjustment:

it were an endless thing,
And too ambitious, to aspire to him [Chaucer],
Weak as we are, and almost breathless swim

12. The Daughter's vision of "the diff'rence of men," to which she alludes at the end of her first scene (2.1.53–54), presumably owes to her upbringing. Note in the preceding lines her father's typically bourgeois attempt to mold her manners to the courtesy of the aristocracy ("leave your pointing. They would not make us their object" [2.1.51–52]). The Jailer's and Wooer's dowry arrangements at the beginning of the scene recall the traffic in women of Pro. 1–3 and anticipate Theseus's negotiation of Emilia's hand with the kinsmen.

13. The Daughter's social climbing parallels Arcite's; for example, "venture" (2.4.30; cf. 2.6.2, 33) echoes Arcite's usage at the end of the preceding scene (2.3.78), and Arcite's defensive affirmation of his own worth at the end of 2.3 cues the Daughter's fear of baseness at the beginning of 2.4. Arcite's success in 2.5 leads to the Daughter's in 2.6, after which Arcite keeps the Daughter's rendezvous with Palamon in the woods. Further parallelisms include 2.3.23 and 2.6.34; 2.3.82 and 2.6.35. Arcite's phrasing at 2.3.21–22 anticipates the rustics' attempts to "make" their fortunes in 2.3 and 3.5 (see note 8, above). If the Daughter's attempt to ennoble herself by daring deeds recalls Arcite's fortune hunting, her hope for a "noble" death in which she dies "almost a martyr" (2.6.16–17) recalls Palamon (e.g., 2.2.263, 276–77). Either way, she escapes the chagrin of social insignificance.

In this deep water. Do but you hold out
Your helping hands, and we shall tack about
And something do to save us.
                              (Pro. 22–27)

Read Palamon for Chaucer, and these lines become a virtual allegory of the Daughter's struggles. Hers, too, is a seemingly endless,[14] too ambitious quest through deep water (she is rescued from drowning by the Wooer), in whose course, helped by father and friends, she tacks about and saves herself. The latter maneuver is glossed by the Daughter's first mad speech, in which she instructs the crew of an imaginary ship to "tack about" or "lose all else" (3.4.9–10) and then follows her own advice. Dismissing the imaginary crew, she tacks deftly in midline (3.4.11), turning to diversions such as the enchanted frog, whose compensatory nature appears in her song of an abandoned girl promised a white horse to seek her faithless lover (3.4.22–23). Again, on her return home, the Daughter retreats into compensatory fantasy; she plans a noble wedding and later recruits a crew of "helping hands" (Pro. 26) to renew her love-quest, even repeating her signature command, "Tack about!" (4.1.152). Nominally, she still seeks "Palamon," but the object of her quest has become generic, permitting a final substitution. If she can accept her Wooer as a kind of Palamon, a realm of bourgeois comforts stands ready to receive her.

This realm is evoked by the Wooer's bustling talk of account keeping, bargaining, and contract sealing, which, following the Daughter's most fevered mad scene, sounds a pastoral note (4.3.66–69): "I . . . would account I had a great penn'-worth on't to give half my state that both she and I . . . stood unfeignedly on the same terms." But because the Wooer lacks verve, the Doctor superimposes on him the romantic figure of her imagined lover, producing a hybrid whose appeal to the Daughter is reflected in a final coinage. Palamon's wondrous horse is "like his master [the actual Palamon], coy and scornful" (5.2.62) and also like the Wooer, symbolizing her acceptance of him. For as her stolid friend "would account" that he and the Daughter had exchanged vows, and now keeps account of their kisses (5.2.6, 109), so the horse "casts himself th' accounts / Of all his hay and provender" (5.2.58–59). Basking in the prestige of Palamon's imagined gift, as Arcite in Emilia's brace of horses, the Daughter feels sufficient to resist the temptation of courtly greatness, as the horse itself has done. For though Theseus's mare has a great crush on Palamon's horse, "he'll ne'er have her"; she is a "poor beast" for all her wealth and stature (5.2.65, 62). On the one hand, the Daughter identifies with the rejected mare; on the other, she exults in *her* stallion, whose discrimination speaks volumes about her own nobility, reconciling her to her place in the social order.

The last we see of the Daughter, she is bargaining for kisses:

14. The desire to make an end is thematic in the Daughter's scenes: see 2.1.18–19; 3.2.21; and her scene-ending remark, "the point is this— / An end, and that is all," 3.2.37–38; also 5.2.72.

Wooer.   Come, sweet, we'll go to dinner,
And then we'll play at cards.
    Daugh.   And shall we kiss too?
    Wooer. A hundred times.
    Daugh.   And twenty?
    Wooer.   Ay, and twenty.
    Daugh. And then we'll sleep together?
    Doct.   Take her offer.
    Wooer. Yes, marry, will we.

                        (5.2.107–11)

In the Prologue's terms, the Daughter gropes her way beyond the desire for "nobleness" to a humble "content" (Pro. 15, 30). Returning to "the old business" of her marital contract with the Wooer (2.1.17) and negotiating for kisses, as she has negotiated with her desire from the onset of her madness, she arrives at a wholesome compromise. Though the Wooer appears comical in Palamon's oversized clothes, he proves worthier of love than his prototype through a gallant willingness to efface his identity, drawing in Palamon's "sequent trace," to save his beloved (1.2.59–60).[15] Settling for this embodiment of the good rather than the honorable, the Daughter divides ways with the kinsmen, who in the final scenes embrace death as the only honorable exchange for love.

In emphasis of the notion of an exchange, the scene in which Palamon prepares to die features both mercantile metaphor and a literal monetary transaction. Pausing in his rehearsal of the benefits of dying young, Palamon fears that his retainers have "sold" their lives "too too cheap" (5.4.15), but they assure him that they die well compensated; apart from gaining "title" to "Fortune," their opponents "A grain of honor / . . . not o'erweigh us" (5.4.17–19). This assurance finds its mark; eager to believe, or reluctant to undermine others' belief, Palamon celebrates the profitable exchange of life for honor with an act of largess. To "quite" the girl who "gave [him] freedom" (5.4.35, 24), he gives the Jailer his purse, touching off a wave of generosity in the assistant knights. In gratitude the Jailer wishes them all a heavenly return on their investment (5.4.36), and they turn cheerfully to the business of dying in sight of their reward: to be well remembered on earth and to sip nectar with the gods.

Although the knights' prodigality buoys their spirits in the face of death, the transparency of their cheer suggests that a more reliable gain lies with the Jailer and his Daughter, materially profiting from the chivalric code. This suggestion is confirmed when the knights are given back their lives. Laying his head on the block, Palamon consoles himself that he dies spiritually solvent. But when his "dream" of *bene moriendi* is broken by the news of Arcite's accident (5.4.48), he appears relieved; moreover, the pathos of Arcite's end underscores Palamon's

---

15. The Daughter's right to broker her own hand at the end of 5.2 contrasts with Emilia's reduction to an exchange object at the beginning of 5.3 and suggests the former's relative good fortune in marriage. This sequence echoes the shift from Emilia and her handmaid's talk of an amorous "bargain," whose negotiators are self-proprietors, to the kinsmen's appraisal of Emilia as a "rare" beauty worthy of acquisition (2.2.152–54).

good fortune in survival. Carried onstage for a final session of account squaring, Arcite gives Palamon Emilia, and with her, he believes, "all the world's joy" (5.4.91), gaining in exchange Palamon's forgiveness. But neither the honor that Palamon promises in annual commemoration of Arcite's death (5.4.98), nor that which Theseus adds to it (5.4.124–26), diminishes the spectacle of foolish waste. Arcite dies indifferent to the glory accruing from his triumph, desiring only a human touch (5.4.91, 94). The survivors understand that life alone may be counted precious, and all quit the stage, fulfilling in their departure the economic prophecy of the Prologue's final line, "Our losses fall so thick, we must needs leave."

IV

In the play's last two scenes, the kinsmen's gains and losses are scrupulously reckoned. As in the practice of double-entry bookkeeping that had recently gained vogue in England, their debits and credits are separately totaled, then balanced against each other in expectation of a zero-sum.[16] The loser hopes to gain honor, repaying his loss of life, the winner to gain pleasure, repaying the death of his friend. In the end, however, this expectation of balance fails. Loss is compounded: Arcite dies without substantial compensation, and his death robs Palamon of desire. Prophesying such a result before the tournament, Emilia interprets Diana's emblem of a rose tree with a single bloom as a sign that "this battle shall confound / Both these brave knights, and I, a virgin flow'r, / Must grow alone, unpluck'd" (5.1.166–68). And if the rose's fall then suggests that she too must "be gather'd" (5.1.170), her prophecy of the men's double loss resulting in a woman's gain fulfills itself not in her own preservation of virginity but in the rise of her alter ego, the Jailer's Daughter. In the final section of this essay, I shall relocate the play's promised balance in the counterpoint of the tragic main plot and the comic subplot. The Daughter's happy ending will appear not just a counterweight to disaster but its mysterious source.

The play's iterative nautical images conveniently illustrate the interdependent fates of the characters of the main plot and the subplot. In the second act, Arcite's and the Daughter's decisions to venture for love evoke seafaring imagery similar to that in the Prologue connected with the players' theatrical enterprise. These images crop up at key points in the action. In the last spoken line of 4.1, the Daughter exhorts her father and friends to "Tack about!"—inverting Theseus's command to the kinsmen that concludes the preceding scene, "hold your course" (3.6.304). Humoring the Daughter by miming a ship's crew, her well-wishers tack sharply; combating falsehoods with falsehoods (4.3.93–94), they participate in madness to achieve a just end. But as a consequence of their swerving, the watery death meant for the Daughter shifts to the main plot.

16. For discussions of English double-entry practice, see A. C. Littleton and B. S. Yamey, *Studies in the History of Accounting* (Homewood, Ill.: Richard D. Irwin, 1956). Allusions to accountancy include 1.1.32–34; 4.3.66–69; 5.2.58–59; 5.3.22–28, 86–89.

Arcite, holding course in his oath to Theseus, his loyalty to Mars, and his equestrian pride, falls heir to the Daughter's escaped fate. Crushed by his horse, he becomes the victim of a metaphorical shipwreck, "a vessel . . . that floats but for / The surge that next approaches" (5.4.83–84).[17]

To conceive the balance of the tragic and comic endings in economic terms is, as I said, to borrow a metaphor from the play's figuration of the kinsmen's interdependent fortunes. Yet an economic model comes to us already adapted to the relationship of main- and subplot characters in the purse-giving interlude staged just before the tragic denouement, in which money passes from the nobles about to die to the Jailer and his Daughter. This scene suggests the structural debt incurred in the larger artistic scheme by the Daughter's happiness. For her to prosper, someone else—either Palamon financially or Arcite mortally—must pay. Although the play does not directly explore class struggle, its contrapuntal plotting thus reveals a proto-Marxian awareness of one class thriving in another's misery, like that of a beggar in an Elizabethan tract smiling at the woes of the rich in plague time when "we poor people have mickle good":

Their loss is our luck; when they do become naked, we then are clothed against their wills; with their doles and alms we are relieved; their sickness is our health, their death our life.[18]

Similarly, the revenge of low on high, implicit in the comedy of the Jailer profiting from the knights' misfortune, reemerges in the play's conclusion. To borrow a phrase from the Daughter, as Palamon has been "kept down with hard meat and ill lodging" (5.2.97), so at play's end certain underclasses, "kept down" by reason of their divergence from a cultural norm of manly nobleness, rise up with Arcite's rearing horse.

That the role of nemesis should fall to the horse is explained by the last speech of the play's first scene. Theseus maps human differences on the difference between the human and the animal: "As we are men, / Thus should we do [support the Theban queens' cause], being sensually subdu'd / We lose our human title" (1.1.231–33). The notion of humanity deformed by insubordination of the beast within recurs frequently, as in Arcite's sneer at Palamon as a

17. The fates of the Daughter and Emilia also form a closed system. In 4.1 the Daughter aspires to Emilia's lot, assuming airs of a great lady preparing for her wedding, after which Emilia takes up the Daughter's refrain, "Would I might end" (4.2.57). Correspondingly, after the Daughter in 5.2 pledges her hand to the disguised Wooer, Emilia expresses a desire to marry her two suitors "metamorphis'd / Both into one" (5.3.84–85).

18. William Bullein, *A Dialogue against the Pestilence* (1564; 2d ed. 1573), excerpted in J. Dover Wilson, ed., *Life in Shakespeare's England* (Cambridge: Cambridge University Press, 1911), 135; cited in Kirby Farrell, *Play-Death and Heroism in Shakespeare* (University of North Carolina Press, forthcoming). Cf. Gloucester on distribution undoing excess, "That I am wretched / Makes thee [Poor Tom] the happier," *King Lear,* 4.1.65–66; and, conversely, *Coriolanus,* 1.1.19–20, in which the sufferings of the poor enhance the satisfactions of the rich. For leveling tendencies in Shakespeare, see Annette Rubinstein, "Bourgeois Equality in Shakespeare," *Science and Society* 41 (1977): 21–35.

"beast" and in Palamon's own fear of lying "fatting, like a swine" (3.3.47; 3.6.12). These slurs culminate in Pirithous's description of Arcite's horse, failing in its aspiration to a noble human identity. "[O]f kind manage," its will an extension of the rider's on its back who has "put pride in him," the horse simulates rational mastery, "counting" the cobblestones it seems to float above (5.4.69, 58). But panicked by a spark, this aristocrat of animals reverts to bestial instinct; realizing Palamon's dread of swinishness by whining "pig-like" (5.4.69), it draws to itself images of a humanity "sensually subdued." Thus, as the snobbish schoolmaster decries the rustics' "[jean] judgments" (3.5.8), pronouncing his loutish wards ineducable, so the horse "Forgets school-doing" (5.4.68). And as the same schoolmaster fantasizes a night-marish phallic woman ("An eel and woman, / . . . unless by th' tail / And with thy teeth thou hold, will either fail" [3.5.48–50]), so the bucking horse brings this caricature to life; its "diff'ring plunges," which seek to "Disroot [Arcite] whence he grew," while Arcite keeps it "'tween his legs" (5.4.74–76), reinforce play-long fears of woman's volcanic sexuality.[19] Epitomizing a degenerate humanity, the horse becomes a screen for slanderous projections, the creation of an oppressor race's bad conscience. All that chivalric man stigmatizes as base, gaining "human title" at the expense of, returns in this beastly incarnation to wreak revenge.[20]

As the horse becomes a repository of calumnious images of fallen humanity, so the Daughter, as a below-stairs denizen of Theseus's court, an advocate of deceived maids, and the leader of the rustics' dance, serves a similar integrative function, amalgamating the dissident energies of the play's outsider factions and channeling them toward release in the horse's violence. In her first scene, her sarcasm about the absurdity of herself "ruling Athens" and her declaration that it is "a holiday to look on" the kinsmen (2.1.38, 53) hints at insurrectionary tendencies, later realized in her assumption of the identity of a spirit of misrule distilling other characters' discontents. Pressured by Theseus to accept Arcite as her master in marriage, Emilia in the second act exits with a mildly insubordi-nate rejoinder; on her heels the Daughter enters, trumpeting rebellion—"Let all the dukes and all the devils roar" (2.6.1)—as though she has become the secret voice of Emilia's resentment. Conversely, the Daughter transmits to others the rebellious energy she attracts; her civil disobedience and subsequent inward departure from the "law and regiment" of sense (4.3.96) cue parallel manifesta-tions—the pandemoniac "disensanity" of the "mad boys" at their country revels (3.5.2, 24), which drives the schoolmaster to spluttering distraction, and the lawless fighting of Palamon and Arcite, which prompts Theseus to roar in echo of Gerrold:

19. Horse (jade) and woman are paired in the rustics' boasting at 2.3.27–33. Also note Arcite's Hotspurian substitution of his horse for Emilia at 2.5.47–48, after the failure of his attempted gallantry. Hippolyta's menace as overturner (1.1.77ff.) and seductress (1.1.175–86) lends ironic point to the etymological meaning of her name ("looser of horses").

20. Page duBois, *Centaurs and Amazons* (Ann Arbor: University of Michigan Press, 1982), discusses the Greek extrapolation of a cultural norm through relations of difference. The subject of the *polis* was not-barbarian, not-female, not-animal.

What ignorant and mad malicious traitors
Are you, that 'gainst the tenor of my laws
Are making battle, thus like knights appointed,
Without my leave and officers of arms?

(3.6.132-35)

Although Theseus charms the kinsmen's "mad" treason into orderly pageantry, the Daughter's madness cannot be so easily contained. Assigned a formal role in the country dance, she returns in the next act madder than ever. Then, almost to the end of the play, her relapse belies main-plot optimism, until finally, after Palamon's prayer to Venus, a version of her frenzy transfers itself to Arcite's horse.

A conspicuous early digression in Pirithous's narrative intimates the kinship of horse and Daughter. Scandalized by the horse's fall from noble breeding, Pirithous speculates on a possible predisposition to savagery, flirting with an explanation that smacks of social stereotyping. Taking the horse's measure in mercantile terms, he comments that in certain circles the horse would lack a purchaser, for its color "Weakens his price, and many will not buy / His goodness with this note" (5.4.52-53). Translated into human terms, this prejudice calls up the exclusionary social system that puts the Daughter at a disadvantage on the marriage market. As a natal accident annuls the horse's "goodness," deterring prospective buyers, so the Daughter's lowly birth undercuts her real value, rendering her ineligible to marry noble Palamon. Fearing rejection, she "run[s] mad" (4.2.12, 48), until Palamon's imagined love token confirms her worth. But if "Palamon's" imaginary horse, keeping accounts and dancing the morris, reflects her growing self-acceptance, then Arcite's horse, "counting / The flinty pavement [and] dancing . . . to th' music / His own hoofs made" (5.4.58-60), runs wild. "Venus" strikes; the "pranks and friskins of . . . madness" lately purged by the Daughter (4.3.80-81) seize on a new victim. Violence enters the main plot both as an incursion of the horse's lower nature and as an upward displacement from the subplot.[21]

As in social revolution, the horse's insurgence has a leveling effect. More than Palamon, who protested much but finally would not "offer / To Mars's so scorn'd altar" (1.2.19-20), Arcite holds his martial course throughout the action. But when his victor's wreath falls from his head, he appears to have mischosen his god. From the bourgeois standpoint of the Daughter and Wooer who attain what Arcite would scorn as a "gain" of "but life and weakness" (1.2.12), the struggle for chivalric eminence is discredited as profitless. Though Palamon gives his cousin a hero's farewell, Emilia eulogizes him, rather, as "a

---

21. Emilia imagines herself running mad for love of Arcite, much as the Daughter runs mad for love of Palamon; more literally, however, running mad is the horse's response to the darted spark. In attempting to explain the horse's violence, Theseus looks upward to the gods, but Pirithous looks downward, insisting on the horse's animal nature and even personifying the "envious flint" on which the horse treads (5.4.61). Similarly, he demotes "old Saturn" to a mere simile (5.4.62), in which disenfranchised condition the father of the gods merges with the play's various underclasses and, arguably, with Chaucer himself, seeking vengeance from "under ground" (Pro. 18).

right good man" (5.4.97), her epithet establishing community, via Palamon's description of the Daughter as "A right good creature" earlier in the scene (5.4.34), with that stratum of common humanity from which Arcite sought to distinguish himself by noble deeds. Pursuing honor through "straying streets" (1.5.15), Mars's votary arrives, as the Third Queen obliquely predicted, and as Pirithous's mundane digression on the horse's price confirms, at "death's . . . market-place" (1.5.16), the inevitable rendezvous of high and low. And there, too, Theseus arrives in his final speech, which denies the distinction between possession and lack, each understood as entailing its opposite:

> For what we lack
> We laugh, for what we have, are sorry, still
> Are children in some kind.
>
> (5.4.132–34)

If winning and losing are kindred states, then heroic striving is vain. The duke is like the Daughter, the noblest of men mere "children in . . . kind." With this downward adjustment of the title notion of noble kinship, Theseus leads his friends from the stage.

Like Arcite's first speech, which extends the Prologue's fear of letting fall Chaucer's nobleness, Theseus's final gesture encompasses the world beyond the footlights: the marketplace of contemporary London invoked by the Prologue and now brought back into view by fifth-act allusions to the theatrical under-pinnings of the action (5.3.134, 5.4.123) and by the Epilogue. Theseus had aspired to stage "deeds of honor in their kind, / Which sometime show well, pencill'd" (5.3.12–13), but finally he accepts the impossibility of modern epic achievement. His last line, which, within the fiction, commends the survivors to a time of mingled joy and sorrow—"Let's go off, / And bear us like the time" (5.4.136–37)—also leads them offstage beyond the fiction to the time of the audience when all must stand in awe of the "fam'd works" of antiquity (Pro. 20). For Theseus at this juncture to confess himself a child in kind is to acknowledge kinship not only with the Daughter but with the rural school-master who, in his epilogue, deferred to Theseus's own greatness, numbering himself among the "good boys" begging for favor (3.5.139). And it is to establish kinship with the speaker who will succeed him at center stage. Relinquishing ambition to produce "a noble work" (5.1.6), Theseus tacks about in chastened spirit, like the Prologue seeking what will bring contentment, and conjures, as an embodiment of his revised self-image, an echo of new self-doubts, the Epi-logue, anxious as a "schoolboy" (Epi. 2) lest philosophical gains prove poor exchange for the noble actions in whose expectation the audience attends the play.

Presumably a single actor plays both Prologue and Epilogue. But no detail can better express the two hours' distance traveled in the course of the play than the difference between these two speakers: the one conscious of debts to a heroic past, the other single-minded in his concern to prevent economic disaster by ingratiating himself with the audience. Although love and war dominate the action of *The Two Noble Kinsmen,* these interests survive the play's final scene only in the faint mimicry of chivalric postures. Recalling the amorous kinsmen, the Epilogue bids the spectator who "has / Lov'd a young handsome wench" to behave decorously, not "hiss, and kill / Our market" (Epi. 5–6, 8–9). For if the audience shows belligerence, then the Epilogue too must assume a martial front: "Have at the worst can come, then!" (Epi. 10; cf. 3.6.131). The Epilogue, however, hopes to avert a confrontation. Acknowledging his vaunt to be out of character, he protests, "mistake me not: I am not bold" (Epi. 11); and, as his swaggering pretense crumbles, he seeks amicable ground:

> If the tale we have told
> (For 'tis no other) any way content ye
> (For to that honest purpose it was meant ye),
> We have our end . . . .
>   (Epi. 12–15)

What contents us, what we "like" (Epi. 1), is often idiosyncratic. That Emilia and Flavina "Lov'd for [they] did" (1.3.61) evidences an ability to covenant meaningfully outside the heroic sphere; and it is such a contract that the Epilogue wishes to strike in the play's final turning from the old ways of honor. Bourgeois pieties abound: though the players fall short of that "endless thing" of imitating Chaucer (Pro. 22), yet to offer "content" is to pursue an "honest . . . end" (Epi. 14–15), in whose perseverance they verge on the heroic. Although, on this occasion, the play may disappoint its audience, "ye shall have ere long / I dare say many a better, to prolong / Your old loves to us" (Epi. 15–17). Not only will new plays someday repay present losses, but the player-patron bond possesses a gratifying feudal solidity, captured in the allusion to "Your old loves." With this obeisance, ennobling the commercial contract that underlies the play's production, the Epilogue brings *The Two Noble Kinsmen* to a complacent close. Pledging his "might" and "service," he enfolds himself within the ranks of the bourgeoisie as in the bosom of a powerful clan: "Gentlemen, good night" (Epi. 17–18).

10 Performance As Criticism
The Two Noble Kinsmen

Hugh Richmond

A paradoxical tension strains relations between literary interpretation of Shakespeare and the production history of his plays, even while there can be no debate over their original and exclusive design as performance scripts. It is well known that some of his plays with mixed critical reputations, such as *Henry VI, Henry V, Measure for Measure, Pericles,* and *Henry VIII,* often achieved considerable popularity and success onstage. Several such plays have suffered critical disfavor from assumptions of incoherence or inferiority because of the possibility of shared authorship between Shakespeare and some lesser, supposedly incompatible playwright. These suspicions of their unity and worth have discouraged the plays' production or speciously justified condescending or openly contemptuous review. For these reasons few major companies have risked production of *The Two Noble Kinsmen;* indeed, it never appeared on the public stage in the eighteenth and nineteenth centuries. It was revived finally by the Old Vic as late as 1928 but since then has reappeared with increasing frequency and a consequent heightening of critical and scholarly interest. Since in this case the theater has fostered a more positive academic approach to the text, it is appropriate to explore the history of the play's productions and to seek such values in them as can be recovered, since they constitute the ultimate test of the text's purposes. I shall first survey the better-known seventeenth- and twentieth-century productions; then briefly explore my own experience in producing the play both live and for television; and lastly review the relevance of the various stagings to some of the major critical issues concerning the text.

The curious production history of *The Two Noble Kinsmen* consists of two periods of substantial activity, in the seventeenth and twentieth centuries, separated by two hundred years of neglect. Hallet Smith argues,

> A number of indications place the play in the year 1613. The Schoolmaster's entertainment in III.v is borrowed from the second antimasque in Beaumont's *Inner Temple and Gray's Inn Mask,* which was presented at Whitehall on February 20, 1613; the same professional dancers probably appeared in both productions. In *Bartholomew Fair* (1614) Ben Jonson refers to a dramatic character named Palamon, and there is reason to believe that Shakespeare was collaborating with Fletcher in 1613 on *Henry VIII* and a lost play called *Cardenio.*[1]

---

1. *The Riverside Shakespeare,* ed. G. Blakemore Evans (Boston: Houghton Mifflin, 1974), 1640. The masque is printed in *The Dramatic Works in the Beaumont and Fletcher Canon,* ed. Fredson Bower (Cambridge: Cambridge University Press, 1966), 1:124–39.

As with many Shakespearean texts, however, the material of this one has a significant pre-Shakespearean production history. A nineteenth-century editor observed:

When Queen Elizabeth visited Oxford in 1566, Wood informs us, "at night the Queen heard the first part of an English play named, *Palamon,* or *Palamon and Arcite,* made by Mr. Richard Edwards, a gentleman of his chapel, acted with very great applause in Christ Church Hall." Another play is mentioned in Henslow's *Diary* under the date of September 1594 of *Palamon and Arsett,* which was cited four times.[2]

This account is amplified in N. W. Bawcutt's Penguin edition, which notes that the earlier play starts with the Kinsmen's imprisonment but includes several virtuoso effects: "a vivid hunting scene, . . . and the burning of Arcyte's body on a funeral pyre, apparently done with a high degree of realism."[3] When the script for *The Two Noble Kinsmen* as we know it was performed around 1613, the story had already clearly transcended its Chaucerian narrative format, with three seemingly successful stage productions. Obviously the practical vindication refutes any modern critical reservations about the romance's fitness for the stage. It appears to have had an early and well-established audience appeal. We may take strong positive reactions to the material in the theater as axiomatic and irrefutable.

This is confirmed by Hallet Smith's further history of the 1613 script: "We know from a scrap of paper from the King's Office of the Revels that the play was in repertory in 1619 and was being considered for performance at court; and two actors' names which have slipped into the text show that there was a revival in the mid–1620's."[4] (This refers to Quarto stage directions at 4.2.70 and the start of 5.3.) Such persistent theatrical interest in the script more than justifies acceptance of the assertion on the title page of the quarto edition (entered in the Stationers' Register on 8 April 1634) that it had been "Presented at the Blackfriers by the Kings Maiesties servants, with great applause." Granted this established popularity under James I and Charles I, it was natural that on the Restoration the play should be revived, albeit in the kind of "revised" and "improved" form typical of many revivals of Shakespeare and his contemporaries in the late seventeenth century. This version was drafted by Sir William Davenant, Shakespeare's godson. Again, the filial revival was a hit, according to Davenant's editor:

The Rivals, a play wrote by Sir William Davenant; having a very fine interlude in it, of vocal and instrumental music, mixed with very diverting dances; Mr. Price introduced the dancing by a short comical prologue which gained him an universal applause of the town. The part of Theocles was done by Mr. Harris; Philander, by Mr. Betterton;

2. William D'Avenant, *The Dramatic Works* (Edinburgh: William Paterson, 1874), 5:216.
3. William Shakespeare, *The Two Noble Kinsmen,* ed. N. W. Bawcutt (Harmondsworth, U.K.: Penguin, 1977), 8–9.
4. *Riverside,* 1639.

Cunopes, the jailer, by Mr. Underhill; all the women's parts admirably acted, chiefly Cel[an]ia, a shepherdess, being mad for love; especially in singing several wild and mad songs - 'My lodging is on the cold ground, etc.' She performed that so charmingly, that not long after it raised her from her bed on the cold ground to a bed royal. [As the actress, Mary Davis, became the mistress of King Charles II]. The play, by the excellent performance lasted uninterruptedly nine days, with a full audience.⁵

On 10 September 1664 Pepys saw what was probably a revival of this 1662 production (without Mary Davis as the Daughter) at the house of the Duke of York: "My wife and I, and Mercer, to the Duke's house, and there saw *The Rivals,* which is no excellent play, but good acting in it; especially [Mrs.] Gosnell comes and sings and dances finely [as the daughter]; but, for all that, fell out of key, so that the musique could not play to her afterwards; so did Harris [Theocles-Palamon] also go out of tune to agree with her."⁶
   The Restoration version of *The Two Noble Kinsmen* may continue to prompt verdicts like Pepys's negative literary evaluation, but it also may suggest production values of the original script, as indicated by Alfred Harbage's analysis of this "very free adaptation":

The basic situation in the older play, the imprisonment and love rivalry of Chaucer's Palamon and Arcite (rechristened by Davenant Theocles and Philander) is retained; but the entire first and last acts are rewritten and extensive alterations are made throughout. For the very diffuse ending of the original play with its tournament . . . a new ending is invented so that both kinsmen may not only remain among the living but also be provided with satisfactory mates. This has been arranged for by substituting Celania, a lady and therefore eligible, for the Jailor's Daughter, whose love madness for one of the kinsmen forms the very extraneous sub-plot of the original play. The altered last act is theatrical but effective, and gives us a heart-warming scene in which the two rivals, bitter enemies in love but true comrades still, defend each other from the slander of outsiders. As a stage play *The Rivals* improves upon its original; it was a popular success [Pepys went to see it again, 2 December 1664], and was revived for the court at least as late as November 1667.⁷

One of the most significant points Harbage makes about this revision is that, far from playing down the choreography of the morris dance, the play developed it by "an elaborate vocal and instrumental interlude representing a cross-country hunt."⁸ Harbage sees such development as a step "towards the development of opera," but historically it clearly sustains the importance of choreography in Renaissance theater. Modern taste has diminished this aspect through the preemption of stage concerns in drama criticism by literary values in the nineteenth and early twentieth centuries. Yet the importance of dance

5. D'Avenant, *Dramatic Works* 5:217.
   6. Ibid., 5:219.
   7. Alfred Harbage, *Sir William Davenant: Poet Venturer 1606-1688* (Philadelphia: University of Pennsylvania Press, 1935), 254.
   8. Ibid., 259, 158.

and choreography is clear in most Shakespeare texts. It is therefore instructive to find that the primary focus in the Restoration versions of the play continued to be on the masque, which was the principal addition to the sixteenth-century script in the 1613 production. By contrast we shall discover that recent performances often skimp this aspect or cut it entirely.

Harbage's attempt, moreover, to suggest that the Jailer's Daughter is "extraneous" is countered by Davenant's preservation of her part and by the ultimate accolade of Charles II, which it won for its performer. The Jailer's Daughter is central; she provides a bridge or modulating note between the aristocratic and low-life elements of the play, as well as offering a contrast for Emilia's sexual difficulties. Harbage's point about the lopping of the beginning and end of the play in Davenant's version also illustrates a narrowing of taste and thematic awareness, reflecting adversely not only on Restoration aesthetics but also on the taste of modern theater critics whose reviews often comment negatively on these supposedly truly Shakespearean sections of the play. The desire for a narrow Aristotelian unity of plot shows how alien to such critics is the multi-layered technique characteristic of Shakespeare. In this spirit Davenant rejects the thematic relevance of the play's opening topic of the costliness of marriage, which the widowed queens urge on the bridegroom Theseus. Davenant's text offers a shallower, more selective topic than sexuality and society—merely the telling of a specific sentimental tale. Any modern production that minimizes the opening theme of the widows' revenge similarly displays a shallower theatrical awareness than the original authors intended: transcendence of empathy for individual characters by a broader analytic thought about the sexual category of social relationships.

There is no record of any substantial performance of *The Two Noble Kinsmen* during the eighteenth and nineteenth centuries, though Davenant's editor mentions that "in the collection of manuscripts presented to the British Museum by Patmore occurs 'Palamon and Arcite; or the Noble Kinsmen, altered from Beaumont and Fletcher. A tragedy in five acts.'"[9] Harold Metz also mentions that "Macready acted the role of Ribemont in a pastiche assembled by Frederick Reynolds from elements of *Philaster, Bonduca,* and *The Two Noble Kinsmen* which was performed twice in January 1828."[10] There is thus good reason to accept the claim made in the program for the Old Vic's revival of *The Two Noble Kinsmen* during its 1927–1928 season: "First recorded Public Performance since XVII Century. Generally accredited to SHAKESPEARE and FLETCHER." This program lists nine performance dates in March 1928. Among the cast were some familiar names: Eric Portman as Arcite, Barbara Everest as Emilia, Jean Forbes-Robertson as the Jailer's Daughter, Rupert Hart Davis as the Jailer's Brother. The producer's note explains the text thus:

9. D'Avenant, *Dramatic Works,* 5:216.
10. G. Harold Metz, "*The Two Noble Kinsmen* on the Twentieth Century Stage," *Theatre History Studies* 5 (1984): 63.

The Play is a dramatic version of The Knight's Tale of Palamon and Arcite from Chaucer's Canterbury Tales, and is essentially a story of medieval chivalry rather than of Greek legend. We are, therefore, presenting it in the costume of Chaucer's time as being in keeping with the hunting and maying, the morris dancing and tilting with which the play abounds.

A version of this play, by D'Avenant, much altered and entitled, "The Rivals," was played by Betterton and his colleagues in the latter half of the seventeenth century. Since then, so far as can be traced, no public performance of the 'Kinsmen' has been given.

Following this note is the credit "Dance arranged by NINETTE DE VALOIS"—an indication of the prominence accorded to choreography in the production. There is also a credit for the orchestra "under the direction of CHAS. CORRI," covering the overture of Thomas's "Raymond" and "Selection [from] Messager's Suite 'The Two Pigeons.'"

Some confirmation of points raised earlier can be drawn from these program statements. The most important to my mind is the prominence given to medieval rituals: the hunt; May Day and the pagan fertility dances now loosely grouped as morris dances associated with that festival; and the competitive jousts or duels that are so often associated with medieval courtship and sexual display. The program's stress on the importance of music and choreography is something that literary scholarship may easily underrate, even if Frederick Sternfeld has explored Shakespeare's musical concerns, and C. L. Barber has made us more aware of the importance of secular festivals, while R. C. Hassel has explored the ritual overtones.[11]

The twenties, unfortunately, were not noted for respecting tradition or for the medievalism associated with the Victorian period, and reviewers of the Old Vic production mostly failed to explore larger thematic issues in the play or its production, preferring to focus on quaint details of characterization such as hair color or eccentric behavior. Far from seeing the piece as a study of archetypes and ritual forms in tension with subjective sentiment, as the program notes invite us to, reviews stressed incidental effects.

In his preface to the Signet edition,[12] Clifford Leech observed that A. G. MacDonell showed the typical "coldness" with which the play's revival was received when he reviewed the production in the London Mercury for April 1928. Admittedly, he praised Jean Forbes-Robertson's performance of the Jailer's Daughter for her "realistic playing of the mad scenes." However, he was also "grateful that he did not have to endure simple nobility in two noble kinsmen," since "Palamon was done comically, in a red wig." Ivor Brown is even harsher in the Saturday Review for March 1928: "that the piece appears to have

11. See Frederick W. Sternfeld, Music in Shakespearean Tragedy (London: Routledge, 1963); C. L. Barber, Shakespeare's Festive Comedy (Princeton: Princeton University Press, 1959); R. Chris Hassel, Renaissance Drama and the English Church Year (Lincoln: University of Nebraska Press, 1979).
12. William Shakespeare, The Two Noble Kinsmen, ed. Clifford Leech (New York: New American Library, 1977), xxxv-vi.

been left unacted since its birth is evidence of wisdom rather than of negligence among actors of the past." He sees the Jailer's Daughter, "a wraith of Ophelia," as the best in the play and notes, "Miss Jean Forbes-Robertson played the Ophelian ghost with exquisite piteousness, but Miss Barbara Everest would only wander amiably through the part of the much desired Emilia. Mr. Eric Portman was a capable Arcite but Mr. Ernest Milton, even in an auburn wig, was not my idea of Palamon." Mr. Milton's judicious levity might have mitigated "the absurdities of a medieval Thebes," if "given greater freedom to play for the laugh." There is a final concession, however, to the production's deeper rhythms in that "Mr. John Garside did much for the play with his Chaucerian decoration: the names are Greek but the matter is romantic and the mode of decoration should be that of the missal."[13] It appears that the stage values were more deeply thought out than this reviewer's sketchy understanding anticipated.

The far more favorable *Times* review on 13 March 1928 agrees with Ivor Brown about "the kinship of the Jailer's Daughter to Ophelia, of the Schoolmaster and his countrymen to Bottom and his." The problem is that, while the play "was intended to be taken with romantic seriousness . . . a modern audience has a natural inclination to be irreverent." The skeptical reviewer attacks the "strangely cowlike" Emilia as a "vague, foolish woman." Each of the Kinsmen is praised, nonetheless, as each won "more laughter than, we will wager, his dramatist bargained for," but "avoided burlesque." Despite its "shallows" the production "was a very wise, a very courageous, and an altogether charming escapade." Above all, this reviewer delights in the pyrotechnics of Jean Forbes-Robertson's Jailer's Daughter: "The stage leaps to life when she approaches it," and she unexpectedly can achieve "genuine splendour," so that even her Wooer has "a brilliant little scene to which he brings fire as well as discretion." In sum, the performance "fills a pleasantly ingenious evening."

Apart from the Old Vic production, as of 1966, Professor Leech knew of only one other revival of the play: eight performances at Antioch College in August and September 1955. Of this version, he reports that "Some cutting had to be done of 'repetitive passages,' but Shakespeare's hand was felt in the 'high imagery'"; that Palamon was "very grand"; and that "the play proved 'very stageworthy,' particularly the scenes involving the Jailer's Daughter."

Antioch was not alone in perceiving the serious values of the play for academic performers and audiences. In addition to the Antioch production, Harold Metz has identified several others by academic institutions,[14] including four performances in 1954 by the Harvard University Dramatic Club; six at the Open Air Theatre Stratford-upon-Avon in 1959 by Reading University Dramatic Society; and five at the Royal Fort by the Drama Department of Bristol University. There were several other runs of the play not noted by Metz, including eight performances directed by Rick Abrams at the University of Texas at

13. Ivor Brown, *Saturday Review* (March 1928): 243–45.
14. Metz, "*Two Noble Kinsmen* on the Twentieth Century Stage," 65.

Austin in 1975 that were done in a bold, geometrical style with back projections of an arresting kind. Abrams followed this in 1979 with a lower-keyed version, also running for eight performances, at Shakespeare Players Incorporated, a regional theater group in Richmond, Virginia. In 1979, I also produced two versions of the play at the University of California, Berkeley. One version was performed in the open air before an invited audience and recorded on videotape. A second, probably the first television version of the play, produced a two-hour videotape shot in a studio and on location, which was later broadcast on California cable networks. Both videotapes are still available from the Educational Television office at the University of California, Berkeley.

Metz notes several more professional productions of the play since the Old Vic revival. The first significant one appears to be that at the York Theatre Royal in 1973 (six performances), followed by the New Shakespeare Company's nine performances in the Open Air Theatre at Regent's Park in London (which inspired my own productions). There were fifteen performances by the Cherub Company at the Edinburgh Festival in 1979 and seventeen in the same year by the Shakespeare Society of America at the Globe Playhouse in Los Angeles. Lastly, Metz notes that in 1981 there were sixteen performances at the Bowery Lane Theatre, New York City, by the Jean Cocteau Repertory Company. Lois Potter has also drawn my attention to an enthusiastic discussion in Spanish of a French-language production of the play directed by Pierre Constant at the Centre Dramatique in La Courneuve, Paris.[15] The Berkeley Shakespeare Festival for 1985 also staged the play in its outdoor theater twenty-one times—one of the play's longest runs, since Renaissance productions were relatively short-lived, if frequently revived. In 1986, the Royal Shakespeare Company introduced the play into its regular repertory for the Swan Theatre at Stratford.

Considering all the productions and revivals covered by Metz and me, we find that (in addition to the initial production) there had been several successful revivals of the play before the Puritans' closing of the theaters in 1643. The Davenant version of the play was produced to acclaim several times in the Restoration. Since the hiatus there have been at least six academic productions and ten professional ones. It is obvious that after substantial and prolonged success in the seventeenth century, the play is now enjoying a marked revival of interest in the late twentieth century for which the various academic productions have led the way after the brave initiative taken by the Old Vic in the twenties. Seemingly, some lost critical response to the play has slowly been recovered less by literary analysis than through experimental and academic efforts to re-create a lost aesthetic via performance and to assemble audiences sufficiently sophisticated and educated to be sympathetic. This favorable shift in taste is one small piece of evidence to back T. S. Eliot's dubious hypothesis of a "dissociation of sensibility" occurring in the late seventeenth century, but only now understood by the more flexible, comprehensive taste in our own time. My

---

15. Manuel Angel Conejero, *La Escena, El Sueno, La Palabra, apunte Shakespeare* (Madrid: Instituto Shakespeare, 1983). The discussion is dated November 1978.

own motives in producing the play certainly included a spirit of antiquarian research and a sense of risk-taking that only an inexpensive academic production might easily attempt. The play suits student performers because, due to its multilayered, thematic approach to issues, there are no dominating, complex major roles requiring major acting expertise and experience. By corollary, however, the academic productions are not as substantial, thorough, and valid in exploring the text's potentialities as fully professional performances, which must be our real test of the text's nature and value.

The next significant professional production after the crucial one by the Old Vic was that at the York Theatre Royal in 1973. This was part of the York Festival of the Arts (which has also revived the Mystery Plays). In his program note the director, Richard Digby Day, identified the play as

almost certainly Shakespeare's last work for the stage. . . . Basically Shakespeare's work can be seen in the first and last acts and Fletcher's in the middle three. . . . On first sight, dramatically it looks, perhaps, as if Fletcher's is the successful part of the play and Shakespeare's the failure and yet it has to be accepted that Shakespeare's failures are often more interesting than other men's successes. The contrasts and conflicts that Fletcher works on in the middle of the play are exciting and entertaining, the Shakespearean parts are laden with pageantry, splendid but static—"they have a deliberate yet vague grandeur, a remote and half exhausted exaltation." They are, I suppose, written by a man who felt old age close upon him. The imagery of the verse is an old man's imagery but underneath all this there is a brilliance, a control and sheer mastery of words that proclaims genius.

This analysis prompted some reviewers, unfortunately, toward conventional negative responses to the text. "H.J." in the *Yorkshire Evening Press* for 5 July 1973 said: "Seeing the play for the first time, one felt that the parts attributed to Shakespeare seemed a little heavy and slow, compared with the lighter and faster-paced scenes by Fletcher. Touches of humor lighten Fletcher's scenes, whereas Shakespeare's seem at times weighted down with the pomp and protocol of medieval spendour." In the *Manchester Guardian* for 5 July 1973, Merete Bates agreed: "The combination of writers doesn't work. A stately, sad, but tiredly formal interpretation of Chaucer's Knight's Tale . . . suddenly turns into the rivalry of two cousins in love. . . . Thus Shakespeare's slow, painful infinite questioning is abruptly dropped. In its uncomfortable, disturbing place pushes an impossibly noble, simplified tale of star-crossed passion with echoes of Ophelia in a sub-plot." The moral of these dubious assertions is that the authorship question remains critically disadvantageous, providing misleading distraction for reviewers, since as Hallet Smith noted in the Riverside edition, the two "incompatible" parts of the play are both in the Chaucerian source.[16] The narrowing of taste reflected in Davenant's revision of the play's scope (and Harbage's preference for it) is still present in these modern commentators.

16. *The Knight's Tale*. Cf. the ceremonial Shakespearean parts of acts 1 and 5 from lines 859 to 999 and 1881 to 3108 and the Fletcherian rivalry of the Kinsmen in the middle acts in lines 1008–1880—though there is no Jailer's Daughter in Chaucer.

The most significant issue in reviewing a production is how well it actually worked. As with so many of the plays bedeviled by disintegrationism (*Henry VI, Measure for Measure, Henry VIII, Kinsmen*), this production in York was certainly a success. Of this Lois Potter has assured me from her own observations of it, and even the negative reviewers concur. There is general agreement that much of this success is attributable to an attempt to break down the effect of the proscenium arch: "P.T." noted in the *Yorkshire Gazette* for 6 July 1973 that the Theatre Royal was "transformed" because "a large apron stage had been constructed to extend over the stalls with flights of steps to the boxes and the front of the dress circle. . . . Some of the audience were seated on the perimeter of the stage." The result was to assimilate the audience more fully into the performance, "giving the effect of an Elizabethan theatre" as the reviewer for *Stage and Television Today* observed (12 July 1973). "H.J." also wrote:

The Theatre Royal's apron stage, which extends into the wings and out to just under the dress circle works superbly, but is not without problems. From the upper circle, parts of the action (and occasionally the dialogue as well) taking place at the front of the stage, are completely lost. But with all seats at 75p it was possible to move during the interval and enter into the spirit of things by sitting along the edge of the stage, as in Shakespearean days. . . . The glossy white finish of the stage, the white baloons hung in the auditorium, and Emilia's and Hippolyta's fashionable white boots make for a sophisticated, almost trendy performance.

The *Guardian* critic agreed: "The audience all but surround the actors. . . . So much change brought excitement." We must recognize the need to approximate to Renaissance conditions of performance if this play is to work well. Its values and interest are not those associated with the realistic tradition behind a proscenium arch: the play depends on stylized, highly artificial approaches to its themes.

One potent element of the original production was missing at York, however, revealing a continued gap in the awareness of the 1970s, for even the Penguin editor, N. W. Bawcutt, approved the cut: "The subplot of the rustics and their dance is evidently the least interesting section of the play. . . . It has no organic function and could without serious loss be omitted (as in fact it was in the York Festival production)." Bawcutt recognizes that "an ingenious attempt could be made to see the dance as a kind of antimasque in relation to the elevated rituals elsewhere in the play," but, he argues, "the argument would hardly be very convincing." Since the play is in many ways a sequel to *A Midsummer Night's Dream* in which *Pyramus and Thisbe* has exactly this function (like the analogous *Pageant of the Worthies* in *Love's Labour's Lost*), it is evident that neither Bawcutt nor the York director has fully recovered the multilayered thematic approach characteristic of Shakespeare and Fletcher. Even Davenant had understood how central the ancient fertility and hunting rituals were to the meaning and spectacle of the play. The ritual significance of such traditional folk dances is not only stressed by Titania but also provides the climax for *The Merry Wives of Windsor.* We have had to wait until 1985 for the National Theater company's version of *The Mysteries* and *Red Noses* to recover fully the assimilation of folk art and ritual to theatrical productions. However, it is only fair to add that the York production did preserve some sense of ritual action "particularly in the early symbolic battle scene" (*Stage and Television Today*). This is "evoked only by a huddle of bodies, pounding hands for hooves, smoke and sudden wild eruption of streamers, yells and the thud of arrows on metal. The jailer's mad daughter hopskotches round her father. Lighting glows or fades to echo mood" (*Guardian*). Nineteenth-century realism has been exorcised to a large degree.

In terms of character interpretation, the reviewers agree on the consistent effectiveness of the performances at York by all the principal characters, a great gain on the skepticism expressed by the Old Vic's reviewers. "As the two noblemen, Arcite and Palamon, Malcolm Armstrong and Philip Bowen give excellent performances bringing out the humour of their rivalry. Lea Dregorn plays the lovely Emilia with great depth of understanding and charm." However: "The highlight of the production is Jean Viner as the jailer's daughter. Her performance has vitality and pathos" (*Stage and Television Today*). The *Guardian* was a little less enthusiastic: "Jane Casson has a luxuriant and sympathetic distinction as Hippolyta, Lea Dregorn is a lucidly beautiful Emilia. Only Jean Viner, as the goaler's daughter, tends to see-saw her lines with more indulgence than sense. And Elizabeth Tyrrel ploughs her grief as a widowed queen. But altogether the production has a radiance that should not be missed." Obviously the women's roles reject many aspects of conventional behavior, a fact that may help to explain the play's revival upon the introduction of actresses on the Restoration stage and that commends it to modern casts for the same reasons.

In 1974, the year following the York indoor production, the New Theatre Company staged an outdoor version of the play in London's Regent's Park, which J. C. Trewin of *Illustrated London News* found "exciting" while regretting that the play's opening song had been dropped—another symptom of modern unease with the stylized opening of the play.[17] At other points, however, this production appears to have followed the Old Vic precedent in its stress on dance and ritual, production values that I noted with appreciation when I attended. Repudiating the scholarly and critical prejudices in favor of the play's incoherence, the program note asserts: "It is a well-arranged play, despite the duality of authorship and the dichotomy of attitude that in this instance is thus imposed." Some kind of meaningful tension had clearly been detected in the text's oscillations of feeling. However, reviewers were not generous to this production, though I found it memorably stylized, even powerfully ritualistic. J. W. Lambert in the *Sunday Times,* 4 August 1974, refused to treat the issues seriously and casually called the play

17. Metz, "*Two Noble Kinsmen* on the Twentieth Century Stage," 66.

a romantic mish-mash. . . . The most interesting matter in it suggests that psychiatrists haven't changed much in 350 years; and the play makes a strong case for unisex friendship as against the confusions of heterosexual love. In the Park it is modestly though energetically acted, the women being altogether superior to the men. The Morris dancers and duellers of the original have been replaced by Japanese (or perhaps Archaic Greek) stampers and stave-tappers.

In a more sustained analysis in the *Times,* Irving Wardle (1 August 1974) "salutes the company's enterprise but must admit that it is a rum evening." Such reviewers refuse to seek any intrinsic values in an alien text, as they might willingly do with a difficult modern one. Wardle cannot come to terms with the way the play "handles its events from contrasted viewpoints," which he ascribes only to its dual authorship, not to any structural rhythm. He is puzzled by the reversal in the Kinsmen's friendship, by Emilia's ambivalence, and by the impossibility of finding any consistency in such "split characters." He sees "unintended absurdities" preferred to "many legitimate occasions for laughter." There is a failure to grasp the significance of such patterns registered in the program notes.

This coherence and general congruence with the dramatic value of the rest of Shakespeare is my overriding impression of the Regent's Park production. We are not, therefore, dealing merely with an antiquarian experience. Though two directors were involved, the Regent's Park production invited us to see *The Two Noble Kinsmen* as the sequel to *A Midsummer Night's Dream* by seemingly deliberate continuities: Theseus was played by the same actor in both productions, as was Hippolyta. The performer of Lysander's role was recast as Arcite; Quince and his associates in *Pyramus and Thisbe* reappeared as the Jailer and the rustic morris dancers who provide the central interlude for *The Two Noble Kinsmen.* The importance of the dancing remains my most marked impression of the Regent's Park production, which was elaborately choreographed. As in the York version, the battles were abstract, in this case stick/sword dances in the morris tradition. This manner is justified, moreover, by the artifice of the particular morris in *Kinsmen,* which Proudfoot notes was "borrowed from the second antimasque in Beaumont's *Masque of the Inner Temple and Gray's Inn,* which was presented at Whitehall before James I on February 20, 1613, during the festivities for the wedding of Princess Elizabeth to Frederick, Elector Palatine."[18] The whole play has preserved many masquelike attributes, heightening its symbolic, even archetypal approach to experience in which music, song, dance, and combat combine to establish a formal, even ritualistic effect that transcends empathy for individual characters. The choreography is merely the core of these efforts.

At this point we reach an interesting conjunction of production values and thematic issues. The play's mode closely follows that of Beaumont's masque,

18. John Fletcher and William Shakespeare, *The Two Noble Kinsmen,* ed. G. R. Proudfoot (Lincoln: University of Nebraska Press, 1970), xii.

which creates a formal counterpoint of social rituals, between dynastic marriage and rustic fertility rites from which folklorists perceive the morris dances to have descended from prehistoric times. This conjunction is intrinsically Shakespearean as we see in the similar configuration of *The Merry Wives of Windsor,* which associates the courtship and marriage of Ann Page with the attempted seduction of the Wives and the primitive folklore of the horn dance. In reading the printed text of *The Two Noble Kinsmen,* one may easily underestimate the pivotal role of the brief stage direction "Knock. Enter the Dance. Music. Dance" (3.5.137). Only by rereading Beaumont's text can one recover the original scale and meanings involved. One of the most complex, meaningful, and powerful production effects in all of Shakespeare, nonetheless, has been the dancing, whether that climaxing the humiliation of Falstaff in *Merry Wives* or the initiatory ball in *Romeo and Juliet* (not to mention the dances in *Much Ado, Tempest,* and *Henry VIII,* with their equally strong implications of courtship and marital rituals).

This ritual recognition of biological forces is another continuity with the elaborate festival references of *Dream,* and these elements of pagan religion may encourage us to stress equally the analogies between Oberon and Titania on the one hand and Mars, Venus, and Diana on the other. The congruity of these forces with the folk rituals is established by such details as Titania's concern with the disuse of "the nine-men's morris" (2.1.98). The conjunction of the *Kinsmen*'s morris with the deer hunt of Theseus and his companions establishes the same configuration as the climax of *Merry Wives,* which is introduced by the theme of "Herne, the hunter" (4.4.28) and developed by Falstaff's apostrophe to the pagan god: "Remember, Jove, thou wast a bull for thy Europa, love set on thy horns. O powerful love, that in some respects makes a beast a man, in some other, a man a beast . . . for me, I am here a Windsor stag" (5.5.3–13). Before the *Kinsmen*'s morris, Gerrold, the schoolmaster and master of ceremonies, evokes "the wrath of Jove," and afterward he ominously salutes the sacrificial stag:

May the stag thou hunt'st stand long,
And the dogs be swift and strong!
May they kill him without lets,
And the ladies eat his dowsets!
(3.5.154–57)

The eating of the dead stag's testicles by the women gives a horrid immediacy to the blending of courtship and marriage with death and mutilation, reminding us of Egeus's initial desire in *A Midsummer Night's Dream* either to force Hermia's martial choice or to have her ritually murdered. *The Two Noble Kinsmen* opens with scenes in which Theseus is constrained by his fiancée and sister to accept the widowed Queens' pleas for revenge before he can be truly married. It is the same obligation Beatrice lays on Benedick as prerequisite for her acceptance, when she commands him "Kill Claudio" (*Much Ado* 4.1.289).

Such a primitive baptism in blood transcends even the affection of Palamon and Arcite, who are both constrained by love to attempt the death of their best friend.

Ironically, the next major professional production cleverly raised the question of the sexual overtones of the original production by the use of an all-male cast. In the Cherub Company's 1979 presentation in the "fringe" of the Edinburgh Festival, at the New Chaplaincy Centre, the text was heavily cut, but the heightened parallelism of the all-male pairings did allow the innate themes of the play to emerge for Gerald Berkowitz, who found "structural patterns in the play that were reflected in the production: the fact that the real couples in the main plot are the two women and the two men, the contrast between Emilia, who can't love either man who wants her, and the Jailer's Daughter, who switches her love from one man to another without ever realizing it; and the ironic parallels between the first and last scenes."[19] When this same production played at the Young Vic Studio, Tony Howard felt that the male cast showed some misogyny, while the leather trousers and bare torsos of the young men in scenes "of tender ferocity" seemed to invite recognition of more than latent homosexuality.[20] This is an issue our own age is now prepared not only to discuss but also to insist on, for Rick Abrams's Texas production seems to have shared the Cherub production's recognition of the play's latent theme of homosexuality and lesbianism. Modern scholars can hardly avoid elaborating these concerns, subordinate though they seem to the play's main concerns with heterosexual courtship and marriage.

It was precisely the heterosexual nature of the play that was stressed in the same year as the Cherub production, when the Shakespeare Society of America produced the play in Los Angeles with highly traditional emphasis on its Elizabethan-style theater. This reversion caused some hints of anxiety about anachronism in the literal-minded reviewer for the *Hollywood Reporter,* Ron Pennington: "The play is set in ancient Greece, but this production, limited by the Globe Theatre replica of SSA space, is played in Elizabethan costume, with garlands strewn around the stage in an attempt at an airy effect." The same reviewer expressed further reservations based on director Walter Scholz's determination in the program notes that "*Kinsmen* was more than likely done as a masque and was performed at Blackfriars rather than the Globe. Essentially, *The Two Noble Kinsmen* is a spectacle with music, dance and ritual. Because of the limits of the Globe stage the conception has been to create this masque with a feeling of unity and harmony by the use of these ritualistic elements." Other reviewers, however, were happy with this emphasis: the *Shakespeare Quarterly* reviewers wrote: "Scholz chose to project plot and character largely through use of dance and ritual, with almost uniformly satisfying results. The play began with the full cast on stage, dancing, while the Prologue was presented. . . . Both the fight choreography (Larry Broyler) and the dance choreography

19. Metz, "*Two Noble Kinsmen* on the Twentieth Century Stage," 66.
20. Ibid.

(G. Oliver King) were superbly wrought."[21] Any implication, however, that such forms distanced the audience would be mistaken: the *Malibu Times* critic (13 July 1979) expressed anxiety about his personal safety "sitting in the front row a few feet from the fiercely dueling combatants," and T. E. Foreman in the *Press Enterprize* (11 July 1979) asserted that the "sword fight in the second act is one of the most frighteningly realistic in recent stage annals."

The production's outstanding emotional impact was achieved by the endearing pathos and charm of Suzanna Peter's performance as the Jailer's Daughter: Foreman called it "particularly moving"; Pennington said it was "the best performance in the production" and "thoroughly charming"; while the *Shakespeare Quarterly* noted, "The most remarkable achievement of this imaginative production was the conception of the Jailer's Daughter." This excellence was confirmed when Peters earned the Los Angeles Drama Critics' Award for her interpretation, presumably the nearest thing to the Restoration's sexual accolade conferred on the charm of Mary Davis for the same role. However, most of the reviewers expressed doubts about the use of an uncut text, which dragged in the later scenes. Most made heavy weather of the authorship issue, and, as too often, the analogy to Ophelia invited further dubious and solemn parallels with *Hamlet*. However, the production obviously succeeded with its audiences, for Sam Birnkrant called it "a highly entertaining evening." It proved "richly satisfying and revelatory" to John C. Mahoney in the *Los Angeles Times* (3 July 1979) and displayed a "naive simplicity that captivates" to Ken Letner (*Independent*, 12 July 1979). By following the traditional stress on choreography and conventional amatory interests, the production vindicated the play's accessibility to general audiences and critical approval.

I have had a more recent personal experience of the text in performance with the production in the Berkeley Shakespeare Festival for 1985 in which it was combined with *Richard III*, seen as a "nightmare," and *A Midsummer Night's Dream*, with which *Two Noble Kinsmen* was linked as "the awakening," by systematic crosscasting of parallel roles. I should declare my interest as a member of the festival's board and artistic committee, which no doubt encouraged the choice of play but did not directly affect the production, which was derived from a previous studio one at the Berkeley Drama Workshop by the same director, Julian Lopez-Morillos. It was unpretentious and traditional in its Elizabethan style of costumes and simple outdoor setting in Hinkel Park.

Like most modern versions, the text was heavily cut, particularly at the start, with some loss to the force, scale, and authority of its serious, ritual aspects. Similarly, the morris dance was perfunctory and marginal in significance compared to the duels, which were elaborately choreographed, as was other business between the Kinsmen, such as their first entry playfully wrestling together in anticipation of Arcite's success in the games. According to the director, this entry was intended to heighten the profound tensions between the kinsmen.

---

21. Lillian Wilds and Joseph H. Stodder, "Shakespeare in Southern California and Visalia," *Shakespeare Quarterly* 31 (1980): 258–59.

The Prologue and Epilogue were spoken by the director with agreeable naturalness in propria persona, which was an effective way of establishing rapport with the audience; but this was somewhat forfeited by the cast's tendency to race through even the heavily cut text without trusting it enough to achieve serious emotional impact. The audience was thus extremely attentive but often quite puzzled about specific meanings, including some of the Rustics' lewd jokes. Though the captured Hippolyta's Amazonian pretensions were intentionally forfeited, the director expressed to me his sense of more modern assertions of women's autonomy in the rejection of traditional feminine obligations by Emilia; but she remained merely charming rather than intense or distressed. By contrast, the Jailer's Daughter was scaled down from a daring sexual adventuress to a disturbed adolescent still clutching her doll. Nevertheless, it was the Daughter who first and best established the audience's amazed rapport with the play's central theme: the comic pathos of humanity's uneasy relationships to the sexual drive that both threatens and ensures the survival of society and its institutions. In this production the key was set when the Daughter wryly exclaimed: "Lord, the diff'rence of men!" (2.1.54). This aside establishes a mood of rueful amusement, which audiences can apply to the oscillations of attitude between the kinsmen in subsequent scenes. There was more jocularity than seriousness in this production; even Emilia tended not to register much intensity, and the intended significance of the magisterial Theseus, facing repeated confrontations with determined female opposition, seemed more comic than disturbing. As a result, the serious implication of the providential overridings of human choices did not emerge so strongly as the play's concluding message. The audience was more curious than challenged by the vagaries of the plot. We underplay the importance of the earlier scenes at our peril if the play is to achieve memorable impact and meaning.

Whatever my personal impressions of this production, it was well received by audiences and enthusiastically reviewed by critics, who welcomed the recovery of an "obscure Shakespeare" text. John McClintock found it "fascinating" and "astonishingly good" (*Times Tribune,* 4 August 1985). Alfred Kay found the performance a "lively and amusing one" and "a worthy and thought-provoking entertainment" (*Monterey Peninsula Herald,* 9 August 1985). It is true that Judith Green asserted the text was that of a "misbegotten melodrama": "*Kinsmen* is full of sound and fury, and most of it signifies nothing, because it is incomprehensible" (*Mercury News,* 29 August 1985). Contradictorily she considered this "a wonderful production almost redeeming [the play] with fine acting, direction and design." The scholarly issue of uncertain authorship perhaps distracted the critic from fully registering the script's excellence in its specific function of performance. It is also significant that the "striking performance" of Nancy Carlin as the Jailer's Daughter and the fine choreography were central to this reviewer's appreciation of the play. The other critics agreed; Alfred Kay also praised Carlin: "This is a juicy role, and Carlin handles it in her own outrageous but highly effective manner" (which included a lot of business with a doll, stressing her quaint and pathetic immaturity). All the reviews unconsciously made clear that the critics were not bringing achieved understanding of the text with them to the theater. They acquired insights by appreciating a stage realization of something they had previously ignored or misunderstood. Performance was the necessary precedent for appreciation in this case.

The Royal Shakespeare Company's version of *The Two Noble Kinsmen* in 1986 (later transferred to London) was noteworthy for giving authoritative sanction to the play's acceptance into the canon. This version had the advantage of inaugurating the Swan Theatre at Stratford: an approximation to the configuration of an Elizabethan outdoor stage moved into the shell of the burnt-out Victorian theater that had previously been used for rehearsals. The resulting blend of intimacy and self-conscious artifice served the play well despite what seemed to me some very willful directorial choices, such as the use of a superficially Japanese kabuki style of acting and stage effects. This had little to do with the text and characterization except to suggest the remoteness of the audience from the subject (which already involved a Renaissance reworking of Chaucer's medieval version of a story involving a legendary, prehistoric, Greek hero). It is curious that a similar, vaguely oriental look had been used in the Regent's Park production, a look that also carried over into the choreography of the morris dance.

In the Royal Shakespeare Company version, the morris dance was highlighted as the ritual focus of the play's interest in sexuality. A massive and grotesque phallus was the central feature, with a mimed orgasm of white silk directed at the female cast members, and the choreography stressed the climactic role of the Jailer's Daughter. She dominated the reviewers' perceptions (even more than in the past) probably because of a modern preoccupation with such proletarian figures. Michael Radcliffe in the *Observer* (11 May 1986) called her "the most interesting character in the play, an eccentric tomboy . . . Imogen Stubbs gives the Jailer's Daughter curiosity, intelligence, pathos, humor, and acrobatic skills, and . . . is the discovery of the night, after the Swan Theatre itself." John Peter in the *Sunday Times* (11 May 1986) considered hers to be "the most appealingly written role in the play," and Irving Wardle's initial reservations about the play in the London *Times* (10 May 1986) as "eccentric" and "peculiar" encouraged him to find the success of this role "the main dramatic surprise" of the evening.

A more searching view of the play by Michael Billington in the *Guardian* (10 May 1986) praised the director, Barry Kyle, who "manages to excavate a hidden theme suggesting the play is about female desperation at masculine competitiveness. . . . *The Two Noble Kinsmen* becomes a play about The Two Lovesick Women . . . a pampered waverer and . . . a shattered, underprivileged victim. . . . He has taken the cobwebs off a theatrically workable piece," despite "some heavy-handed phallic rustic revelry." Michael Radcliffe corrected this proletarian fixation by seeing that "the complexities of the [kinsmen's] honorable antagonism provide the tragicomical core of the plot," though John Barber in the *Daily Telegraph* (10 May 1986) censured "this gallimaufry" for the "odd device of making one of the cousins black and the other white, maybe to conceal their total lack of individuality." Yet Irving Wardle asserts the opposite: that the production seems to "abandon the traditional moral equity of the two lovers in presenting Palamon and Arcite as violently contrasting figures. . . . Arcite is a magnanimous, strong-nerved realist," while Palamon "erupts into feverish jealousy."

Perhaps John Peter's verdict that the play was "full of intense feeling impersonally expressed" is the most resonant. Despite many eccentricities of direction, of which the Japanization was only the most distracting, the production did catch the basic power of the play and its humorous, rueful charm. Imogen Stubbs merited her acclaim, not only because of her many talents but also because she responded sympathetically to the vitality of the part—perhaps Shakespeare's last study of the attractively comic yet pathetic ingenue. There were also fascinating glimpses via recasting of actors from the production of *A Midsummer Night's Dream* that was also part of this company's season: Emilia reappeared as Hermia, Egeus alternated as the Jailer, and the passionate Palamon doubled as Oberon. Unfortunately, the potentialities of such interconnectedness were not exploited to indicate how closely one play serves as the sequel for the other. My residual impression is, however, that the script called forth the substantial talents of the company and thus transcended the occasional willfulness of the director, who otherwise worked hard to put across a script that has its own theatrical values (as the best reviewers and most audiences recognized on this occasion).

The overall impression left by this performance history remains that actors and directors have been more seriously committed to the themes in this text than have reviewers and critics, perhaps because theater people correctly perceive all successful drama as aesthetically dependent on collaboration. The planned new editions in the Arden, Cambridge, and Oxford series are tardy scholarly explorations compared to the numerous stagings of the play over the last fifty years. As we have seen, this change of taste reverses that recorded by Pepys at the Restoration, but it has still not fully restored to academic favor the minor plays of Shakespeare and his contemporaries. Such late and elusive plays as *Cymbeline* and *The Winter's Tale* are still too often regarded as alien, difficult, and indeed defective. Even less approval has been extended to texts of debated authorship: *Pericles, Henry VIII,* and *The Two Noble Kinsmen* have remained subjects of critical suspicions that have discouraged interest and performance. Only with the emergence of self-confident professional theaters with a concern to develop a national repertory, such as the Old Vic, the Royal Shakespeare, and the National Theatre, have daring revivals begun to recover the production values of the Jacobean and Caroline stages through plays such as *The Revenger's Tragedy, The Changeling, Philaster, The Maid's Tragedy,* and similar works of uncertain or collaborative authorship. As such plays continue their slow climb to respectability and scholarly appreciation, we may expect *The Two Noble Kinsmen* to acquire the same critical respect as the *Henry VI* plays have recovered with their triumphant production at Stratford-upon-Avon after languishing in obscurity from similar doubts concerning their authorship.

Nevertheless, potential performers remain apprehensive that the aesthetic anxieties felt by critics over the divided authorship of *The Two Noble Kinsmen* may be justified. Unintended inconsistencies of plot, characterization, style, and tone may lead to poor audience response. In practice this has proved to be a fallacy for the play, just as it has proved with *Pericles* and *Henry VIII*.[22] Geoffrey Bullough's *Narrative and Dramatic Sources of Shakespeare* shows how many of Shakespeare's plays verge on collaborative reworkings of successful existing scripts, as Greene bitterly observed to their writers. The age excelled in shared endeavors, such as the Authorized Version of the Bible, to be tested not by wondering which parts are written by whom, but by noting whether the whole achieves a genuine aesthetic and conceptual coherence.

These considerations of supposed discontinuity bring us to the heart of the play's distinctive performance values and fascination even for modern audiences. Despite its often stately verse, the text frequently introduces elements of violent melodrama and uncouth harshness, as with the opening intrusion of the three Queens lamenting the gruesome fate of their spouses. The quarrels of the kinsmen reevoke such brutal effects in their confident expectation of death, while the Jailer's Daughter provides us with equally bizarre explorations of suicidal sexual mania. Such situations allow language and attitudes that are shockingly perverse, holding the audience's attention by sheer unpredictability in terms of plot expectation and textual prefigurings. Of all Shakespearean plays, this is perhaps the one that most avoids preconditioning the audience's expectations: even the other romances establish a mood of positive expectation for their outcomes that this one refuses to concede. Nevertheless, these seemingly arbitrary reversals of the plot are less random than most reviewers recognize, and not necessarily degrading and shaming to the characters. The supernatural forces in both *A Midsummer Night's Dream* and *The Two Noble Kinsmen* may initially seem only mischievous, but in the end they approach that "something of great constancy" that I believe Shakespeare's divinities share with the Euripidean ones (even while they seem callously indifferent to the expectations of conventional human understanding). The movement toward acceptance of this enigma is the subtext of any successful performance of the play and invalidates the critical reader's resistance to its outcome, a resistance often resulting from lack of recognition of theatrical affect through performance.

If there is any critical consistency in recent performance history, it seems to lie in the need to recognize a deeper, less "realistic" level of interest than picturesque characterization and ingenious plotting. The play aspires to that higher (or at least more abstract) level of interest recognized in Douglas Peterson's study of other romances, *Time, Tide, and Tempest*.[23] Like so many of Shakespeare's plays, this one illustrates the medieval world view that limited human

---

22. See William Shakespeare, *Henry VIII*, ed. H. M. Richmond (Dubuque: W. C. Brown, 1971); Hugh M. Richmond, "Shakespeare's *Henry VIII*: Romance Redeemed by History," *Shakespeare Studies* 4 (1968): 334-49; Hugh M. Richmond, "The Feminism of Shakespeare's *Henry VIII*," *Essays in Literature* 5 (1979): 11-20.

23. Douglas L. Peterson, *Time, Tide and Tempest: A Study of Shakespeare's Romances* (San Marino, Calif.: Huntington Library, 1973).

reason can only stoically submit itself to the unpredictable, but not arbitrary, decisions of Providence. This hitherto unfashionable view of life is best evoked by a deliberately archaic style of production that excludes the realistic expectations of modern, humanistic scholarship. The play establishes initially a higher level of idealism than most moderns can tolerate, but then it systematically frustrates that vision without collapsing into the nihilism that many critics seem to perceive in its conclusion. It cannot adequately be defined as hopelessly fragmented and incoherent. In rehearsal and performance any perceptive reading subtly elicits a unique and memorable rhythm, as I have observed in two productions, and I would now like to explore exactly how this distinctive rhythm crystallizes in the course of production.

In my own two Shakespeare Program productions at the University of California, Berkeley, *The Two Noble Kinsmen* provided an excellent occasion for exploring the adverse affects of its supposedly divided authorship. We approached it both as a modest live performance in the open air corresponding to an Elizabethan traveling production and as a more analytical television version allowing more detailed presentations of character through close-ups and nuanced speech. If our goal was to vindicate the sustained interest of the text (albeit a drastically cut one, as Irwin Smith argues was often originally the case),[24] then both productions were successful, for we found our audiences remarkably attentive; first puzzled, they were then fascinated by the recurrent zigzags of the action and its humorous irony. In production the play systematically features an arresting permutation of plot reversals, of which the climax favoring the seemingly defeated suitor is only the last. This characteristic rhythm establishes a virtuous expectation among each group of characters, which is then abruptly frustrated by irresistible and compulsive drives, often involving physical violence, but which ultimately allow for the survival of the community through socially sanctioned procreation.

Though dealing with amatory rather than political issues, the play's affective structure is similar to that of *Henry VIII*, as I have argued for that text's coherent orchestration: the recurrent defeat of rational, moralistic expectations by a kaleidoscope of forces approximating the pagan pantheon. The images of the opening marriage song are paradoxical: the conventional rose that has lost its thorns reminds us of the bizarre nature of Hippolyta's courtship on the battlefield. A little later the song anticipates the Queens' entry by its seemingly inappropriate allusion to "marigolds, on death beds blowing," and "the boding raven." The disruption of the festive marriage pageant by the ominous trinity of widows should be staged as melodramatically as Richard of Gloucester's disruption of the very different funeral cortege of Lady Anne with the corpse of Henry VI. Indeed, the scene in *The Two Noble Kinsmen* in which a mourning challenge is made to a sexual ritual is a witty reversal of that in *Richard III* in which a sexual challenge is made to a mourning celebration. The working out

---

24. Irwin Smith, *Shakespeare's Blackfriar's Playhouse: Its History and Its Design* (New York: New York University Press, 1964), 260–61.

of this abrupt dichotomy neatly occupies the whole of the first act. After the shock effect of the three Queens' hysterical pleas, the audience pays silent and serious attention to the resolution of the situation.

The second act, despite its supposedly split authorship, follows a parallel path in tracing disruptions both of the marriage of the Jailer's Daughter and of the intense friendship of Palamon and Arcite. If the assignment of 2.2 to Fletcher is correct, he shows an astounding intuitive understanding of the play's overall structure (just as he must have in *Henry VIII* if he detected its analogous rhythms). Act 2 scene 1 shows us a low-life analogue to the first act in the disruption of the marital plans of the Jailer's family by outside forces. More-over, this brief interlude changes the tone as dexterously as does the Porter scene in *Macbeth*. Our audience was highly amused by the naive fixation of the Daughter on the aristocratic prisoners, and we also got a significant and appre-ciative laugh on her exit line: "It is a holiday to look on them. Lord, the diff'rence of men!" (2.1.54).

This humorous sense of sexual volatility (echoing that of *A Midsummer Night's Dream*) subtly conditions our response to 2.2, which is an elegant exercise in emotional reversals. From sentimental alliance against societal adversity, the kinsmen progress to murderous sexual rivalry. The comic note set by the Daughter ensures that the audience can savor the delicate ridiculousness of the kinsmen's reversal of feelings, so similar to that in *A Midsummer Night's Dream*. The scene was highly approved by all our audiences, earning the live production's first marked applause. If the planning of this audience reaction is Fletcher's, it is as effective onstage as anything in the play assigned to Shake-speare, and totally true to his skeptical vein.

The plot now moves into its archetypal phase—the return to a "wood near Athens," that green world so favored by Shakespeare, yet in scenes here par-tially assigned by disintegrationists to Fletcher. Any audience readily recognizes that now we are moving to the farcically ominous mood of *Pyramus and Thisbe* with the grotesque preparations for the morris on which the neurotic Daughter intrudes with her compulsive masochism, clearly modeled not only on the pathos of Ophelia but also on the quaint emotional excesses of Helena. As did the Berkeley Shakespeare Festival, we recast our Helena from an earlier produc-tion of *A Midsummer Night's Dream* as the Daughter. The tone here is a bizarre mixture of intense commitment, violent frustration, and comic ob-scenity, also recalling the brothel scenes in *Pericles*. After slowly exploring vicissitudes of feeling in the nearly three hundred lines of 2.2, we now experi-ence a brisk series of action-oriented scenes involving similar mood changes. The audience is fully instructed and able quickly to savor the humorously para-doxical blend of the sentimental and the sinister. The Daughter laments:

I love him beyond love and beyond reason,
Or wit, or safety. I have made him know it.
I care not, I am desperate.

                    (2.6.11–13)

The rustic's reactions are coarser: "There's a dainty madwoman, master." "A mad women? We are made, boys!" (3.5.72, 76). More abrupt paradoxes characterize the genial preparations of the kinsmen for mutual assassination: "I would have nothing hurt thee but my sword" (3.6.87).

We found, in the portrayal of Emilia's anxiety, reversals, and resentment, a depth of awareness that deeply moved audiences. Her agonized meditations delicately set off yet reinforce the Daughter's antithetical problem. The Daughter involuntarily loves what she cannot have; Emilia will not choose between two ideal suitors, neither of whom she prefers. Each woman is denied rational motivation, and both are reduced to stoical acceptance of what is made available. This repudiation of meaningful human volition is stressed in the Epilogue—ostensibly a didactic note on which to end the play. But, after the amusing eccentricities it so ingeniously evokes, we found our audiences accepted this conclusion as obediently as the women characters. There was a very positive mood at the end. Like the plot permutations of *Cymbeline* and *The Tempest,* the oscillations of mood and reversals of plot in *The Two Noble Kinsmen* seem to generate humorously rueful agreement that "Pardon's the word to all" (*Cymbeline,* 5.5.422).

In reading *The Two Noble Kinsmen,* one cannot easily detect this dexterous evolution of mood. As producer, I found that my main function was to convince the participants that our experiment was a significant attempt to discover whether such an effect could be made accessible to audiences. We found that it was less readily detectable initially because the wordiness of the text requires the kind of editing invited by the conventional two-hour playing time for Shakespearean performances. When first rehearsing the script, the actors found the scenes bewilderingly incoherent and elusive: the characters seemed abstract, impersonal, stylized, and inaccessible to modern approaches. Indeed, all participants had initially reconciled themselves to a performance limited to conscientious recitation of alien and stilted sentiments likely at best to be received with polite curiosity.

There was a remarkable divergence from such anticipations in actual performance: as one incredulous actor wrote afterward, "All I can say is—Goddam—it works!" The audience was far more intensely involved in the quaint vicissitudes of the idealistic characters than could have been predicted, and the delicacy with which the audience was conditioned to accept and savor the humorous pathos of the narrative reversals proved illuminating to everyone. The play has a unique stage effect, a ruefully humorous pathos for which it has been dexterously, consciously, and systematically designed by its author(s). This conclusion allows a producer to arbitrate on the importance of the question of authorship in terms both of styling and of critical impact. The issue of divided goals or methods is not relevant to performance of the play, which reflects a consistent rhythm of feeling independent of the varied authorship assigned to particular scenes. In staging there is no easily detected divergence stylistically: the range is well within that shown in earlier Shakespeare plays experimenting with a variety of conventional styles (such as *Love's Labour's*

Lost and *Henry IV*). The play has a well-designed cumulative effect on the audience, generating a kind of rueful amusement at the paradoxical frustration of human sentiment, expectation, and conventions by impersonal forces manipulating human wills. In the absence of irrefutable evidence, any concerns about authorship should always be subordinated to the play's intrinsic value as a distinctive illustration of Shakespeare's last experiment in controlled stagecraft. However much, or little, Fletcher contributed to it, he clearly worked alertly to realize consistent effects rising out of Shakespearean concerns evident in the oscillation of feelings exploited in the earlier plays.

Experience with such productions of Shakespeare also suggests that they provide a convenient testing ground for interpretations, particularly those highly sophisticated ones derived from the close textual scrutiny encouraged by the New Criticism. The risks of overexplicating nuances are corrected by the fact that an ingenious argument derived from the printed page may be invalidated by practical issues of stage structure and blocking, limits of communicable intent, or audience resistance to oversophisticated interpretation. Granted this option of testing critical ideas against not only actual productions but also possible ones, we may find it salutary to review some of our current views of *The Two Noble Kinsmen* as production concepts. One disconcerting issue for the literary critic is to recognize the discrepancy between a dramatist's first "literary" draft and a revised script tuned to performance needs. It is axiomatic that Elizabethan performances at least aspired to two hours of uninterrupted performance time and that most modern productions avoid greatly exceeding this limit for audience attention. If we accept this almost unavoidable pressure to streamline a wordy text such as that of *The Two Noble Kinsmen,* then significant interpretations should not be narrowly based on local analysis of imagistic overtones or verbal minutiae. Indeed, these remain mostly unperceived by audiences or, if they are perceived, may well be reevaluated. Palamon's sententiousness proved in our performance to be a sympathetic, youthful trait that won him consistent audience approval and applause, rather than contemptuous alienation.

Many critics subjectively describe their alienation from the abrupt and sententious conclusion of the play without allowing for the normally positive audience affect, one that tends to soften awareness of the characters' seeming hubris on the printed page to a charming pathos on the stage. Studiously severe reading produces a false negative impression of characters that is uncharacteristic of most audience empathy with the actual actors. In performing *The Two Noble Kinsmen,* we found a consistently more positive response than that given by the critics: seeming moral defects or plot limitations proved challenging or amusing. This vastly greater positive impression in performance is characteristic of most significant productions of Stuart plays that I have seen and helps to explain the discrepancy between critical condescension to Beaumont and Fletcher and their consistent success with audiences in the theater.

The need to correct negative interpretations in the study against positive reactions in the theater extends to characterization in general. The intensely positive response of most audiences to the Jailer's Daughter is a case in point: in practice she is more humorous, more dynamic, and more significant than can easily be perceived on the printed page—a fact of staging confirmed by most reviewers. Similarly, there is a serious weakness in modern critics' views of tensions between latent homosexual relations in the play and its heterosexual concerns. Just as our modern anxieties over ethnic differences have encouraged perhaps morbid responses to *Huckleberry Finn, The Merchant of Venice,* and even *Othello,* so our attentions to homosexuality and lesbianism may have unbalanced our reaction to historical same-sex relationships (as Leslie Fiedler has argued in *Love and Death in the American Novel*). Our inclination to polarize the issues in *The Two Noble Kinsmen* into a confrontation between homosexual and heterosexual passion oversimplifies it. Some modern critics insist on an overtly homosexual intent in Shakespearean friendships, whether in the sonnets, *The Winter's Tale,* or even *Othello.* Should we accept the lesbianism of Emilia, for example, on the evidence of casual remarks such as her inquiry if her maid wishes to have a bedmate? (2.2.151–52). In production, this proves too slight to establish so major a theme; if noted, it seems merely playful. Her account of her friendship with Flavina is endearing precisely because of its innocence and lack of proto-Freudian sexual precocity. This innocence is shared by the girlish friendship of Hermia and Helena in *A Midsummer Night's Dream,* where the inexpert Helena makes a desperate effort to arrest her friend's disruptive growth into active sexual life. Both plays are surely not explorations merely of sexual alternatives but of the pathos when friendships within one sex are preempted by heterosexual compulsions that serve the genetic needs of the species to the disadvantage of other feelings.

In staging, this issue is crucial because it allows us to distinguish between two approaches: a superficially arresting stress on the provocative aspects of our own concerns with homosexual issues, and a more tragic, or at least pathetic, involvement in the loss of asexual innocence in the interest of a higher social gain. The universe of the Elizabethan and Jacobean audience was ultimately a providentially Christian one, as was Chaucer's. Modern agnostic critics seem to resent the play's stoic conclusion; but, in performance, any overt resistance to it constitutes not only an anachronism but also a violation of the artistic rhythm of the text both overall and in detail. Much as we may wish to disagree with the authors' seeming goal of rueful reconciliation with inhuman forces governing human destiny, any attempt to force the audience to resist a tone of acceptance is a dogmatic violation of the mood not only of the romances but of Shakespeare's plays generally—in which the vagaries of human will are reconciled (albeit at a cost) to a providential outcome for human society as a whole.

A Select Bibliographical Guide
to *The Two Noble Kinsmen*

Will Hamlin

The purpose of this bibliography is to provide a survey of major scholarship and criticism on *The Two Noble Kinsmen* from the early eighteenth century through 1987. In the interests of clarity I have separated the annotations into five sections: (1) editions (including general introductions) and textual commentary; (2) studies of authorship and date; (3) source study; (4) criticism; and (5) accounts of recent performances. Within each section the annotations are arranged chronologically. I realize that the section headings themselves are somewhat arbitrary, inasmuch as they by no means represent mutually exclusive categories; they do, however, serve to indicate the primary emphases of the commentaries summarized within them.

Since this is a selective bibliography, a number of articles about *The Two Noble Kinsmen* have been excluded, principally on the grounds that they add little or nothing to the evolving critical discussion of the play. Among the exclusions are studies that dismiss the play as undramatic or unworthy of critical attention and studies that consider the play's subplot inferior, unintegrated, immoral, or obscene. Also excluded are works that seek to deny Shakespeare's or Fletcher's partial authorship of the play. Finally, attempts to prove Shakespeare's presence through metrical tests or studies of diction, syntax, or image clusters are for the most part omitted, except when they offer other commentary of interest or when they have been frequently cited by critics and editors. An exhaustive annotated bibliography of midcentury (1928–1980) studies of *The Two Noble Kinsmen* may be found in G. Harold Metz, *Four Plays Ascribed to Shakespeare* (New York: Garland, 1982).

I have included those critical studies that examine political, philosophical, moral, and psychological themes in the play, studies that situate the play within contexts of Renaissance history and cultural production, and studies concerned with collaboration as a fact of life in the theater of Elizabethan and Jacobean England. I have also provided a short section on the play in recent performance (1979–1986); accounts of earlier performances are cited in G. Harold Metz's "*The Two Noble Kinsmen* on the Twentieth-Century Stage" (*Theatre History Studies* 4 [1984]: 63–69). My hope is that this bibliography will serve as a useful starting place for those interested in thinking and writing about *The Two Noble Kinsmen*.

Reference Sources

Bibliographic Articles and Single-Volume Bibliographies

Bevington, David. *Shakespeare*. Goldentree Bibliographies. Edited by O. B. Hardison, Jr. Arlington Heights, Ill.: AHM Publishing, 1978.

Ebisch, Walther, and Levin L. Schucking. *A Shakespeare Bibliography*. Oxford: Clarendon Press, 1931.

———. *Supplement for the Years 1930–1935 to A Shakespeare Bibliography*. Oxford: Clarendon Press, 1937.

Erdman, David V., and Ephim G. Fogel. *Evidence for Authorship: Essays on Problems of Attribution*. Ithaca: Cornell University Press, 1966.

Jaggard, William. *Shakespeare Bibliography*. Stratford-upon-Avon: The Shakespeare Press, 1911.

Littledale, Harold. "Introduction." In *The Two Noble Kinsmen*, rev. ed., pt. 2. London: New Shakspere Society, 2d ser., no. 15, 1885.

McManaway, James G., and Jeanne Addison Roberts. *A Selective Bibliography of Shakespeare*. Charlottesville: The University Press of Virginia and The Folger Shakespeare Library, 1975.

Metz, G. Harold. *Four Plays Ascribed to Shakespeare*. New York and London: Garland Publishing, 1982.

Proudfoot, G. R. "*Henry VIII, The Two Noble Kinsmen,* and the Apocryphal Plays." In *Shakespeare: Select Bibliographical Guides,* edited by Stanley Wells. London: Oxford University Press, 1973.

Smith, Gordon Ross. *A Classified Shakespeare Bibliography, 1936–1958*. University Park and London: The Pennsylvania State University Press, 1963.

Annual Bibliographies and Indexes

American Humanities Index. Troy, N.Y.: The Whitston Publishing Co.

Annual Bibliography of English Language and Literature. Leeds: W. S. Maney and Son, for The Modern Humanities Research Association.

Arts and Humanities Citation Index. Philadelphia: Institute for Scientific Information.

British Humanities Index. London: The Library Association.

Deutsche Shakespeare-Gesellschaft West Jahrbuch. Bochum: Verlag Ferdinand Kamp.

Humanities Index. New York: H. W. Wilson Co.

MLA International Bibliography. New York: Modern Language Association of America.

World Shakespeare Bibliography. *Shakespeare Quarterly*. Washington, D.C.: The Folger Shakespeare Library.

The Year's Work in English Studies. London: John Murray for The English Association.

1. Editions and Textual Commentary

Littledale, Harold. "Bibliography." In *The Two Noble Kinsmen*. Reprint of the 1634 Quarto. London: New Shakspere Society, 2d ser., no. 7, 1876.

This bibliography serves as a preface not only for the Quarto reprint but also for the revised edition of *The Two Noble Kinsmen* prepared by Littledale and published by the New Shakspere Society in the same year. The Quarto reprint, as Littledale accurately remarks, is "virtually a facsimile reproduction" (p. v); the revised text, based largely on that provided by Alexander Dyce in his 3d edition of Shakespeare (1876), is the play's first critical edition. Among other things, it retains the old spelling and offers the student abundant notes, a collation of textual variations, and a commentary on the ten previous editions of *The Two Noble Kinsmen*.

Littledale, Harold. "Introduction." In *The Two Noble Kinsmen*, rev. ed., pt. 2. London: New Shakspere Society, 2d ser., no. 15, 1885.

Published nine years after Littledale's edition of *The Two Noble Kinsmen*, this general introduction further refines the speculations of William Spalding and Samuel Hickson as to the respective shares of Shakespeare and Fletcher in the play's composition. With regard to external evidence, Littledale agrees with Spalding that there are no decisive grounds for believing that Shakespeare did not contribute to the play. As for internal evidence, Littledale asserts that his belief in Shakespeare's part-authorship "is threefold: metrical similarities, artistic handling (regardful of character and motives rather than situations and scenic effects), and style of thought and imagery" (p. 18). On the first two of these grounds, Littledale spends relatively little time, merely recapitulating conclusions derived by other critics from metrical tests measuring "light- and weak-endings," "stopt and unstopt lines," and "double-endings" (pp. 19–22) and claiming that the characterization in the play and the general handling of the plot appear to be Shakespeare's, even though the choice of the story is "injudicious" (p. 27). However, Littledale devotes nearly forty pages to his third criterion and compiles an impressive number of parallels—both verbal and thematic—between the Shakespearean passages of *The Two Noble Kinsmen* and passages from undisputed Shakespeare plays, "especially from the plays of the fourth period" (p. 68).

Littledale's conclusion as to the division of authorship is that Shakespeare wrote all of act 1 except scene 5 and lines 1–37 of scene 1; only the first scene of act 2; most of act 3 scene 1 and all of scene 2; nearly all of act 4 scene 3; and all of act 5 except lines 1–17 of scene 1, part of scene 3, and lines 86–98 of scene 4 (p. 13). Fletcher wrote everything else, including the "trash of the underplot" (p. 13). In general, then, Littledale's division is much closer to Hickson's than to Spalding's, particularly in that it assigns three of the subplot's scenes to Shakespeare. But Littledale differs from Hickson in attributing a greater overall share of the verse to Fletcher. He gives 1.5 to Fletcher, for example, in contrast to both Spalding and Hickson; and he is much more willing than they are to see a hand other than Shakespeare's in 1.1, 3.1, 5.1, and 5.3.

Littledale dismisses the idea that *The Two Noble Kinsmen* was based on either *Palaemon and Arcyte* (1566) or *Palamon and Arsett* (1594)—both of which have been lost—arguing instead, "We have the strongest grounds for supposing that our play was a new play, based directly on the *Knightes Tale* [of Chaucer]" (p. 12). For one thing, the Prologue plainly states that the play is new and that its story is derived from Chaucer. Moreover, "the very simplicity of the underplot" (p. 12) is convincing evidence of its "origination by Shakspere" (p. 12). As for the play's date, Littledale places "the Shaksperian portion about 1609, and the Fletcherian portion about 1613" (p. 68). Like Hickson, he is inclined to think Fletcher finished a play that Shakespeare began but gave up due to lack of time or interest.

The introduction concludes with a "synoptical History of Opinion" (p. 81) regarding *The Two Noble Kinsmen*. This is a useful compilation of critical commentary on the play (mostly on the question of authorship) from the end of the seventeenth century until the time at which Littledale was writing. It is invaluable for anyone doing research on early criticism of *The Two Noble Kinsmen*.

Kittredge, George Lyman, ed. *The Two Noble Kinsmen*. In *The Complete Works of Shakespeare*. Boston: Ginn and Co., 1936.

Kittredge's text is based on the 1634 Quarto.

Noting that there is "substantial agreement" (p. 1409) among scholars about the division of the play between Fletcher and Shakespeare, Kittredge adds that the two writers probably "worked in active collaboration, as was perhaps also the case in *Henry VIII*" (p. 1409). "Some of the Shakespearean scenes may have been touched up by Fletcher, and possibly Fletcher's work includes a bit of Shakespeare here and there. Exact details are beyond the scope of sane criticism" (p. 1409).

Kittredge arranges the plays in the same order they are found in the First Folio; thus, *The Two Noble Kinsmen,* along with *Pericles,* appears at the end and is not categorized as a "romance" or "tragicomedy." Kittredge says little about the play itself but does defend its subplot against those who have found it trivial and/or obscene: "Apart from one or two characteristic Fletcherian touches, there is nothing in the underplot to justify the heroics with which some critics have assailed it" (p. 1410).

Waller, Frederick O. "Printer's Copy for *The Two Noble Kinsmen.*" *Studies in Bibliography* 11 (1958): 61–84.

Waller questions the common belief that the 1634 Quarto text of *The Two Noble Kinsmen* was based on a theatrical prompt book. While it is true that the Quarto contains a number of prompter's annotations and the names of two actors associated with the King's Men in 1625–1626, it is also true that the non-Fletcherian portions of the play present several textual tangles that one would not expect to find in a prompt book. Moreover, the presence of several imperfect jointures in the play (for instance, that between 2.1 and 2.2) suggests that a systematic revision and transcription of the play was never carried out (pp. 72–73), although Waller admits Fletcher may have made a few additions to the scenes written by his collaborator. In short, Waller conjectures that the Quarto text was based on "annotated foul papers" (p. 61) rather than on a prompt book or an authorial fair copy. Responding to the objection that the Fletcherian portions of the Quarto text exhibit far fewer instances of such Fletcherian trademarks as the use of "ye" and "'em" than one would expect in light of Fletcher's other plays, Waller hypothesizes that Fletcher's foul papers were transcribed while his collaborator's were not. In any case, "whether the printer's copy was an intermediate transcript, foul papers, or a mixture of the two, it seems clear enough that foul papers are the ultimate basis for Q" (p. 80).

Waller accepts the division of *The Two Noble Kinsmen* between two authors, though he doesn't attempt to make a strong case for Shakespeare's having been one of them. He does point out that the textual difficulties occur for the most part in those sections of the play normally assigned to Shakespeare: one feature "invariably mentioned in discussions of the non-Fletcherian parts is their denseness or 'knottiness'" (p. 69). As for collaboration, Waller believes with Chambers that the play is a collaborative effort and not "the completion by Fletcher of a Shakespearean fragment" (p. 73). At the same time, Waller doubts that Shakespeare and Fletcher worked closely together; if they had, such dislocations as that between 2.1 and 2.2 would not have occurred.

Leech, Clifford, ed. *The Two Noble Kinsmen.* In *The Signet Classic Shakespeare.* New York and Toronto: New American Library, 1966.

This is a modern-spelling critical edition based on the text of the 1634 Quarto.

Although Leech has no doubt that Shakespeare and Fletcher collaborated on the play, it seems likely to him that "the final putting together of the manuscript was left to Fletcher" (p. xxiv). Resemblances to Shakespeare's romances abound in the play: like *Pericles* and *The Winter's Tale,* it has a Hellenistic setting (p. xxvi) and its characters are "subject to divine power," though "more disturbingly" (p. xxvii) than in the previous romances; and like *Pericles,* it is based on a story told by an earlier English poet. But there are also resemblances to earlier plays in the canon—notably *The Two Gentlemen of Verona* and *A Midsummer Night's Dream*—suggesting "a disposition to recall and to look upon with a changed vision" (p. xxx) themes and situations treated before. In general, according to Leech, the division of authorship is most apparent (apart from considerations of verse) in the play's dichotomy of attitude: Shakespeare treats the story of the two kinsmen with high seriousness and probably found the story's "sense of the inscrutable" (p. xxxvii) attractive; Fletcher saw the "essential, often painful, but never overwhelming, absurdity" (p. xxxvii) of the story and thus treats it primarily as a comedy, frequently employing his "deflating hand" (p. xxxii). Leech believes the play "has some good verse and a fairly realistic picture of the onset of madness" (p. xxxvi) and also thinks the play's subplot is strongly linked to the main plot, since both Emilia and the Jailer's Daughter are deprived of choice and "neither girl has, ultimately it seems, the power to differentiate" (p. xxxiii). Moreover, the country entertainment provided in 3.5 is "a comic counterpart to, and an anticipation of, the final tournament" (p. xxxiii). Leech stresses the play's "recurrent irony" (p. xxxix), citing examples from the subplot and from conversations between Palamon and Arcite, Hippolyta and Emilia, and Theseus and his petitioners. Finally, Leech notes that up to 1963 only two modern productions of *The Two Noble Kinsmen* had been mounted, one at the Old Vic in 1928 and one at Antioch, Ohio, in 1955. "It is more than time that a further attempt was made to see it in action" (p. xxxvi).

Proudfoot, G. R., ed. *The Two Noble Kinsmen.* Regents Renaissance Drama Series. Lincoln: University of Nebraska Press, 1970.

This is a modern-spelling critical edition based on a collation of twelve copies of the 1634 Quarto.

Proudfoot sees no reason to doubt the traditional division of authorship of the play; "readers of *The Two Noble Kinsmen* have always been aware that the play contains passages in two markedly different styles" (p. xvi). But in addition to stylistic evidence for dual authorship, there are also inconsistencies in the play that clearly result from "differing aims and differing conceptions of the characters" (p. xviii). For example, while 2.2 and 3.3 are "written for immediate effects of pathos and excitement" (p. xix), 2.1 and 5.1 are "more concerned with a wider scheme of ideas and values" (p. xix). Also, the variant spellings and scannings of the name *Pirithous* suggest that the play's two authors learned the name from different sources (p. xix). In any case, "whatever the mode of collaboration, the final text, as we have it, would seem to have been overseen by Fletcher rather than Shakespeare" (p. xvii).

Proudfoot believes that *The Two Noble Kinsmen* "belongs to the vogue of tragicomedy that began about 1609" (p. xxi). He sees evidence for this in the play's mastery of tragicomic effects, especially "pathos and suspense" (p. xxiii). However, *The Two Noble Kinsmen* differs from the majority of tragicomedies in that it sustains to its end "a somber note" (p. xxi) that the others dispel at their conclusions. The play's central theme is the destructive power of sexual love (p. xxi); Proudfoot agrees with Philip Edwards that the design of the play emphasizes that human growth involves an inevitable movement away from innocence and joy (p. xxii). On the whole, the "impressiveness" (p. xxiii) of *The Two Noble Kinsmen* lies not in its portrayal of human character but "in its success, against the odds, in persuading us that its story, which teeters constantly on the verge of absurdity, is a fit vehicle for a poetic exploration of the inscrutability of the gods and of the dangerous power of love" (p. xxiii).

The primary source of *The Two Noble Kinsmen* is, of course, Chaucer's *Knight's Tale*, but other minor sources include North's *Plutarch*, Boccaccio's *Teseida*, Statius's *Thebais*, Sidney's "Lady of May," Beaumont's *Masque of the Inner Temple*, and Shakespeare's *A Midsummer Night's Dream*, *Love's Labour's Lost*, *Hamlet*, and *Pericles* (pp. xix-xxi). Proudfoot thinks the 1634 Quarto text of the play "was set by a single compositor from a scribal manuscript" (p. xxiv), doubting the theories of both Waller and Bertram that the manuscript was authorial. The play's first performance was "by the King's Men at their private theater in the Blackfriars, probably during the winter of 1613-14" (p. xii).

Ribner, Irving, and George Lyman Kittredge, eds. *The Complete Works of Shakespeare*. Waltham, Mass., and Toronto: Xerox College Publishing, 1971.

The text follows Kittredge's in his 1936 edition of Shakespeare, which in turn is based on the 1634 Quarto.

Although he places *The Two Noble Kinsmen* among Shakespeare's romances and accepts the dual-author attribution of the 1634 Quarto, Ribner remains more skeptical than most other recent editors of Shakespeare's participation in the play, claiming, "The work is so different in its general tone and effect from anything we know him to have written, that it is difficult to believe that he could have had more than a slight hand in a few scenes" (p. 1587). Ribner points out some of the deficiencies in Paul Bertram's argument that the play is entirely Shakespeare's. He also notes that the similarity of some characters in *The Two Noble Kinsmen* to characters in *The Two Gentlemen of Verona*, *A Midsummer Night's Dream*, *Love's Labour's Lost*, *Hamlet*, and *Macbeth* "may merely demonstrate that Fletcher was deliberately imitating the most distinguished of his masters in the Elizabethan theatre" (p. 1588).

While he admits that *The Two Noble Kinsmen* "has much in common with the romances Shakespeare wrote at the end of his career" (p. 1588), Ribner emphasizes the differences: the romances stress "the final benevolence of the divine plan" (p. 1588), "reconciliation and forgiveness for ancient evils" (p. 1588), "restoration of universal harmony after chaos and disorder" (p. 1588), and "emergence of young lovers" (p. 1588). *The Two Noble Kinsmen*, on the other hand, is concerned with "codes of behavior rather than with what validity in terms of human experience these codes may have" (p. 1588) and provides "no exploration of what either love or friendship may mean in a world of real men and women" (p. 1588). Moreover, the episode of the Jailer's Daughter "tends to reinforce the play's conception of love between man and woman as an emotion without real substance, and such a conception is entirely alien to the treatment of love in virtually every play we know Shakespeare to have written" (p. 1588).

Ribner argues that the differences between *The Two Noble Kinsmen* and the other romances suggest "the fallacy of the commonly-held notion that their Blackfriars performance did more than any other single factor to shape the special quality of Shakespeare's final plays" (p. 1589). *The Two Noble Kinsmen* is "exactly the kind of play to which we might expect a Blackfriars audience to have enthusiastically responded" (p. 1589), but it lacks "those special qualities of Shakespeare's last plays that cannot be limited or created by the specific requirements of any theatre" (p. 1589).

Smith, Hallett. "Introduction" to *The Two Noble Kinsmen*. In *The Riverside Shakespeare*, edited by G. Blakemore Evans. Boston: Houghton Mifflin Co., 1974.

This is a modern-spelling critical edition based on the 1634 Quarto.

Smith accepts *The Two Noble Kinsmen* as a collaborative effort by Shakespeare and Fletcher and places it among the romances. It has "many links" (p. 1640) to these plays, among them the fact that "the gods are invoked and their favors are granted" (p. 1640) and the similarity in setting—"Thebes and Athens are as remote as Antioch, Tharsus, Mytilene, and Ephesus" (p. 1640). Moreover, in *The Two Noble Kinsmen* "Nothing is too strange or improbable to be accepted, not the interruption of Theseus' wedding ceremony for a military expedition, nor the courtesy of two deadly foes who arm each other before conflict, nor the gratuitous accident which kills the victor before he can claim his prize" (p. 1640).

In considering the subplot involving the Jailer's Daughter, Smith finds, "The extended sentimentality of the daughter's situation and the coarseness of the doctor's suggested cure by seduction are far more characteristic of Fletcher than of Shakespeare" (p. 1640). On the whole, the play "deals in a curious way with the theme of innocence and experience, and the conflict between sexual desire and duty" (p. 1641). The characters move from presexual innocence into "an area of experience where the will seems totally irrelevant to the way things will come out" (p. 1641).

Bawcutt, N. W., ed. *The Two Noble Kinsmen*. New Penguin Shakespeare. Harmonds-worth: Penguin, 1977.

This is a modern-spelling critical edition based on the 1634 Quarto.

Bawcutt proposes that we approach *The Two Noble Kinsmen* seriously and sym-pathetically. He plays down the importance of ascertaining which parts of the play are by Fletcher or Shakespeare, claiming that it ought to be possible "to make a critical approach to *The Two Noble Kinsmen* which accepts the fact of collaboration with all its consequences, and treats the play as a work of art (not merely a repository for some passages of authentic Shakespearean blank verse), but without desperately trying to impose on it a unity it does not possess" (pp. 15–16). Bawcutt stresses the emphasis on ritual ceremony found in the play—both in Shakespearean and Fletcherian scenes—noting the "rich spectacle of sight and sound was no doubt provided partly for its own sake, but it also helps to surround the characters with an atmosphere of ceremony and mystery" (p.12).

Bawcutt takes issue with the common complaint that Palamon and Arcite are hardly distinguishable: "From Act III onwards Palamon is clearly presented as the lover, the follower of Venus, and Arcite as the soldier, the follower of Mars, as in Chaucer" (p. 23). He admits, however, that in the play's earlier scenes there is "some degree of confusion or clumsiness" (p. 23) in the characterization of the two young men. More striking, though, is the difference in the portrayal of Emilia by the respective authors. "Fletcher's concep-tion of her as a girl with a streak of sensuality, who is quite willing to 'run mad' for a man and whose only problem is to make up her mind which of two handsome young men to choose, is surely less impressive than Shakespeare's conception of her as a virgin by temperament who is reluctantly forced into marriage by fate" (p. 35). In general, Fletcher's handling of events "lacks the largeness and resonance of Shakespeare's presen-tation" (p. 28).

The episode of the Jailer's Daughter, in Bawcutt's opinion, "is related to the main plot and throws light on it" (p. 36). Like Palamon and Arcite, the Jailer's Daughter loves someone who hardly knows of her existence. Through all three of them, love is pre-sented "not as a mutual relationship based on acquaintance but as one-sided obsession which may lead to madness or death" (p. 37). Moreover, the Jailer's Daughter ends up accepting her wooer instead of Palamon, just as Emilia ends up with Palamon rather than Arcite. "Shakespeare and Fletcher are not, however, trying to argue that personal iden-tity is unimportant or that one lover is as good as another; the point is rather that destiny frequently does not allow us to choose for ourselves, and nobility lies in an unselfish acceptance of the role we have been alloted" (p. 37).

Bawcutt admits that *The Two Noble Kinsmen* has moments of "inconsistency and incoherence" (p. 45). But he believes Shakespeare and Fletcher "were trying to say something of value" (p. 46), and he calls for the play to be pushed more into the mainstream of thinking about Shakespeare (p. 46).

The Two Noble Kinsmen: A programme/text with commentary by Simon Trussler. Swan Theatre Plays Series. London: Methuen by arrangement with the Royal Shakespeare Company, 1986.

The Royal Shakespeare Company first performed *The Two Noble Kinsmen* on 26 April 1986. The roughly 350 lines cut by RSC director Barry Kyle are indicated by square brackets in this edition; the text used is that of N. W. Bawcutt for the New Penguin Shakespeare (Harmondsworth, 1977).

The commentary by Simon Trussler includes brief discussions of such topics as collaborative authorship of plays, tragicomedy as a genre, and the debate over the complexity of Palamon and Arcite as dramatic characters. In addition, Trussler provides a brief chronology of the lives of Shakespeare and Fletcher and their interaction with The King's Men. He also intersperses critical pronouncements on *The Two Noble Kinsmen* by such writers as Philip Edwards, Richard Proudfoot, and Una Ellis-Fermor.

Commenting on *The Two Noble Kinsmen*'s relation to Chaucer's *Knight's Tale,* Trussler remarks that in the play "the thematic emphasis shifts from suffering patiently endured to the workings of chance and fortune" (p. 7). As for the common observation that the characterizations of Palamon and Arcite are inconsistent—shifting from nobility to "vain salacity" (p. 14)—Trussler argues that this "inconsistency" shows a "precise knowledge of how the male human being adapts his sexual persona to circumstances and pressures" (p. 14). Trussler is interested above all in supporting the thesis of the dramatic unity of *The Two Noble Kinsmen*. He readily admits the collaboration of Fletcher and Shakespeare and claims, "The main impulse for collaboration was surely an unconscious recognition that the playwright had the very spelling of his occupation in common with other makers of goods: he was concerned with a shared theatrical craft, not an exclusive literary art, and saw no reason to be ashamed of that" (p. 8).

2. Authorship and Date

Pope, Alexander. Preface to *The Works of Shakespeare.* London, 1725. Reprinted in *Shakespeare: The Critical Heritage,* edited by Brian Vickers, vol. 2. London and Boston: Routledge and Kegan Paul, 1974.

Pope concludes that Shakespeare was "conversant with the Ancients of his own country from the use he has made of Chaucer in *Troilus and Cressida* and in the *Two Noble Kinsmen,* if that play be his, as there goes a tradition it was (and indeed it has little resemblance of Fletcher, and more of our author than some of those which have been received as genuine)" (p. 408).

Warburton, William. Preface to *The Works of Shakespeare.* London, 1747. Reprinted in *Shakespeare: The Critical Heritage,* edited by Brian Vickers, vol. 3. London and Boston: Routledge and Kegan Paul, 1975.

Warburton asserts that "The whole first Act of Fletcher's *Two Noble Kinsmen* was wrote by Shakespeare, but in his worst manner" (p. 227).

Steevens, George. *Supplement to the Edition of Shakespeare's Plays*. London, 1780. Reprinted in *Shakespeare: The Critical Heritage*, edited by Brian Vickers, vol. 6. London and Boston: Routledge and Kegan Paul, 1981.

Steevens cites thirty-eight verbal parallels between *The Two Noble Kinsmen* and various canonical plays of Shakespeare but concludes that the play is not Shakespeare's but was "written by Fletcher in silent imitation of our author's manner" (p. 301). Dryden and Rowe, as Steevens point out, are other authors who have imitated Shakespeare in their plays.

Lamb, Charles. *Specimens of English Dramatic Poets*. London, 1808. Reprinted in *The Life, Letters, and Writings of Charles Lamb*, edited by Percy Fitzgerald, vol. 4. London, 1895; Freeport, N.Y.: Books for Libraries Press, 1971.

Lamb includes three passages from *The Two Noble Kinsmen* among his "specimens": 1.1.25–218, 1.3.49–82, and 2.2.1–110. The first two of these "give strong countenance to the tradition that Shakespeare had a hand in this Play" (p. 250). Lamb is skeptical of Steevens's theory that Fletcher wrote *The Two Noble Kinsmen* in "silent imitation" of Shakespeare; he believes it unlikely that Fletcher could have copied Shakespeare's style with "such facility" (p. 250). Moreover, "If Fletcher wrote some scenes in imitation, why did he stop? or shall we say that Shakespeare wrote the other scenes in imitation of Fletcher?" (p. 251). Lamb is the first critic to attempt to characterize the respective styles of Fletcher and Shakespeare as they appear in this play. Fletcher's "ideas moved slow; his versification, though sweet, is tedious, it stops every moment; he lays line upon line, making up one after the other, adding image to image so deliberately that we see where they join" (p. 250). Shakespeare, on the other hand, "mingles everything, he runs line into line, embarrasses sentences and metaphors; before one idea has burst its shell, another is hatched and clamorous for disclosure" (p. 251).

Schlegel, Augustus Wilhelm von. *A Course of Lectures on Dramatic Art and Literature*. Translated by John Black. London, 1846.

In Lecture 27 (delivered in Vienna during the spring of 1808), Schlegel calls *The Two Noble Kinsmen* "the joint production of Shakespeare and Fletcher" (p. 471). He sees no reason for doubting Shakespeare's participation in the work: "What could be the motive with the editor or printer for any deception, as Fletcher's name was at the time in as great, at least, if not greater celebrity than Shakespeare's?" (p. 471). Moreover, "a certain ideal purity" (p. 472) distinguishes the play from others known to be Fletcher's, and the "conscientious fidelity" (p. 472) with which the play follows Chaucer's *Knight's Tale* is a further indication of Shakespeare's collaboration. Indeed, Schlegel emphasizes the idea of collaboration, reminding us that "it was then a very general custom for two or even three poets to join together in the production of one play" (p. 472), and adding, "With regard to theatrical effect, four eyes may, in general, see better than two, and mutual objections may be of use in finding out the most suitable means" (p. 472).

Coleridge, Samuel Taylor. *Lectures and Notes on Shakespeare and Other English Poets*. Compiled by T. Ashe. Vol. 1. London: George Bell and Sons, 1890.

Coleridge is quoted by J. Payne Collier (in a journal entry for 13 October 1811) as saying, "There is the clearest internal evidence that Shakespeare importantly aided

Fletcher in the composition of [*The Two Noble Kinsmen*]" (pp. 10-11). However, Coleridge doubts the subplot was Shakespeare's because "the mad scenes of the Jailor's daughter are coarsely imitated from *Hamlet;* these were by Fletcher, and so very inferior, that I wonder how he could so far condescend" (p. 11). He concludes, "There is no finer, or more characteristic dramatic writing than some scenes in *The Two Noble Kinsmen*" (p. 11).

Coleridge, Samuel Taylor. *Literary Remains.* Vol. 2. London, 1836; New York: AMS Press, 1967.

Touching on *The Two Noble Kinsmen* in an 1818 lecture, Coleridge compares the dialogue between Palamon and Arcite in 1.2 with that in 2.2 and finds that he "can scarcely retain a doubt as to the first act's having been written by Shakespeare" (pp. 320-21). But his main argument for Shakespeare's participation lies in "the construction of the blank verse, which proves beyond all doubt an intentional imitation, if not the proper hand, of Shakespeare" (p. 321). Still, the "harshness" (p. 321) of many passages, along with "the want of profundity in the thoughts" (p. 321), keeps Coleridge from certainty that Shakespeare contributed to the play.

Shelley, Percy Bysshe. Letter to Mary Shelley, 20 August 1818. In *The Works of Percy Bysshe Shelley,* edited by Harry Buxton Forman, vol. 8. London, 1880.

Shelley writes that *The Two Noble Kinsmen* disappointed him. "The Jailer's Daughter is a poor imitation and deformed. The whole story wants discrimination and modesty. I do not believe that Shakespeare wrote a word of it" (pp. 31-32).

Hazlitt, William. *Lectures on the Literature of the Age of Elizabeth.* London, 1840; London: George Bell and Sons, 1880.

Hazlitt's lecture on Beaumont and Fletcher, delivered in 1820, argues that while the first act of *The Two Noble Kinsmen* contains poetry "in the manner of Shakespeare" (p. 120), it also contains "bravura speeches" (p.121) and verse in which "the sentiment is overdone, and the style merely mechanical" (p. 120). He therefore concludes that "the first part of this play was written in imitation of Shakespeare's manner" (p. 121) by Fletcher, and "The subsequent acts are confessedly Fletcher's" (p. 122). Hazlitt was not impressed by the subplot: "The jailor's daughter, who falls in love with Palamon, and goes mad, is a wretched interpolation in the story, and a fantastic copy of Ophelia" (p. 125). Hazlitt notes that Chaucer's *Knight's Tale* was the source Fletcher drew on but claims that the latter part of the story, "which in Chaucer is full of dramatic power and interest, degenerates in the play into a mere narrative of the principal events, and possesses little value or effect" (p. 125).

De Quincey, Thomas. *Thomas De Quincey's Works.* Edited by Adam Black and Charles Black. Vol. 10. Edinburgh, 1862.

In a lengthy note in his essay "Rhetoric" (originally published in *Blackwood's Magazine,* December 1828), De Quincey claims, "The first and the last acts, for instance, of the *Two Noble Kinsmen,* which, in point of composition, is perhaps the most superb work in the language, and beyond all doubt from the loom of Shakespeare, would have been the most gorgeous rhetoric, had they not happened to be something far better" (p. 49).

Coleridge, Samuel Taylor. *Specimens of the Table Talk of the Late Samuel Taylor*

Coleridge. Edited by Henry Nelson Coleridge. Vol. 2. New York: Harper and Brothers, 1835.

In a conversation dated 17 February 1833, Coleridge is quoted as saying "I have no doubt whatever that the first act and the first scene of the second act of *The Two Noble Kinsmen* are Shakespeare's" (p. 63). This appears to be the first claim that part of the play's subplot was written by Shakespeare.

Spalding, William. *A Letter on Shakespeare's Authorship of The Two Noble Kinsmen*. Edinburgh, 1833; London: New Shakspere Society, 8th ser., no. 1, 1876.

Spalding, a Scotsman, appears to have written this lengthy letter as much to establish his reputation as to convince his readers that *The Two Noble Kinsmen* belongs within the Shakespearean canon. He acknowledges that other writers (Pope, Warburton, Farmer, and Schlegel) have previously reached the same conclusion, but he insists, "The discussion of the questions cannot be needless, so long as this fine drama continues excluded from the received list of Shakespeare's works" (p. 2).

Dealing first with external evidence, Spalding echoes Schlegel in pointing out that a deceptive use of Shakespeare's name on the 1634 Quarto would by no means have guaranteed an increase in sales, since Shakespeare had by then "fallen much into neglect" (p. 4). Moreover, the claim on the Quarto's title page that the play was acted by the King's Servants at the Blackfriar's Theatre tends to confirm the idea that Shakespeare and his company were involved. As for collaboration, Spalding thinks it likely that Shakespeare and Fletcher worked together: "Such partnerships were very generally formed by the dramatists of that time; both the poets were likely enough to have projected some union of the kind, and to have chosen each other as the parties to it" (p. 5). Spalding dismisses the idea that the absence of *The Two Noble Kinsmen* from the First Folio is an argument against Shakespeare's authorship, since the Folio provides clear evidence "that profit was its aim more than faithfulness to the memory of the poet" (p. 7). In addition, it contains two plays (*1 Henry VI* and *Titus Andronicus*) that Spalding believes are not Shakespeare's and omits two others (*Pericles* and *Troilus and Cressida*) that clearly are. (Spalding claims *Troilus and Cressida* was "only found appended, like a separate work, to some copies" of the Folio [p. 8].) In short, the absence of *The Two Noble Kinsmen* from the First Folio "is of itself no proof whatever that Shakespeare was not the author of it" (p. 9).

Turning to internal evidence, Spalding outlines what he sees as the "distinctive differences" (p. 11) between Shakespeare and Fletcher. Shakespeare's versification is "broken and full of pauses, . . . sparing of double terminations"; Fletcher's is "of a newer and smoother cast, . . . abounding in double endings" (p. 11). Shakespeare's style is "always energetic," "concise," and tends toward "obscurity" (p. 13); Fletcher's is "diffuse" (p. 14) and "often reaches the verge of feebleness" (p. 15). Shakespeare is "scarcely ever vague" (p. 15), Fletcher "often vague and deficient in precision" (p. 16); Shakespeare's style is "metaphorical to excess" (p. 16), Fletcher's "poor in metaphor" (p. 17). Shakespeare is adept at classical allusion; Fletcher is not. Shakespeare's writing is characterized by wit and abundant wordplay, Fletcher's by "slow elegance and want of pointedness" (p. 23). Finally, Shakespeare has a "tendency toward reflection" (p. 20); Fletcher has "very little of Shakespeare's practical, searching, worldly wisdom, and none of that solemnity of thought with which he penetrates into his loftier themes of reflection" (p. 20). With these differences in mind, Spalding carries out a scene-by-scene analysis of the play and concludes that all of act 1, the first scene of act 3, and all of act 5 except the second scene are Shakespeare's; the remaining scenes are Fletcher's. Spalding dismisses the idea that Fletcher wrote the play in imitation of Shakespeare because Shakespeare's "dissimilar powers . . . make it next to impossible, even in short and isolated passages, to produce an imitation which shall be mistaken for his original composition: but there is not even a possibility of success in an attempt to carry on such an imitation of him throughout many entire scenes" (p. 58).

Having established Shakespeare's "subsidiary authorship" (p. 60) beyond any reasonable doubt, Spalding turns to the question of the overall design of the play. Although he believes the "tragi-comic underplot" (p. 60) is Fletcher's because of its "inferiority in the execution" (p. 60) and its weak imitations of scenes in *Hamlet, Lear, Macbeth, Love's Labour's Lost,* and *A Midsummer Night's Dream,* he maintains that with regard to the play as a whole, Shakespeare "was the poet who chose the story, and arranged the leading particulars of the method in which it was handled" (p. 60). Shakespeare, after all, habitually dramatized stories already known to his audience; Fletcher tended to create his own plots. Moreover, few writers in the early seventeenth century apart from Shakespeare were interested in dealing with historical drama or chivalrous subjects. But the fact that two earlier English plays—*Palaemon and Arcyte* (1566) and *Palamon and Arsett* (1594)—treated essentially the same subject as *The Two Noble Kinsmen* appears to Spalding convincing evidence that Shakespeare was involved in the play's creation, since such reworking of earlier drama was one of his trademarks. Spalding also considers the simplicity of the plot of *The Two Noble Kinsmen* a sign of Shakespeare's hand in designing it: "Fletcher either would not have chosen so bare a story, or he would have treated it in another guise" (p. 76). And such scenes as 1.2 and 1.3, containing "no activity of incident" (p. 77), reveal Shakespeare's controlling influence in the play in their focus on the principal characters.

In short, the story of *The Two Noble Kinsmen* "is ill-suited for the dramatic purposes" (p. 107) of Fletcher, while it is clear that if "the execution of the plan" (p. 108) is any indication that Shakespeare was connected with the work, "we can hardly avoid the conclusion that it was by him that the subject was chosen" (p. 108). Spalding believes he is the first critic to point this out. In conclusion, he writes of *The Two Noble Kinsmen,* "Imperfect as it is, however, it would, if it were admitted among Shakespeare's acknowledged works, outshine many, and do discredit to none" (p. 109).

Dyce, Alexander, ed. *The Works of Beaumont and Fletcher.* Vol. 1. London, 1843-1846.

After reviewing the opinions of such writers as Lamb, Coleridge, Hazlitt, Spalding, and Knight, Dyce states that he believes "Shakespeare undoubtedly wrote all those portions of *The Two Noble Kinsmen* which are assigned to him by Mr. Spalding, though I apprehend that in some places they have suffered by alterations and interpolations from the pen of Fletcher" (p. lxxxii). He thinks it impossible that any writer could have imitated Shakespeare in passages such as 1.1.77-98, 1.1.175-186, 5.1.49-68, or 5.4.65-73. But he disagrees with Spalding on the issue of collaboration, arguing that since the "distraction" (p. lxxxvi) of the Jailer's Daughter is in some places "a direct plagiarism of Ophelia's madness in *Hamlet*" (p. lxxxvi), it is "highly improbable that, if the two dramatists had worked together on the tragedy, Fletcher would have ventured to make so free with the poetical property of Shakespeare" (p. lxxxvi). Instead, Dyce envisions Shakespeare, around 1610, altering the *Palamon and Arsett* of 1594, and Fletcher, years later, adding the "underplot" (p. lxxxvi) and various other minor changes. Like Spalding and Knight before him, Dyce finds the subplot "of a nature not to be conceived by Shakespeare, and further not to be tolerated in any work with which he was concerned" (p. lxxxvi).

Hickson, Samuel. "The Shares of Shakspere and Fletcher in *The Two Noble Kinsmen*." *Westminster and Foreign Quarterly Review* 67 (April 1847): 59–88. Reprinted in *New Shakspere Society's Transactions*, 1st ser., no. 1 (London, 1874): appendix, pp. 25–61.

Hickson's article, like Spalding's *Letter,* argues that Shakespeare wrote a large part of *The Two Noble Kinsmen* and that Fletcher was responsible for the remainder; but Hickson differs from Spalding in maintaining that the play's subplot has intrinsic value and that scenes 2.1, 3.2, and 4.3 were composed by Shakespeare.

In the fourteen years between the publication of Spalding's *Letter* in 1833 and Hickson's article in 1847, *The Two Noble Kinsmen* was published twice in editions of the plays of Beaumont and Fletcher and once in an edition of Shakespeare. The latter, Charles Knight's *Pictorial Edition of the Works of Shakespeare* (1839–1841), contains a bowdlerized version of *The Two Noble Kinsmen* that Hickson clearly regards as of little value to anyone. But Knight later changed his mind and decided that the non-Fletcherian scenes of *The Two Noble Kinsmen* were by George Chapman—an idea Hickson completely dismisses. As for the two editions of Beaumont and Fletcher, Hickson says nothing about one of them (George Darley's, 1840) but takes issue with claims in the other (Alexander Dyce's, 1843–1846) that Shakespeare had nothing to do with the subplot of *The Two Noble Kinsmen* and probably did not write the play in collaboration with Fletcher.

Comparing the first two scenes in which Palamon and Arcite appear (1.2 and 2.2), Hickson claims that while the second has the potential for considerable dramatic effect, it is nonetheless a failure: "Between the characters of Palamon and Arcite there is positively no distinction; and the speeches of one might be given to the other without the least injury to the plot" (p. 27). In the first of these scenes, on the other hand, Hickson sees a marked distinction between Palamon and Arcite and thus concludes, "The individuality of character drawn by one author [Shakespeare] was not preserved by the other [Fletcher]" (p. 28). Hickson considers this lack of follow-through a predominant trait of the play and a sure sign that its authors were indeed Shakespeare and Fletcher.

The treatment of the subplot is Hickson's most notable contribution to critical opinion regarding this play. Claiming that Spalding was too quick to dismiss the subplot on the grounds of its inferiority to the remainder of the play, Hickson examines it more carefully and finds that parts of it are neither gross nor crudely imitative—these being the two most common complaints. In particular, Hickson believes that 2.1 is "delicately managed" (p. 38) and agrees with Coleridge that it is Shakespeare's; that 3.2 "displays a depth of insight into the psychological character of this state [the incipient madness of the Jailor's Daughter] only excelled by Shakespeare himself, in *King Lear*" (p. 43); and that 4.3 is "the most important scene of the whole play" (p. 47). Dismissing the notion that the Jailer's Daughter bears any resemblance to Ophelia, Hickson asserts that the true resemblance is to Lear: "Between this person and the jailor's daughter, there is a certain degree of parallelism that altogether fails in the other case; there is a similarity in the language; and we see in the latter as in the former, the different gradations from a 'mind diseased' to madness" (p. 47). Fletcher, however, was unable to sustain what Shakespeare had begun; this accounts for the relative inferiority of 3.4 and 5.2.

With regard to the question of collaboration, Hickson rejects "the idea of anything like equal co-operation" (p. 58) between Shakespeare and Fletcher but finds Dyce's supposition of complete noncollaboration improbable. Far more likely, he thinks, is the notion that Shakespeare planned the entire play—including the subplot—and wrote a good deal of it, but "perhaps for want of time to complete it by a day named, and probably by way of encouragement to a young author of some promise, he availed himself of the assistance of Fletcher to fill up a portion of the outline" (pp. 60–61).

Ward, Adolphus William. *A History of English Dramatic Literature.* Rev. ed. Vol. 2. London: Macmillan and Co., 1899.

Ward begins by sketching a brief history of opinion regarding the authorship of *The Two Noble Kinsmen* but refrains from making any claims of his own. He believes, for example, "Nothing in the general treatment of the story, or of the personages concerned in it, can, so far as I see, be set down as beyond Fletcher's dramatic powers" (p. 240). Nonetheless, he admits that dual authorship seems probable. He agrees with Dyce that a collaboration between Shakespeare and Fletcher is unlikely. In the first place, Fletcher was too young to have been a suitable coauthor with Shakespeare; in addition, "the frequent change of scene and the abundance of soliloquies" and "the want of inner connection between the under-plot and the main story" (p. 241) indicate to Ward that Shakespeare is not likely to have been associated with the composition of this play. In short, Ward is skeptical regarding Shakespeare's involvement but unwilling to endorse the theories of other critics that such writers as Chapman or Massinger composed the non-Fletcherian scenes.

Leaving aside the question of authorship, Ward claims that "besides abounding in poetic beauties" *The Two Noble Kinsmen* "solves, on the whole most successfully, the difficult problem of transforming an epical narrative into a drama" (p. 744). It does this primarily by "developing the characterisation" (p. 744)—particularly of Palamon, Arcite, and Emilia—but also by condensing the time lapse, omitting lengthy descriptions, abbreviating the catastrophe, and leaving aside the supernatural machinery found in Chaucer's tale. Moreover, it introduces several new characters, in particular the Jailer's Daughter, whom Ward considers "pathetic or rather hyper-pathetic" (p. 746). The play's primary flaw lies in "the dramatic insufficiency of the close, of which we cannot here, as with the aid of Chaucer's opportune philosophy in the poem, lay the blame on the unequal dealings of Destiny" (p. 746).

Thorndike, Ashley Horace. *The Influence of Beaumont and Fletcher on Shakspere.* Worcester, Mass.: Oliver B. Wood, 1901.

Thorndike's main contribution to the critical debate regarding the authorship of *The Two Noble Kinsmen* is his argument for "direct collaboration" (p. 37) between Fletcher and Shakespeare. In opposition to Hickson and Littledale, who propose that Fletcher completed a play left unfinished by Shakespeare, Thorndike examines all the play's scenes and finds that "so intimate is this inter-relation of the two parts that we safely conclude that each author was well acquainted with the plan of the whole action and the arrangement by scenes and situations" (p. 54). In regard to the play's "two parts," however, Thorndike follows Hickson and Littledale almost unquestioningly; in fact, his "'em/them test" (p. 24), which shows the ratio of the use of "'em" to that of "them," confirms Littledale's division of scenes between Fletcher and Shakespeare (p. 40).

As to the date of *The Two Noble Kinsmen,* Thorndike seconds Littledale's observation that the dance at 3.5.136 is an imitation of the antimasque in Beaumont's *Masque of the Inner Temple and Gray's Inn,* performed at Whitehall on 20 February 1613. "Mr. Littledale's conjecture, then, that the play dates shortly after the performance of the masque, is almost certainly correct" (p. 47).

Farnham, Willard. "Colloquial Contractions in Beaumont, Fletcher, Massinger and Shakespeare as a Test of Authorship." *PMLA* 31 (1916): 326–58.

Using the statistical methods made popular in the late nineteenth century by F. G. Fleay and Robert Boyle, Farnham notes the frequency of three types of colloquial contractions in *The Two Noble Kinsmen* and claims that his results provide "strong evidence that the non-Fletcherian parts of *The Two Noble Kinsmen* are not by Massinger or Beaumont, and that they are by Shakespeare" (p. 327).

Bradley, A. C. "Scene-Endings in Shakespeare and in *The Two Noble Kinsmen.*" In *A Miscellany*. London: Macmillan and Co., 1929.

Bradley argues that the relative abundance of "part-line endings" (p. 219) of scenes in *The Two Noble Kinsmen* is strong evidence that Shakespeare composed these scenes, since he "was increasingly addicted to these endings as time went on" (p. 221). But laying aside this sort of metrical evidence, Bradley concludes, "I cannot for a moment doubt the presence of [Shakespeare's] hand in most of the scenes not obviously Fletcher's, though it does not appear to me improbable that Fletcher revised these scenes" (p. 222).

Chambers, E. K. *William Shakespeare: A Study of Facts and Problems*. Vol. 1. Oxford: The Clarendon Press, 1930.

Chambers has no doubt about dual authorship: "Clearly there are at least two hands in the play" (p. 531). Dismissing theories that attribute the non-Fletcherian parts of the play to Massinger, Chapman, Tourneur, or Rowley, Chambers argues that "the constant use of coined words, of archaistic words, of vigorous unliterary words" and "the characteristic involutions of the sentence-structure" (p. 531) all point to Shakespeare as Fletcher's collaborator. Moreover, the "distribution of the Shakespearean matter shows that it is a case of collaboration and not of the completion by Fletcher of a Shakespearean fragment" (p. 532). In this respect Chambers differs from Littledale and Hickson. The source of the play is Chaucer's *Knight's Tale;* Chambers is skeptical of the idea that *The Two Noble Kinsmen* is a reworking of either *Palaemon and Arcyte* (1566) or *Palamon and Arsett* (1594).

Hart, Alfred. "Shakespeare and the Vocabulary of *The Two Noble Kinsmen.*" *Review of English Studies* 10 (1934): 274–87. Reprinted in his *Shakespeare and the Homilies,* chap. 5. Melbourne: Melbourne University Press, 1934.

Hart begins by dividing *The Two Noble Kinsmen* into two parts, Part A being those sections traditionally attributed to Shakespeare (all of act 1, the first scene of act 3, and all but the second scene of act 5) and Part B being the remainder of the play, normally assigned to Fletcher (p. 242). He then does a series of elaborate word counts, showing in tables that the incidence of rare words and neologisms is much higher in Part A than in Part B and much more consistent with Shakespeare's tendency in plays such as *Antony and Cleopatra, Coriolanus, Cymbeline, The Winter's Tale,* and *The Tempest*. In short, Hart demonstrates that in addition to "differences in characterization, moral tone, treatment of subject-matter, style and metre" that have forced critics to affirm dual authorship of *The Two Noble Kinsmen,* the play also reveals striking differences in vocabulary—differences that support the theory of two authors, "one of whom has a less copious and more commonplace vocabulary than the other" (p. 244). Hart concludes that his evidence "strongly supports the claim made by many critics that *The Two Noble Kinsmen* should be included in the Shakespeare canon" (p. 256).

Mincoff, Marco. "The Authorship of *The Two Noble Kinsmen.*" *English Studies* 33 (June 1952): 97–115.

Like many earlier commentators, Mincoff is primarily interested in arguing that Shakespeare was a coauthor of *The Two Noble Kinsmen;* he assumes without question that Fletcher wrote the non-Shakespearean passages. The external evidence for collaboration is "extraordinarily strong" (p. 98), in Mincoff's opinion; but even without it we would be forced to regard Shakespeare's participation in the play as highly probable, since the "style and language" (p. 103) of the non-Fletcherian scenes lead to the conclusion that "there is really no case for doubting his authorship" (p. 103). The aspects of style and language Mincoff selects for discussion are "richness of imagery" (p. 105), neologisms (p. 109), circumlocutions (p. 110), and juxtapositions of "high-sounding terms" with "colloquialisms and provincialisms" (p. 109)—all of which point to Shakespeare's coauthorship. In addition, Mincoff stresses that the "supposed poverty of the portraiture" (p. 101) of Palamon and Arcite is no ground for arguing that Shakespeare didn't write the parts: "The question is not whether Palamon and Arcite in the Shakespeare scenes are as full of life as Othello and Macbeth, or even as Benedict and Claudio, but are they markedly worse than the puppets of *Cymbeline?*" (p. 101). He notes in addition that *All's Well That Ends Well, Romeo and Juliet, Julius Caesar, Othello, King Lear,* and *Macbeth* all exhibit dramatic shortcomings apparent in *The Two Noble Kinsmen* (pp. 100-101). Indeed, Mincoff attributes much of the resistance to admitting *The Two Noble Kinsmen* to the Shakespeare canon to "bardolatry" (p. 97), and he regards arguments assigning the non-Fletcherian parts of the play to authors other than Shakespeare "too fanciful to need refutation" (p. 115).

Hoy, Cyrus. "The Shares of Fletcher and his Collaborators in the Beaumont and Fletcher Canon (VII)." *Studies in Bibliography* 15 (1962): 71-90.

Hoy accepts the assumption that Fletcher and Shakespeare collaborated on *The Two Noble Kinsmen;* arguments for Shakespeare's participation based on external evidence and stylistic features are, in his opinion, persuasive. Arguments based on linguistic evidence, however, are much less satisfying: "Shakespeare uses no language forms which, either in themselves or by virtue of their rate of occurrence, can serve to point immediately and unmistakably to his presence in a play of doubtful authorship" (p. 72). For example, though Fletcher generally uses "'em" more frequently than Shakespeare, its rate of occurrence in *Women Pleased* and *The Mad Lover* is hardly distinguishable from that in *Timon of Athens* or *The Tempest.* Still, Hoy is able to show that Shakespeare's use of "hath" and "doth" and his avoidance of "ye" contrast markedly with Fletcher's practice. Largely on this basis, he claims that linguistic evidence in the play confirms the division of authorship as follows: Shakespeare; 1, 2.1, 3.1 and 2, 5.1.137-173, 5.3 and 4; Fletcher; 2.2-6, 3.3-6, 4, 5.1.1-136, and 6.2 (p. 71).

Hoy finds Waller's theory that the 1634 Quarto of *The Two Noble Kinsmen* was printed from annotated foul papers "altogether untenable; the linguistic evidence will not support any such conjecture" (p. 75). But he believes that Waller's alternative suggestion—that the printer's copy was an intermediate scribal transcript—"meets the conditions demanded by the linguistic facts of the case more satisfactorily than any other theory about the nature of the printer's copy for the quarto edition of the play" (p. 76).

Bertram, Paul. *Shakespeare and The Two Noble Kinsmen.* New Brunswick: Rutgers University Press, 1965.

Bertram's study, still the only book-length examination of *The Two Noble Kinsmen,* seeks to demonstrate that the play is entirely the work of Shakespeare. It is a thorough piece of scholarship and has lived up to Bertram's claim that whether or not readers accept his thesis, they will find his book "the most comprehensive and detailed examination of the relevant historical and textual evidence ever published" (p. vi).

Central to Bertram's argument is the fact that from the late eighteenth century until the middle of the twentieth century scholars have taken it for granted that Fletcher is one of the two authors whose presence is discernible in the play. This unquestioning assumption derives both from external evidence (the play's original title page) and from critical tradition (Lamb, Coleridge, Spalding, Hickson, and others); however, Bertram proposes to examine the evidence afresh. He points out, for example, that the metrical tests—so popular in the late nineteenth century—that supposedly proved the play's two authors were Fletcher and Shakespeare were in fact applied to "inaccurate texts" (p. 32) and thus must be dismissed. Indeed, Bertram takes "Victorian literary science" (p. 33) to task for ignoring the assumptions upon which it based its conclusions. He adds that once the Fletcher tradition was firmly established, it allowed Victorian scholars with their "puritan attitudes" (p. 43) to attribute anything that struck them as morally impure to Fletcher rather than to Shakespeare. In short, Bertram claims, "The common assumptions about divided authorship and Fletcher's presence in *The Two Noble Kinsmen* rest in part upon very shaky evidence" (p. 56).

In chapter 2 Bertram provides a careful study of the quarto text of 1634 and argues that this text allows us to infer that the manuscript the printer worked from was a fair copy of the play written in Shakespeare's own hand. If this is the case, "whether or not there had been dramatic collaboration, Shakespeare was responsible for the final draft of the play" (p. 6). As for the absence of *The Two Noble Kinsmen* from the First Folio of 1623, Bertram speculates that the manuscript/promptbook of the play was temporarily lost—as was that of *The Winter's Tale*—and not recovered until after the Folio was published. But, as Spalding pointed out more than a hundred years earlier, Bertram stresses that the First Folio is by no means the ultimate authority for our decision as to what constitutes the Shakespearean canon.

In seeking to prove that *The Two Noble Kinsmen* is solely the work of Shakespeare, Bertram takes several tacks. He points out, for instance, a continuity of imagery that cuts across the traditional divisions of authorship (p. 53). He argues that if we examine the play's subplot carefully (especially passages in 2.1 and 4.3) "we are forced to assume that the shape and direction" are wholly Shakespeare's (p. 229). He claims that the "underlying conception" of the role of the Jailer's Daughter throughout the play is "coherent" (p. 233). He demonstrates that the play follows Chaucer's *Knight's Tale* closely, often borrowing exact words, as at 1.4.28–29, 1.5.13–16, and 4.2.94–95 (p. 245). Such lexical congruence is by no means characteristic of Fletcher. Moreover, Bertram shows that the progress of the *Knight's Tale* is carefully reflected in such scenes of *The Two Noble Kinsmen* as 2.5, 3.1, 3.3, and 3.6, even though these scenes straddle the traditional division of authorship (pp. 246–58).

A further indication of single authorship, according to Bertram, is the fact that the play may be seen as falling into three movements: "the war against Creon (Act I), the May Day contests (Acts II and III), and the final tournament (Acts IV and V)" (p. 265). The first two of these are relatively simple, but the third, with its "sharply contrasted scenes and cross-rhythms" (p. 266), clearly points to "a single imagination at work" (p. 268). Bertram states that none of the play's scenes is "easily detachable" from the others (p. 268) and argues that "the general likeness of Palamon and Arcite to one another" (p. 281), far from being a dramatic defect and a piece of evidence for dual authorship, is "obviously deliberate" (p. 281).

In the rare cases when scholars have attempted to show that the supposedly

Fletcherian passages of the play are in fact by Fletcher, the general tendency, according to Bertram, has been to point to passages from canonical works by Shakespeare in order to corroborate the old theories (Steevens, Hazlitt, Halliwell-Phillips) that Fletcher is imitating him (chapter 5). Littledale, it is true, did *not* do this; but, as Bertram points out, he did something almost equally inconclusive, by citing *Henry VIII* and *The Lover's Progress* (primarily Massinger's) in his attempt to adduce verbal parallels proving Fletcher's presence in *The Two Noble Kinsmen* (pp. 234–35). On the whole, Bertram dismisses as misguided the theories that propose Fletcher wrote part or all of *The Two Noble Kinsmen* in imitation of Shakespeare; he asserts, "To search in Fletcher's work for passages whose language seriously resembles that of passages assigned him in *The Two Noble Kinsmen* is to come to appreciate the fact that the traditional scholarship on the play has failed to bring them forward because there aren't any" (p. 240). Scenes such as 4.1 contain passages superior to anything known to have been written by Fletcher (pp. 220–22).

Bertram believes that the Prologue's reference to a single writer (Pro. 19) should be taken at face value because such prefatory speeches "were frequently used to acknowledge collaboration or revision" (p. 259). A false claim that the play had only one author "would be an especially puzzling piece of deception, unlikely to be attempted and unlikely if attempted to succeed" (p. 260). Against the authority of the 1634 Quarto's title page, which attributes the play to both Fletcher and Shakespeare, Bertram poses the testimony of "a respected Oxford scholar" (p. 261), Leonard Digges, who claimed, in a dedicatory poem to the 1640 edition of Shakespeare's poems, that Shakespeare never collaborated in his plays. "Document for document, the poem by Digges would surely seem to outweigh the authority of a title-page written to be displayed as an advertisement on posts about the city" (p. 261).

Bertram coincides with other scholars in dating the composition of *The Two Noble Kinsmen* to 1613 and holding that the play's first performance was "at Blackfriars in the autumn of that year" (p. 13). The play's sources, besides *The Knight's Tale,* are the Plutarch-North *Life of Theseus* (p. 253), Barnaby Barnes's *Foure Bookes of Offices* (p. 258) and Sidney's *The Lady of May* (p. 258), but Bertram is skeptical about either *Palaemon and Arcyte* (1566) or *Palamon and Arsett* (1594).

In general, Bertram's book is excellent in its demonstration that *The Two Noble Kinsmen* possesses internal coherence and structural integrity; it also does a fine job of pointing out the weaknesses of many of the earlier (especially late-nineteenth-century) arguments for dual authorship of the play. However, Bertram consistently undervalues theories of collaboration, and his failure to adequately confront this possibility seems the book's major flaw.

Hoy, Cyrus. Review of *Shakespeare and The Two Noble Kinsmen,* by Paul Bertram. *Modern Philology* 67 (August 1969): 83–88.

Hoy disputes Bertram's claim that *The Two Noble Kinsmen* was written solely by Shakespeare. In the first place, Bertram's argument that the 1634 Quarto was printed from a manuscript in Shakespeare's hand is "distinctly dubious" (p. 84). Moreover, Bertram's attempt to explain away the disjunction between 2.1 and 2.2 is unconvincing; Hoy reaffirms the traditional view that it provides "telltale evidence" (p. 87) that the two scenes were written by separate authors. Bertram's reference to Leonard Digges's claim that Shakespeare never collaborated is inconclusive, and the claim itself is as "naive" (p. 88) as another well-known claim about Shakespeare—that he never revised. Hoy has no doubt that Shakespeare collaborated on *The Two Noble Kinsmen* and that his collaborator was indeed Fletcher, as the Quarto's title page asserts. While Hoy agrees with Bertram that most of the nineteenth-century metrical studies were "badly interpreted" (p. 84), he insists that the non-Shakespearean passages in the play are marked by "a number of syntactical and rhetorical qualities" that are "highly distinctive—not to say integral—features of Fletcher's verbal manner" (p. 84).

3. Sources and Influences

Thompson, Ann. *Shakespeare's Chaucer*. Liverpool: Liverpool University Press, 1978.

Accepting the "orthodox position on the division of scenes" (p. 167) between Fletcher and Shakespeare, Thompson finds that Shakespeare treats the story of Palamon and Arcite much more seriously than Chaucer does, while Fletcher "adopts a much lighter tone" (p. 166) without copying Chaucer's irony. Indeed, the contrast between the two dramatists' attitudes is the most interesting aspect of their "free adaptation" (p. 166) of Chaucer's story: "Shakespeare and Fletcher clearly saw completely different things in *The Knight's Tale* and dramatized it in quite independent ways" (p. 167). Fletcher, in essence, "was trying to turn *The Knight's Tale* into a tragicomedy like *Philaster*" (p. 210), which is evident in the way that he extracts situations from Chaucer's poem, then "proceeds to elaborate with maximum sensational effect" (p. 211). Moreover, "he omits Chaucer's ironic perspective because his kind of tragicomedy requires its pathos to be taken seriously" (p. 212). Shakespeare, on the other hand, was writing a romance. While *The Two Noble Kinsmen* is "grimmer than the other romances" (p. 213), its characters, particularly Palamon and Emilia, acquire the kind of self-knowledge that is "one of the more characteristically 'tragic' elements of the romances and which gives them a level of meaning which is quite alien to the Fletcherian conception of tragicomedy" (p. 213). Thompson points out that while the story of Palamon and Arcite is "more obviously suited to a narrative medium than to a dramatic one" (p. 167), it has potential as a play if one is willing to allow "stylization, ritual and symmetry the dramatic power on stage that they can achieve in religious contexts" (p. 168). Thus, given that "Shakespeare was not concerned with the same type of 'drama' at this stage of his career as he had been earlier" (p. 169), it is hardly surprising that he would choose to dramatize this "curiously impersonal story which takes an absurd yet tragic plot as the basis for a meditation on the wider implications of love, friendship and human destiny" (p. 168). Like Philip Edwards, Thompson sees a fundamental skepticism in *The Two Noble Kinsmen,* and she attributes at least part of it to the source from which Shakespeare and Fletcher drew their story (p. 215).

Donaldson, E. Talbot. *The Swan at the Well: Shakespeare Reading Chaucer*. New Haven and London: Yale University Press, 1985.

Pointing out that *The Two Noble Kinsmen* represents Shakespeare's "most direct and unquestionable use of a Chaucerian source" (p. 50), Donaldson shows how Shakespeare adapts the "heavy strain of pessimism underlying *The Knight's Tale*" (p. 53) to the purposes of his play. Like Philip Edwards, Donaldson sees Venus as a major disruptive force in the lives of the play's characters, but he stresses that Mars is equally disruptive: "Shakespeare's Theseus, Palamon and Arcite, and Hippolyta all represent Mars come down from the temple walls in Chaucer and into their hearts" (p. 68). Or, somewhat differently put: "Venus may be the most malignant influence in the play, [but] the world in which she works is wholly Mars's" (p. 56).

Donaldson devotes a good deal of space to comparing how various characters are portrayed by Chaucer and by Shakespeare. He finds, for example, that while Palamon is essentially the same in the play as he is in the poem, Arcite "suffers a good deal of change" (p. 57), losing some of his common sense and acquiring an inflated ego (p. 58). Emilia is "more fully developed and more interesting" (p. 60) than Chaucer's Emelye, and Shakespeare "seems to suggest that her resistance to sexual love is mature and valid, and that the entanglement of marriage is not an inevitable prescription for all women's happiness" (p. 63). As for Theseus, Donaldson finds him "a harsher, more remote, more prideful, more bullheaded figure than his forebear" (p. 66). Moreover, though "Shakespeare must have been aware that his play, unlike Chaucer's poem, was not about the chance-laden interaction of gods and mortals; yet he allows Theseus to pretend that it was" (p. 72), thus giving him the speech at 5.4.131-36 that suggests the existence of divine justice, even though the play doesn't sanction it (p. 3). In the end, it is only Emilia who questions the principals of the world she lives in, a world "willing to settle unquestioningly for such second-rate deities" (p. 73) as Mars and Venus.

4. Criticism

Spencer, Theodore. "*The Two Noble Kinsmen.*" *Modern Philology* 36 (1939): 255-76. Reprinted in *The Two Noble Kinsmen,* edited by Clifford Leech. The Signet Classic Shakespeare. New York and Toronto: New American Library, 1966.

Accepting the traditional division of authorship between Fletcher and Shakespeare, Spencer moves at once into a discussion of how the two authors differ in their treatment of a story that is "intrinsically feeble, superficial, and undramatic" (p. 218). Fletcher, in Spencer's opinion, makes "first-rate theater" (p. 219) of the parts he dramatizes; Shakespeare, on the other hand, fails dramatically because his passages "are static, and though with splendor, stiff" (pp. 219-20). Both playwrights realized that for the story to work at all, Palamon and Arcite would have to be "colorless and indistinguishable" and Emilia "a passive, if beautiful, doll" (p. 219), but while Fletcher makes the most of the contrasts and conflicts available in the story, Shakespeare emphasizes its ritualistic aspects. Thus, Spencer concludes—after examining the play's first scene—that "we see gesture rather than action. Drama has returned to its womb, and has once more become ritual" (pp. 226-27). The writing is not that of someone "interested in process or in change" (p. 240) but that "of a man who has come out on the other side of human experience, and who, looking back, can no longer be interested in what he has once seen so vividly and so passionately felt" (p. 227). Further evidence of this may be found in the Shakespearean passages that deal with friendship—especially 1.3.55-82—and in Palamon's prayer to Venus, which in Spencer's opinion shows us a Shakespeare uninterested "in writing for Palamon the kind of speech which Palamon—eager and ardent with young love—should speak" (p. 239). In short, the Shakespearean passages of *The Two Noble Kinsmen* illustrate more clearly than anything in *Henry VIII* or *The Tempest* that Shakespeare was "no longer interested in the development of character . . . no longer fully interested in what he was doing" (p. 240).

Bentley, Gerald Eades. "Shakespeare and the Blackfriars Theatre." *Shakespeare Survey* 1 (1948): 38-50. Reprinted in *The Two Noble Kinsmen,* edited by Clifford Leech. The Signet Classic Shakespeare. New York and Toronto: New American Library, 1966.

In the context of a discussion of Shakespeare's association with the Blackfriars Theatre, which was acquired by Shakespeare's company in 1608, Bentley suggests that "the association between Fletcher and Shakespeare from 1608 to 1614 was closer than has usually been thought" (p. 214), since Fletcher was experienced in writing for the more sophisticated Blackfriars audience. Bentley thinks it certain that the two dramatists collaborated on *The Two Noble Kinsmen, Henry VIII,* and *Cardenio* and suggests that Shakespeare may have been "at least an adviser" (p. 214) in the preparation of *Philaster, A King and No King,* and *The Maid's Tragedy.*

Pettet, E. C. *Shakespeare and the Romance Tradition.* London: Staples Press, 1949.

Pettet places *The Two Noble Kinsmen* among Shakespeare's romances but states that while it "belongs to the same dramatic type" as the four earlier plays, its "substance and spirit derive more completely than any of them from the oldest layer of the romantic tradition" (p. 170). Its setting, for example, is "consistently medieval," and its story is "unique among the plays in which Shakespeare had a hand for its dependence upon and fidelity to the chivalric code" (p. 170). In fact, unless we temporarily accept the conventions of chivalry, "the plot is absurdly impossible" (p. 172). But Pettet stresses that Shakespeare and Fletcher do at times depart from the precedent set by Chaucer, most notably in the portrayal of Emilia, who is "a far more sensitive creature" (p. 173) than Chaucer's Emelye. Pettet concludes, "What has made Emilia so different from her earlier incarnation is largely the growth and the change in the doctrines of romantic love" (p. 174).

Muir, Kenneth. *Shakespeare as Collaborator.* London: Methuen and Co., 1960.

Muir contends that the repeated testimony of such writers as Pope, Lamb, Coleridge, De Quincey, Bradley, Chambers, and Spencer that Shakespeare was a coauthor of *The Two Noble Kinsmen* cannot be lightly dismissed; he adds that this belief is substantially reinforced by the conclusions of nineteenth-century metrical tests, Bradley's "part-line ending" test, Hart's vocabulary tests, Mincoff's study of iterative imagery, Armstrong's study of image clusters, and various compilations of verbal parallels to other plays in the Shakespearean canon (pp. 98–122). To Armstrong's "kite" and "hum" clusters Muir adds a new cluster consisting of images of dirt, lust, crime, and death (p. 115). Muir believes that Shakespeare wrote all of act 1, the first scene of act 3, and all of act 5 except scene 2, and on this basis claims that *The Two Noble Kinsmen* "has as much right to be included in editions of Shakespeare as *Sir Thomas More* or *The Passionate Pilgrim,* and perhaps as much as *Titus Andronicus, 1 Henry VI,* and *Pericles*" (p. 122).

In contrast to Theodore Spencer, Muir finds that the verse of the Shakespearean parts of *The Two Noble Kinsmen* shows "no sign of tiredness or flabbiness" (p. 128). In fact, only in the characterization is there evidence of "a definite falling off" (p. 128), some of which can be attributed to the dramatic exigencies of the story. The Fletcherian passages of the play are generally characterized by fewer and less significant references to Fortune and the gods, as well as by poetry that is "manifestly inferior" (p. 130) to Shakespeare's. Moreover, the play's underplot is "bungled" (p. 131), not only by the "artificiality and unreality" of the Jailer's Daughter's speeches but also by "the way in which the madness is used to arouse laughter, and the disparity between the speaker of courtly prose in Act II and the girl in Act V who has one 'poor petticoat and two coarse smocks'" (pp. 132–33). Muir corroborates Spencer's observation that Palamon's prayer to Venus in 5.1 is "very strange" (p. 140) but offers several reasons for the satirical nature of this speech, among them the idea that "Palamon has indeed found Venus's yoke heavier than lead, more stinging than nettles" (p. 142). On the whole, Muir finds that *The Two Noble*

Kinsmen leaves us "with a sense of mystery, the impossibility for man to understand the workings of providence, and of gratitude for life" (p. 145).

Muir says little about collaboration other than that he suspects that Shakespeare was asked to provide a new play for the Blackfriars Theatre but was able only to sketch it out and write parts of it before he had to return to Stratford. "Fletcher, who may have collaborated with him already in *Henry VIII,* would write the remaining scenes, and make any necessary alterations in the parts written by Shakespeare" (p. 147).

Edwards, Philip. "On the Design of *The Two Noble Kinsmen.*" *A Review of English Literature* 5 (1964): 89–105. Reprinted in *The Two Noble Kinsmen,* edited by Clifford Leech. The Signet Classic Shakespeare. New York and Toronto: New American Library, 1966.

After quickly reviewing the standard complaints about *The Two Noble Kinsmen*—its undramatic quality, its wordy speeches, its intellectual unrespectability—Edwards claims that "there is much more purposeful thought in the play than Brooke and Spencer saw; we really need not be ashamed of it" (p. 245). Edwards focuses on the play's treatment of love, taking his cue from Clifford Leech, who "has been the only critic to remark on the curious division of view which belittles the love in the play, and on the insistence that 'mature' love means abandoning something more worthwhile" (p. 245). For Edwards, the play demonstrates that human growth involves an inevitable progression from innocence to experience, from "the impulsive life of youth with its friendship" to sexual love and "the contained life of marriage" (p. 253). This progression may be seen in Theseus and Hippolyta and Emilia as well as in Palamon and Arcite, but it is in the lives of the latter two where we most clearly perceive that reaching the stage of sexual passion and love necessarily entails a deterioration of the noble bonds of youthful and innocent friendship (p. 260). As Edwards puts it, "to gain the new love is to destroy the old" (p. 257).

The address of Palamon to Venus is, in Edwards's opinion, "the center of the play" (p. 249). It not only emphasizes the deforming power of love but also interprets for us the behavior of the Jailer's Daughter, whose plight "gives a particularly unpleasant picture of what happens when sexual desire gets hold of one" (p. 249). Indeed, sexual desire and Venus are one and the same thing in the play: the Venus who debases Palamon and Arcite "as they struggle with each other for Emilia is of course their own sexual nature" (p. 257).

The play's design, particularly in the first three scenes, reinforces the notion that human beings are deformed and redirected—sometimes in very ironic ways—by forces beyond their control. Just as the marriage of Theseus and Hippolyta is interrupted by the Queens from Thebes, the mutual resolve of Palamon and Arcite to abandon their city is destroyed by the news of Theseus's invasion. In both cases, "the action of each scene is basically the action of change of cherished purpose under the pressure of unexpected events. It is, I think, a Chaucerian view of the frailty of our determinations which comes across" (pp. 253–54). In light of these events Edwards suggests that Emilia's vow, in 1.3, that she will never "love any that's call'd man" is likely to be undermined both from without (unexpected events) and from within (her own desires). The absurd ending of the play, in which Emilia must accept the tournament's loser because its winner has died, "is the clinching of the case against Venus and the poverty of the relationships which she provides" (p. 259).

The Two Noble Kinsmen differs from other romances in that it seems to deny that sexual love is "the natural and beautiful fulfillment of an otherwise immature innocence" (p. 260). On the whole, Edwards finds this play "the most cynical assessment of the progress of life since the writing of *Troilus and Cressida*" (p. 261). Still, even if its "vision is rather sweeping and careless of detail" (p. 261), Edwards has no doubt that it is Shakespearean.

Hartwig, Joan. *Shakespeare's Tragicomic Vision*. Baton Rouge: Louisiana State University Press, 1972.

While Hartwig acknowledges that *The Two Noble Kinsmen* shares "many of the premises of Shakespeare's 'tragicomic action'" (p. 184), she states that it differs from the "four tragicomedies" in that its ending provides "no release from anxiety" but rather confirms the "sorrowful recognition that the gods will have their way despite man's efforts" (p. 188). The play's subplot also emphasizes this theme of "the chance which governs man's destiny" (p. 188). Its resolution, in which the Jailer's Daughter prepares to marry her wooer—who has disguised himself as Palamon—implies that "love of a particular person is not so important as the fancy suggests" (p. 189). Joy, which figures prominently in *Pericles, Cymbeline, The Winter's Tale*, and *The Tempest*, "seems to have lost its climactic place" (p. 189) in *The Two Noble Kinsmen*.

Bradbrook, M. C. *The Living Monument: Shakespeare and the Theatre of His Time*. Cambridge: Cambridge University Press, 1976.

Bradbrook stresses the "dual character" of *The Two Noble Kinsmen*, calling it "an old, native heroic setting for an avant-garde hit" (p. 241). The "hit" is the morris dance in act 3—based on the antimasque from Beaumont's *Masque of the Inner Temple and Gray's Inn*—in which the Jailer's Daughter plays a prominent role. Bradbrook speculates that *The Two Noble Kinsmen* was "perhaps only commissioned to provide a setting for the antimasque. It is said that in performance the Jailer's daughter turns out to be the star part" (p. 236).

The funeral of the eighteen-year-old Henry, Prince of Wales in December 1612—just two months before his sister's wedding—is perhaps reflected in *The Two Noble Kinsmen* when the wedding of Theseus and Hippolyta is "crossed by the dark pageant of three mourning queens" (p. 236). Indeed, the play proceeds largely "by spectacle rather than debate" (p. 237). And the play's "masque-like concern with roles rather than characters, allows the topic of homosexuality [Palamon/Arcite; Theseus/Pirithous; Emilia/Flavina] to become pervasive without being acknowledged" (p. 237). This topic "reflects what everyone knew to be the habits of the monarch himself" (p. 237).

Bradbrook concurs with the majority opinion in believing that *The Two Noble Kinsmen* was written by Shakespeare and Fletcher in collaboration. "The reasons for collaboration may have been, first, speed; secondly, to emphasize variety by engaging the two best authors of the King's Company" (p. 241). Moreover, if "the whole town were talking of the antimasque, it would be profitable to put it on quickly" (p. 241). Bradbrook claims, however, that "since the main design was Fletcher's and hardly amounted to a drama," the play's exclusion from the First Folio may represent a choice Shakespeare would have made had he been alive (p. 241).

Rabkin, Norman. "Problems in the Study of Collaboration." *Research Opportunities in Renaissance Drama* 19 (1976): 7–13.

Rabkin finds that Elizabethan dramatic collaboration "submerges brilliance or its lack as much as it does idiosyncrasy" (p. 12). He claims that if *The Two Noble Kinsmen* is indeed a collaboration—in spite of Paul Bertram's argument—then "Shakespeare has found it appropriate, fresh from *The Tempest,* to submit himself to a Fletcherian decorum" (p. 12).

Brownlow, F. W. *Two Shakespearean Sequences.* Pittsburgh: University of Pittsburgh Press, 1977.

Brownlow calls *The Two Noble Kinsmen* "a very beautiful play, revealing an artistic intelligence in complete control of its material" (p. 216). He rejects Theodore Spencer's assessment of the play as the work of a writer "turning away from life" (p. 202). He argues that the play is characterized by the fictional deities who rule it, Venus and Mars: "The contrast between those two deities of love and war, or, in our blunter jargon, sex and aggression, their attraction for one another, their common origin in human appetites, were favorite themes of Renaissance art" (p. 202). Brownlow sees these two forces eventually being "subdued to necessary ends," "their driving energy turned to the forms of civility" (p. 202).

In opposition to critics who question the relevance of the first act to the main action of the play, Brownlow points out that it is in the first act that we learn "Shakespeare has preferred to give Theseus and Hippolyta each a dual allegiance to Venus and Mars tempered by reason embodied in the institution of marriage" (p. 207), in contrast to Palamon and Arcite, each of whom has a single allegiance. This foreshadows the eventual resolution in the play, where we see "the gods themselves subdued to the order of a large design" (p. 215). Theseus, whose "absoluteness is mitigated by his reasonableness," is the spokesman throughout the play "of limitations upon human potentiality" (p. 211), and his awareness of this contributes both to a feeling of "melancholy" (p. 211) and to the sense that his city, Athens, has a "temperate beauty" (p. 215) due to its control of destructive passions. At the play's end we are left with impressions of "civility and graciousness, of irregularity tamed by ceremony and justice, of Providence acknowledged" (p. 215).

Leech, Clifford. "Masking and Unmasking in the Last Plays." In *Shakespeare's Romances Reconsidered,* edited by Carol McGinnis Kay and Henry E. Jacobs. Lincoln and London: University of Nebraska Press, 1978.

Leech notes that masques-within-plays became frequent in Jacobean drama, though often they were not true masques due to their brevity and irony. The country dance presented in 3.5 of *The Two Noble Kinsmen,* for example—long recognized as an adaptation of the second antimasque from Beaumont's *Masque of the Inner Temple and Gray's Inn*—is distinctive in that it is basically comic but at the same time touched with sadness due to the presence of the Jailer's Daughter, whom we know to be mad. Leech suggests that our sympathies are with her rather than with the rustics and that "It may be better, though less pleasant, to be mad with her than to be wise with the Schoolmaster" (p. 46).

Frye, Northrop. "Romance as Masque." In *Shakespeare's Romances Reconsidered,* edited by Carol McGinnis Kay and Henry E. Jacobs. Lincoln and London: University of Nebraska Press, 1978.

In the context of an article on Shakespearean romance in the light of New Comedy and the masque, Frye classifies *The Two Noble Kinsmen* as a romance and points out its reliance on rituals such as Theseus's wedding and the petitions of the mourning Queens (p. 33). The ritualistic elements in the play define its themes: "Just as death takes precedence of marriage, so a destructive and enslaving passion destroys the freedom of friendship" (p. 33). Frye considers the action of the play to be dominated by a Venus "as menacing as the Indian Kali" (p. 34) and finds the "only 'natural,' spontaneous, and apparently free-willed action" of the play to be the freeing of Palamon from prison by the Jailer's Daughter—an action that ends up being "totally disastrous" for her (p. 34).

Wickham, Glynne. "*The Two Noble Kinsmen* or *A Midsummer Night's Dream, Part II?*" In *The Elizabethan Theatre VII*, edited by G. R. Hibbard. Hamden, Conn.: Archon Books, 1980.

Following M. C. Bradbrook's suggestion that *The Two Noble Kinsmen* owes much of its form and content to two historical events—the death of Henry, Prince of Wales, in November 1612 and the wedding of his sister, Princess Elizabeth, to Count Frederick V, Elector Palatine of the Rhine, in February 1613—Wickham argues that the play's central characters correspond to members of the royal family: "Emilia becomes the dramatic emblem for the Princess in the Court hieroglyphics of *The Two Noble Kinsmen,* Palamon the emblem for the Palsgrave [Count Frederick], Arcite for Prince Henry. By the same token Theseus and Hippolyta represent, in this world of the play, James I and Queen Anne" (p. 178). Wickham then claims the play "is not only superficially related in its external forms to the events it marks, as Professor Bradbrook suggested, but is organically connected to the emotional relationships of the five principal characters of the real-life funeral and marriage ceremonies" (p. 178).

Wickham then turns to *A Midsummer Night's Dream,* the "only previous play in the Shakespeare canon that is generally acknowledged to have been written to celebrate a wedding" (p. 178). After pointing out structural similarities between this play and *The Two Noble Kinsmen* (p. 181), Wickham notes that comparing the two plays is "a perfectly legitimate exercise" (p. 180) and concludes that while "the earlier play adopts a youthful and optimistic approach to the conflicting dictates of lust and love, and urges an orthodox approach to the social institution of marriage, the later one approaches both problems from a far more detached, contemplative and even cynical standpoint; it is a reverie rather than a dream" (p. 182). The disenchantment experienced, in one form or another, by all four of the young lovers—Palamon, Arcite, Emilia, and the Jailer's Daughter—reflects "the very events that occasioned the writing of this play—the Princess Elizabeth's loss of her brother and closest friend . . . and the crude, diplomatic bargaining that for four years had been conducted by the King and Queen over her person as if that were some form of merchandise" (p. 186).

The Two Noble Kinsmen is thus a second version of *A Midsummer Night's Dream,* and the differences between the two plays "teach us what aspect of love and marriage had come to interest Shakespeare some twenty years after writing" the earlier play (p. 181). In place of "youthful exuberance and optimism" we find "the disenchantment of experience matched with a fortitude compounded of Christian acceptance and stoic resignation" (p. 194). The "fairy world" (p. 194) of *A Midsummer Night's Dream* has been replaced by "the all-pervading presence of Hymen, Diana, Mars and Venus, supernatural powers of a much harsher and more realistic school" (p. 195).

Frey, Charles. "'O sacred, shadowy, cold, and constant queen': Shakespeare's Imperiled and Chastening Daughters of Romance." In *The Woman's Part: Feminist Criticism of Shakespeare,* edited by Carolyn Ruth Swift Lenz, Gayle Greene, and Carol Thomas Neely. Urbana: University of Illinois Press, 1980.

Discussing Shakespeare's "post-romance attitude" (p. 307) and "the evolution of his heroines toward virgin faith" (p. 306), Frey finds that *The Two Noble Kinsmen* "simultaneously attacks and defends romantic imagination" (p. 309). It attacks it in the sense that the devotions of Palamon and Arcite to their respective deities are revealed as "debased, decadent visions of chivalric and courtly ideals"; they serve to develop and expand "Shakespeare's critique of patriarchalism and the potential murderousness and sterility that often accompany its political, social, and sexual hierarchies" (p. 307). But the play also defends romantic imagination—not so much through the action of Emilia, who marries Palamon, as by the presence of the Jailer's Daughter, who "makes the union of Palamon and Emilia acceptable" (p. 308). Emilia, by herself, lacking a father or a brother, exemplifies a tendency in daughters "to resist marriage or to see it as especially troublesome" (p. 307); but the Jailer's Daughter, with her "creative passion" (p. 308) and her "warmer eagerness" (p. 309) toward Palamon and love itself, legitimizes and supports the "aim and function" (p. 309) of Emilia's union. In short, the Jailer's Daughter—a character from the subplot—is at the heart of the play, and "the development of the main plot lies secretly" (p. 311) in her hands.

Frey notes that *The Two Noble Kinsmen,* in one sense, is a satire: "The state of mind that overcomes the impasse of love which is split into effete worship and Mars-like rapacity is a state of mind represented as madness, an unthinkable dedication of unified mind and heart, spirit and flesh" (p. 311). But he suggests that behind this satire Shakespeare has "the secret project of resuscitating the romance-ic spirit" (p. 311). *The Two Noble Kinsmen* shows us "the beleaguered maiden's often-instinctive retreat to Diana," but it also honors, through the passion of the Jailer's Daughter, "the unquenchable desire of romantic will to purge and renew itself toward some version, no matter how strangely won, of ongoing and productive love" (p. 311).

Williams, Gwyn. *Person and Persona.* Cardiff: University of Wales Press, 1981.

In a chapter titled "The Loneliness of the Homosexual in Shakespeare," Williams notes that with the exception of Achilles and Patroclus and *Troilus and Cressida,* "homosexual affection is not reciprocated in the plays and poems of Shakespeare, and this accounts for the loneliness of Antonio the sea captain [*Twelfth Night*], of Antonio of Venice, of Emilia, since Flavina is dead, and possibly of Palamon, whose thoughts at the end of the play are only of Arcite" (p. 141). Williams refers to Emilia as "a high-minded lesbian" and suggests that she, like the two Antonios, is "yet another person banished by emotional inhibitions to the periphery of normal social relationships, a bride who doesn't want to be married but has marriage thrust upon her" (p. 141).

Waith, Eugene M. "Shakespeare and the Ceremonies of Romance." In *Shakespeare's Craft: Eight Lectures,* edited by Philip H. Highfill, Jr. Carbondale and Edwardsville: Southern Illinois University Press, 1982.

Waith demonstrates that the ceremonial scenes of *The Winter's Tale, Cymbeline, Henry VIII,* and *The Two Noble Kinsmen* show the influence of epic and romance traditions from religious ceremony and earlier drama. *Henry VIII* and *The Two Noble Kinsmen,* he claims, are "the most insistently ceremonious of all Shakespeare's plays" (p. 121). In *The Two Noble Kinsmen,* ceremony generally expresses "the struggle for self-transcendence" (p. 124). For example, the first scene of the play—with its emphasis on the begging of the three mourning Queens and the active participation of Hippolyta and Emilia in the supplication—ends with a display of pity by Theseus: "A hard-won triumph of courtesy over self-interest, a movement toward more god-like behavior" (p. 131).

Waith agrees with Philip Edwards that "the central idea of the play is a movement from innocence to experience" (p. 136) and claims the play's final ceremonies are "consonant with this interpretation" (p. 137). He believes, however, that the play's earlier ceremonies, such as the one in the first scene, add a new dimension to Edwards's interpretation: "In this play, as in *Pericles,* what makes disillusionment affecting is the effort to behave nobly. The most memorable ceremonies give a brilliant visual immediacy to moments in which Theseus, Palamon, and Arcite make the choice of 'honorable deeds and generous behavior'—'honour' and 'curteisye'" (p. 137).

Berggren, Paula S. "'For what we lack, / We laugh': Incompletion and *The Two Noble Kinsmen." Modern Language Studies* 14:4 (Fall 1984): 3–17.

Berggren notes that the play "is beginning to attract the attention it deserves" (p. 3). In contrast to the romances, which celebrate fresh love and wise reflection, *The Two Noble Kinsmen* explores dilemmas of early adult life but never suggests the possibility of confident growth through life stages. In comparison to Chaucer's *Knight's Tale, The Two Noble Kinsmen* presents a "disorienting labyrinth that mocks direction" (p. 5). For example, "Theseus' test of superiority demands not straightforward expression of individual skill but the imposition of one will on another. To touch the center, to make essential contact, is here to fail; the loser yields his self-determination, but the winner is denied the touch of the pillar. An extraordinary retreat from simplistic phallic assertion lies at the heart of this contrivance and of *The Two Noble Kinsmen* as an entity, however divided its authorship" (p. 7). The play, furthermore, continually denies the audience the release of action or of intimate soliloquy. Shakespeare suggests that the heroes are impetuous and uncontrolling, that "the gods do punish wrongly" (p. 12), and that any faith in ennobling sexuality deserves to be subverted. Still, "had Shakespeare told us everything he knew at the end of his career, it might have been too much to bear" (p. 15).

Abrams, Richard. "Gender Confusion and Sexual Politics in *The Two Noble Kinsmen.*" In *Themes in Drama 7: Drama, Sex and Politics,* edited by J. Redmond. Cambridge: Cambridge University Press, 1985.

In contrast to the identity confusion portrayed in *A Midsummer Night's Dream, The Two Noble Kinsmen* shows us gender confusion: "strict differentiation of sexual kind breaks down, becoming as fluid as in King James's openly homosexual court" (p. 69). Abrams points out, for example, the "sapphic orientation" (p. 69) of Emilia as displayed in her conversation with her handmaiden (2.2.135-52)—a conversation "which ends in the women going to bed together" (p. 70). He notes, too, that Emilia's "delight in similars" (p. 72) helps to explain both her youthful love for Flavina and her later heterosexual attraction to both Palamon and Arcite. But this attraction soon fades, and "after a brief flirtation with the men's pictures, she prays to remain a virgin, continuing in Diana's band, while the right to deflower her is contested by Palamon and Arcite" (p. 73). Indeed, the two kinsmen, who "represent, almost heraldically, the male and female sexual principles" (p. 73), care little about Emilia, and this lack of concern "suggests the moral inequality of the traditionally powerful (men) vs. the politically disenfranchised (women)" (p. 74). Thus, the play's psychosexual themes open up into moral and political questions.

Abrams concludes by arguing, "The play's deepest conflict is not between the kinsmen, but between Theseus, as patriarchal ruler of Athens, and Emilia as representative of 'The powers of all women'" (p. 74). In opposition to the thoroughgoing "misogyny" (p. 74) of Theseus we have "the healing superiority of Emilia's values" (p. 75); in the end, Palamon and Arcite and Theseus, along with the chivalric world they represent, "are less civilized and insightful than the helpless girl for whom they compete" (p. 75).

Waith, Eugene M. "Shakespeare and Fletcher on Love and Friendship." *Shakespeare Studies* 18 (1986): 235-50.

Waith's concern is with the "shifts of emphasis in Shakespeare's and Fletcher's dramatization of the story of Palamon and Arcite" (p. 237), a story previously told by both Chaucer and Boccaccio. Waith agrees that Shakespeare and Fletcher collaborated in writing *The Two Noble Kinsmen* and accepts the authorship divisions given by G. R. Proudfoot in his 1970 edition of the play. *The Two Noble Kinsmen,* in Waith's opinion, is "better unified than is often granted" (p. 237).

After demonstrating how the play's first act creates a thematic context by "emphasizing the extraordinary worth of true friendship and comparing its value with that of true love" (pp. 238-39), Waith moves to 2.2—normally attributed to Fletcher—and argues that even though the professions of ideal friendship of Palamon and Arcite might seem to verge on absurdity, it is probable that Renaissance audiences accepted them at face value. These audiences may well have been familiar with the idealized friendships presented in popular romances; they may also have read Montaigne's essay "Of Friendship" in the 1603 John Florio translation. Waith claims that "Montaigne's sincerity is a reliable guide to the seriousness with which such a profession of friendship might be taken in the seventeenth century" but adds that Fletcher, like Shakespeare, was capable of "looking with amused detachment" at characters and incidents—which might account for the "element of playfulness" in the rhetoric of the two cousins (p. 241).

Waith goes on to provide other examples of the play's means of stressing the value of friendship, concluding, "Shakespeare and Fletcher, in contrast to both Boccaccio and Chaucer, make the friendship of the two cousins their central concern" (p. 247). Love, on the other hand, "does not score very high. The only happy love between a man and a woman is that of Theseus and Hippolyta. Emilia comes to it reluctantly; the Jailer's Daughter is driven mad by it; . . . To the kinsmen it is like a bolt of lightning, totally disrupting their lives" (p. 248). Interestingly, Waith does not attend to the resolution of the play's subplot, in which the Doctor attempts to cure the madness of the Jailer's Daughter by reuniting her with her Wooer, who is disguised as Palamon.

Waith concludes that "The Boethian wisdom of making a virtue of necessity, preached by Theseus just before the conclusion of *The Knight's Tale,* takes a curious turn" in *The Two Noble Kinsmen* (p. 249). The emphasis in the play is not on the practical value of this wisdom but on "bewilderment at the plight of human beings who must pay so dearly for their innocence" (p. 249). This results in a rather "somber" mood at the end of a play that nominally, at least, is a tragicomedy; the "predominant feeling is the loss of friendship" (p. 249).

Edwards, Philip. *Shakespeare: A Writer's Progress.* Oxford and New York: Oxford University Press, 1987.

Accepting without dispute that *The Two Noble Kinsmen* was a collaborative effort between Shakespeare and Fletcher, Edwards comments that this collaboration was "not a great success. Fletcher was an excellent dramatist with an outstanding stage sense, but he was not inconvenienced by seriousness of mind. *The Two Noble Kinsmen* might have been better if left entirely to him" (p. 24).

Edwards claims that *The Two Noble Kinsmen* was Shakespeare's last play (p. 35) and classifies it as a tragicomedy, grouping it with *All's Well, Measure for Measure, Pericles,*

Cymbeline, The Winter's Tale, and *The Tempest* (p. 160). The tragicomedies, like the early comedies, have "little use for verisimilitude," but their improbabilities "seem much more striking because they occur in plays which contain serious and extended treatment of grave moral problems" (p. 160).

Commenting on *The Two Noble Kinsmen*'s "celebrations of perfect friendship between people of the same sex" (p. 34), Edwards suggests that Emilia's speech about her affection for Flavina "seems to echo Montaigne's great essay 'On Friendship' (arguing its superiority to sexual love)" (p. 35).

Lief, Madelon, and Nicholas F. Radel. "Linguistic Subversion and the Artifice of Rhetoric in *The Two Noble Kinsmen.*" *Shakespeare Quarterly* 38 (1987): 405–25.

Lief and Radel argue that a "consistent undercutting of the language of invocation" (p. 406) in *The Two Noble Kinsmen* is a characteristic technique of the play, one practiced by both Shakespeare and Fletcher. This "linguistic subversion," combined with Fletcher's manipulation of the subplot, "reflects a cynical and problematic world view emerging in Shakespeare's late plays and in non-Shakespearean drama of the early seventeenth century" (p. 406).

Noting Fletcher's familiarity with the "new verisimilitude" (p. 408) advocated by Giambattista Guarini in his discussion of tragicomedy, Lief and Radel point out the coincident development in England of the empirical tradition championed by Bacon, and they suggest that these influences contributed to "a skeptical drama that plays on the tension between reality and the attempt of the characters to impose order on that reality" (p. 410). In particular, Fletcherian tragicomedy evidences "a comical, even cynical, detachment of language from characters who are engaged in serious actions" (p. 410). In such scenes from *The Two Noble Kinsmen* as 2.2, we see Fletcher employing rhetoric to expose the failure of characters to live up to their words. Fletcher reveals these characters as "small, absurd creatures, interesting not as they grapple with great ideas, morality, and ethics, but, rather, as they are unable to do so" (p. 413).

Turning to sections of the play conventionally attributed to Shakespeare (for instance 1.1, 1.3, and 5.1), Lief and Radel find further examples of linguistic subversion, most of them raising questions as to "man's ability to comprehend fully his place in the cosmos" (p. 414). In particular, the speeches of the two knights to their respective deities (in 5.1) differ substantially from their predecessors in Chaucer's *Knight's Tale;* Shakespeare's Arcite "perceives the world as a struggle for survival, and hence views Emilia as a prize that he must win" (p. 416), while Palamon—far from the speaker of a "humble love lament" whom we remember from Chaucer—becomes self-righteous and "boasts of his virtues as a man and lover" (p. 417).

But it is in the play's subplot that "the seeds of skepticism" (p. 419) are planted, particularly in Fletcher's scenes in act 3. Lief and Radel point to the shortsightedness of Shakespeare's and Fletcher's Theseus (especially in 3.6) and contrast him with the Physician who in 5.2 treats the Jailer's Daughter, dismissing "ethics and morality in favor of life and sanity" (p. 421). The schoolmaster Gerrold also provides an example of rhetorical insipidity that exposes "the sterility of Theseus's rhetoric of order" (p. 421). In short, the play's subplot "reminds us of the inadequacy of Theseus's decorous and ritualistic imposition of order on his world" (p. 424), which, in turn, reinforces the authors' idea that *The Two Noble Kinsmen* is concerned with "an unsettling kind of realism," a mimesis that considers "the empirical nature of things, not the ideal reflection of them" (p. 425).

5. The Play in Performance

Howard, Tony. "Census of Renaissance Drama Productions." *Research Opportunities in Renaissance Drama* 22 (1979): 73–85.

Howard briefly reviews a production of *The Two Noble Kinsmen* mounted by the Cherub Company at the Young Vic Studio in London during November and December 1979. The cast was all male, "probably to the play's disadvantage"; the resulting "emphatic sexuality seemed an anti-feminine joke, capped by the comic playing of the doctor" (p. 75). Numerous cuts, including the removal of "the morris men, the Six Knights and even the kinsmen's recollections of 'the wenches we have known,'" provided a "sense of consistency" to the play; the most striking moment was the "tender ferocity of the arming scene" (p. 75). The speaking was "musical," but, "in the denser Shakespearean passages, incomprehensible" (p. 75).

Berkowitz, Gerald M. "Shakespeare in Edinburgh." *Shakespeare Quarterly* 31 (1980): 163–67.

Berkowitz reviews the all-male Cherub Company production of *The Two Noble Kinsmen* presented at the New Chaplaincy Centre in Edinburgh during August and September 1979. Noting that the play was "heavily cut" (p. 165), Berkowitz nonetheless found that "Palamon and Arcite were effectively differentiated—the one intense and suspicious, the other open and rational" (p. 166)—and that the actor playing Emilia succeeded "in conveying her turmoil and unhappiness at being a pawn in a game she didn't want to play any part of" (p. 166). Moreover, the cuts illuminated not only "the fact that the real couples in the main plot are the two women and the two men" but also the action of the Jailer's Daughter, "who switches her love from one man to another without even realizing it" (p. 166).

Stodder, Joseph H., and Lillian Wilds. "Shakespeare in Southern California and Visalia." *Shakespeare Quarterly* 31 (1980): 254–74.

Stodder and Wilds review the Shakespeare Society of America's production of *The Two Noble Kinsmen,* mounted at the Globe Playhouse of Los Angeles in June and July 1979. The play's director, Walter Scholz, "chose to project plot and character largely through use of dance and ritual, with almost uniformly satisfying results" (p. 258). For instance, the appearance of the three mourning Queens—all dressed in black—"was a persuasive example of the power that ritual could achieve when blended effectively into the action of the play" (p. 166). But the play's "most remarkable achievement" (p. 166) was its portrayal of the Jailer's Daughter, with her "Ophelia-like tenderness" and "the stunning enactment of her mad fantasy by the Jailer and others" (p. 167).

Metz, G. Harold. "*The Two Noble Kinsmen* on the Twentieth-Century Stage." *Theatre History Studies* 4 (1984): 63–69.

Metz reviews the production history of *The Two Noble Kinsmen,* pointing out that after two revivals in the seventeenth century the play was not performed again until 1928 at the Old Vic Theatre in London. From then until 1984 there were nine additional productions of the play, four in the United States and five in Britain. For the most part, according to Metz, reviewers and audiences alike have been enthusiastic about the play. Its production, among other things, "invites spectacular effects, especially in the opening scene with its inter-mingling processions and in the theophanies and the tournament sequence in the final act" (p. 67). Moreover, the play has "masque and song elements and the folk-quality of the morris-dance that can be made to contrast nicely to the more stately elements of the play presented through the aristocratic characters" (pp. 67–68). Though the play is obviously not sparking "a great rush of enthusiasm," its recent productions stand out "against the dark background of the preceding three centuries of total neglect" (p. 68). Metz foresees further interest and more productions of *The Two Noble Kinsmen* in the future (p. 68).

Maguire, Nancy Klein. *"The Two Noble Kinsmen." Shakespeare Bulletin* 4:4 (July/ August 1986): 8–9.

Maguire reviews the Royal Shakespeare Company's first production of *The Two Noble Kinsmen,* which opened at the Swan Theatre in Stratford-upon-Avon on 28 April 1986. Directed by Barry Kyle, this production emphasized "exotic symbolism," employed "heavily stylized" stage props, and stressed "the motif of bondage" (p. 8)— especially with regard to the Jailer's Daughter. Maguire finds the relationship between Palamon and Arcite "emotionally unconvincing" and concedes that one general reaction to the production would be that it "misses conviction" (p. 9). However, she admits that by another reading, the production is "a deliberate attempt to draw a contrast between the regulated and unnatural posturing of the main-plot characters, shaped by the forces of chivalry and bereft of any interior life, and the liveliness of the subplot characters, who are psychologically viable" (p. 9). The Jailer's Daughter, for example, "is capable of sexual response and of commitment to a single man; her wooer demonstrates unselfish dedication" (p. 9).

Collier, Susanne. "The Inauguration of the New Swan Theatre with *The Two Noble Kinsmen* and *Every Man in His Humour,* Stratford-Upon-Avon." *Journal of Dramatic Theory and Criticism* 1:2 (Spring 1987): 163–67.

Collier stresses the "disparity of treatment of the two plots" (p. 165) of *The Two Noble Kinsmen* as produced by the Royal Shakespeare Company in April 1986. On the one hand, director Barry Kyle chooses to dress Theseus and his court in "Japanese Noh fashion," thereby creating a "chiaroscuro effect of white-face and black wigs" that emphasizes the play's "overtones of symbolic activity" and is consonant with its "mythic elements" (p. 165). On the other hand, Kyle employs "typically English rustic details" (p. 165) in those parts of the play pertaining to the Jailer's Daughter and the Schoolmaster's entertainment. The result is that "faced with a difficult and mediocre play to open a theatre dedicated to such experiments, Kyle has succumbed to the temptations of gimmickry and gingered up an evening of patchy interest" (p. 165).

About the Contributors

RICHARD ABRAMS, associate professor of English at the University of Southern Maine, has published essays on Shakespeare and Dante in *English Literary Renaissance, MLN,* and other journals. He is writing a book titled *"Strange Art": The Achievement of "The Two Noble Kinsmen."*

MICHAEL D. BRISTOL, professor of English at McGill University, is the author of *Carnival and Theater: Plebeian Culture and the Structure of Authority in Renaissance England.*

CHARLES H. FREY, professor of English at the University of Washington, is the author of *Shakespeare's Vast Romance: A Study of "The Winter's Tale"* and *Experiencing Shakespeare: Essays on Text, Classroom, and Performance.*

SUSAN GREEN is assistant professor of English and Humanities at Virginia Polytechnic Institute and State University.

WILL HAMLIN, a doctoral candidate at the University of Washington, is completing a dissertation that treats Renaissance ethnography as a context for representations of savagery and civility in Montaigne, Spenser, and Shakespeare.

DONALD K. HEDRICK, professor of English at Kansas State University, is currently the O'Connor Professor of Literature at Colgate University and Visiting Fellow with the Western Societies Program of the Center for International Studies at Cornell University. He has been a Fellow at Cornell's Society for the Humanities and has published on Shakespeare and Renaissance drama, modern poetry, language philosophy, and Renaissance architectural theory.

HUGH RICHMOND, professor of English at the University of California, Berkeley, directs the performance-oriented Shakespeare Program at Berkeley. He heads the U. C. Shakespeare Forum and the U. S. A. Advisory Board for rebuilding Shakespeare's Globe Theatre. His performance history of *Richard III* will be published by Manchester University Press in 1989.

JEANNE ADDISON ROBERTS, professor of literature at The American University, is author of *Shakespeare's English Comedy: "The Merry Wives of Windsor" in Context.* She is finishing a book on *The Shakespearean Wild: Geography, Genus, and Gender.*

BARRY WELLER has edited Byron's dramas for Volumes VI and VII of the Oxford University Press *Complete Poetical Works of Lord Byron.* He is preparing a book on character and theatrical representation in Shakespeare's comedies. He teaches at the University of Utah where he also edits the *Western Humanities Review.*

PAUL WERSTINE, co-editor of the New Variorum *Romeo and Juliet* and associate editor of *Medieval and Renaissance Drama in England,* has published on analytical bibliography in *Studies in Bibliography, The Library, Papers of the Bibliographical Society of America,* and *Analytical and Enumerative Bibliography.* Currently he is applying critical theory to Shakespearean textual criticism.

Index